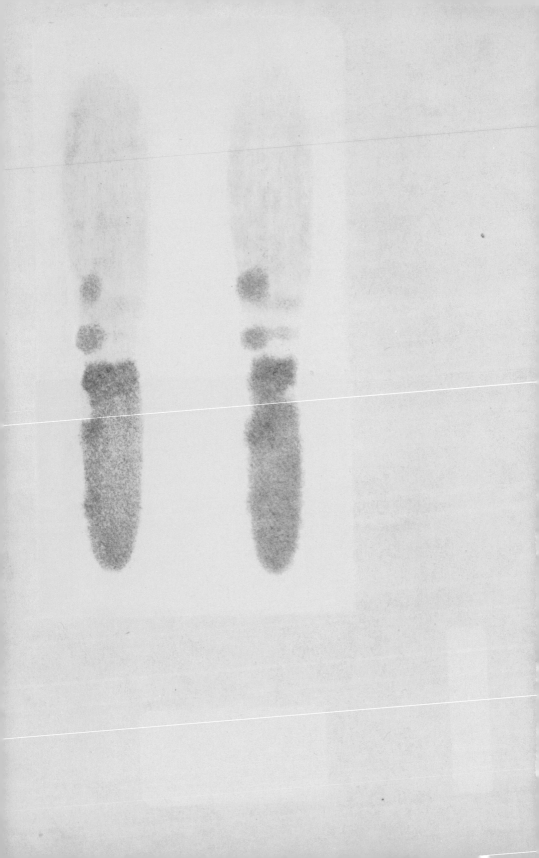

Conversations with Lillian Hellman

Literary Conversations Series

Peggy Whitman Prenshaw
General Editor

Conversations with Lillian Hellman

Edited by
Jackson R. Bryer

University Press of Mississippi
Jackson and London

Copyright © 1986 by the University Press of Mississippi
All rights reserved
Manufactured in the United States of America
89 88 87 86   4 3 2 1
The paper in this book meets the guidelines for permanence and durability of the Committee
on Production Guidelines for Book Longevity of the Council on Library Resources.

Library of Congress Cataloging-in-Publication Data

Hellman, Lillian, 1906–
  Conversations with Lillian Hellman.

  (Literary conversations series)
  Includes index.
  1. Hellman, Lillian, 1906–   —Interviews.
  2. Dramatists, American—20th century—Interviews.
  I. Bryer, Jackson R.   II. Title.   III. Series.
  PS3515.E343Z467   1986   812'.52 [B]   85-31473
  ISBN 0-87805-293-3
  ISBN 0-87805-294-1 (pbk.)

Books by Lillian Hellman

The Children's Hour. New York: Alfred A. Knopf, 1934.

Days to Come. New York: Alfred A. Knopf, 1936.

The Little Foxes. New York: Random House, 1939.

Watch on the Rhine. New York: Random House, 1941.

Four Plays [*The Children's Hour, Days to Come, The Little Foxes, Watch on the Rhine*]. New York: Modern Library, 1942.

The North Star. New York: Viking Press, 1943.

The Searching Wind. New York: Viking Press, 1944.

Another Part of the Forest. New York: Viking Press, 1947.

Montserrat. Adapted from the French play by Emmanuel Roblès. New York: Dramatists Play Service, 1950.

The Autumn Garden. Boston: Little, Brown, 1951.

The Selected Letters of Anton Chekhov. Edited by Lillian Hellman. New York: Farrar, Straus and Cudahy, 1955.

The Lark. Adapted from the French play by Jean Anouilh. New York: Random House, 1956.

Candide. Book by Lillian Hellman, score by Leonard Bernstein, lyrics by Richard Wilbur, Dorothy Parker, and John Latouche. New York: Random House, 1957.

Six Plays [*The Children's Hour, Days to Come, The Little Foxes, Watch on the Rhine, Another Part of the Forest, The Autumn Garden*]. New York: Modern Library, 1960.

Toys in the Attic. New York: Random House, 1960.

My Mother, My Father and Me. Adapted from the novel *How Much?* by Burt Blechman. New York: Random House, 1963.

The Big Knockover: Selected Stories and Short Novels by Dashiell Hammett. Edited by Lillian Hellman. New York: Random House, 1966.

An Unfinished Woman: A Memoir. Boston: Little, Brown, 1969.

The Collected Plays [*The Children's Hour, Days to Come, The Little Foxes, Watch on the Rhine, The Searching Wind, Another Part of the Forest, Montserrat, The Autumn Garden, The Lark, Candide, Toys in the Attic, My Mother, My Father and Me*]. Boston: Little, Brown, 1971.

Pentimento: A Book of Portraits. Boston: Little, Brown, 1973.

Scoundrel Time. Boston: Little, Brown, 1976.

Three [*An Unfinished Woman, Pentimento, Scoundrel Time*]. Boston: Little, Brown, 1979.

Maybe: A Story. Boston: Little, Brown, 1980.

Eating Together: Recollections and Recipes. By Lillian Hellman and Peter Feibleman. Boston: Little, Brown, 1984.

Contents

Introduction

Speaking with Lewis Funke in 1968, Lillian Hellman remarked, "I think I'm a bad person to interview." On numerous other occasions, beginning as early as 1941 when she warned Robert Van Gelder that "I'm difficult . . . I can't think good quotes," she complained that she didn't like giving interviews and didn't, as she explained to Christine Doudna in 1976, like "talking about myself." Despite these reservations and characteristically modest comments, Miss Hellman allowed herself to be interviewed often and extensively during the fifty years which began with her first Broadway play, the controversial and highly successful *The Children's Hour,* in 1934, and ended with her death in 1984. The twenty-seven interviews included in this volume were selected from some one hundred fifty which were located; numerous others probably remain buried in the files of local newspapers around the world. It is also safe to assume that few interviewers left her presence agreeing that she had been "a bad person to interview." She may well have not enjoyed talking about herself; but she did so entertainingly and often very openly and directly. And she was usually ready to offer her opinions on a wide variety of social, political, and literary subjects, almost always in outspoken terms which produced extremely "good quotes." From the moment that she burst upon the Broadway scene at the age of twenty-nine with a play which included suggestions of a lesbian relationship between two of its characters until the day she died, when her defamation suit against Mary McCarthy remained unresolved, Hellman was seldom far from controversy; and she never was shy about confronting it.

The interviews are arranged chronologically; and because this volume tries to be representative and comprehensive, it begins with a sampling of the many brief newspaper interviews Hellman gave, usually to theatre critics or correspondents from New York dailies, either just before or just after one of her plays opened on Broadway or about the time a film she had written was released. While these early pieces are certainly slight and generally focus almost entirely on the work recently completed, on the circumstances of its composition, and on her future plans, there are as well occasional hints of an individual who even then did not hesitate to speak her mind—as when she tells Lucius Beebe in 1936, while comparing movies to plays, "They wouldn't know an idea if they saw it on the Coast, and if by any chance they should recognize it the film people would be frightened right out of their suede shoes."

These early interviews are also interesting because they give us what Hellman thought of her plays and film scripts right after completing them; it is worth comparing what she has to say about *The Little Foxes* in 1939 a month after it opened with remarks made about the same play thirty and forty years later. Sometimes, opinions expressed early contrast with or are echoed in later interviews. In 1936, she describes the theatre to Lucius Beebe as "a place for the expression and exchange of ideas"; in later years she would deny that her plays began with ideas but rather were based on characters. Her admission to Irving Drutman in 1943 that "I think of things in terms of novels, then I have to transpose my ideas into play form" resonates intriguingly with her contention, in several later interviews, that she never considered herself a "natural" playwright and in fact didn't know why or how she began writing for the stage.

The Drutman interview also stands as an expression of Hellman's feelings about Hollywood and the film industry early in her career, when she was dividing her time quite evenly between movies and plays, before her first blacklisting and her bad experience with *The Chase* (1966) kept her from working on screenplays ever again. Similarly, the 1949 Murray Schumach interview documents the brief period when she directed productions of her plays and felt that directing "required something less than genius." Twenty years later, she confides to Fred Gardner that, in 1949, she "found out that I didn't make a good director" and "didn't even like it very much." Several of these early interviews also mention the amount of back-ground research Hellman did in preparing her plays and filmscripts; this desire for accuracy and authenticity not only is reflected in the dramas and movies themselves but also in her ability to resurrect specific details from her memory when, later in her life, she began writing her four volumes of memoirs. Finally, it is worth noting that her view of *The Autumn Garden* as her favorite among her own plays is first articulated on the eve of its Broadway opening in 1951 and never changes from that moment to the end of her life.

But perhaps the most important reason for including so many of these early newspaper interviews becomes apparent when one stands back from the full range of interviews presented in this volume and notes that they divide into three stages. The first consists of these newspaper interviews focused primarily on the plays and films and ends with Richard G. Stern's long and important 1958 piece (printed here in its entirety rather than in the heavily edited and cut version which was published in *Contact* in 1959). It centers on *Toys in the Attic,* then in the process of being written (the version which Hellman presents to Stern differs in fascinating ways from the produced play), dwells briefly on *The Little Foxes,* and concludes prophetically with her positive comments on Samuel Beckett and her uncomplimentary ones on the contemporary American theatre. The Stern interview also contains the first mention of Dashiell Hammett; in the pre-1960s period he is coyly referred to as "her friend."

The second stage of Hellman interviews begins dramatically with the headline of Thomas Meehan's long 1962 *Esquire* article: "Q: Miss Hellman, What's Wrong With Broadway? A: It's a Bore." Here we are introduced to the Hellman of the caustic, pithy, and always frank retort who finds the American theatre wanting in virtually every respect. She is ready to offer her views on playwrights (William Inge: "He's a skillful man. The plays aren't up my alley."); actors (Marlon Brando: "I wish he'd cut out the high jinks and get down to work."); and directors (Elia Kazan: "He's very wise about the theatre—maybe too wise."). Apparently the fact that Hellman, one of America's foremost dramatists, found most of contemporary theatre uninteresting was sensational news; because Meehan's interview inaugurates a series of long articles which abruptly shift the focus from Hellman's plays to her views on the state of the American theatre and film industries and to discussions of aspects of her life, principally her relationship with Hammett (now discussed far more openly as a love affair in which they "lived together" but never married) and her 1952 appearance before the House Un-American Activities Committee. Hammett, in fact, becomes so central to the 1964 *Paris Review* interview that Hellman herself notes, "Dash comes into this interview very often, doesn't he?"

This shift can even be seen in the titles of the interviews. Where earlier ones were called "Miss Hellman Talks of Her Latest Play, *The Little Foxes*" or "Miss Hellman and Her First Screen Venture," now they have titles like "A Playwright Looks at the Theater Today" or "Lillian Hellman Reflects upon the Changing Theater." To be sure, such topics as how she began writing plays, why she stopped, her feelings about having her plays labeled "well-made," and why she never wrote a third play about the Hubbard family of *The Little Foxes* and *Another Part of the Forest* do recur; but in the 1960s, interviewers more often asked Hellman about matters other than her own work. Lewis Funke, for example, spends a lot of time on Hellman as a teacher (after Hammett's death in 1961, she taught occasional brief courses at Harvard, Yale, M.I.T., Hunter College, and the University of California at Berkeley). The interviewers for *Yale Reports* focus her attention on the reasons for the low quality of American theatre, why she likes films more than plays, and why the United States has produced so few women playwrights.

Fred Gardner's late 1968 interview (published here for the first time) was conducted after Hellman had completed her first book of memoirs, *An Unfinished Woman,* but before it was published. It provides the same sort of bridge between the second and third stages of Hellman interviews as the Richard G. Stern one does between the first and second stages. Gardner begins in the same mode as Meehan and *Yale Reports* by getting Hellman to lament the condition of the American theatre and her lack of interest in it and he gets her as well to talk some about her career as a playwright and screenwriter. But about two-thirds of the way through the interview, he alters its focus when he observes, "In 1944 during the war you accepted an invitation to the Soviet Union." This leads Hellman to read an excerpt from the new book; and most of the rest of the interview alternates between events in her life and details about her writing career.

What seems to have happened in this third stage of interviews is that, as the memoirs appeared, interviewers became so fascinated by the events of her life as told therein that they virtually forgot that she had ever written plays or films. Hellman continues to be asked about social and political issues; in fact, with the advent of the women's movement and Watergate, her outspoken independence and defiance of the Un-American Activities Committee as depicted in the memoirs (which became best sellers) make her what Christine Doudna calls "an icon in an age of iconoclasm." Her living arrangement with Hammett, hardly mentioned in the 1940s and 1950s, now becomes, in the more tolerant 1970s, an emblematic romantic saga of two difficult human beings finding a basis on which they can coexist comfortably most of the time (and uncomfortably a certain amount of the time). The retelling, embellishing, and augmenting of sections of the memoirs totally dominate the later interviews, along with such evidence of Hellman's continuing "newsworthiness" as her helping to found the Committee for Public Justice in 1971, her posing for a fur coat advertisement in 1976, and her 1980 suit against Mary McCarthy. Her status as a "media star" is confirmed by the fact that several of these late interviews were originally conducted on television (they are published here for the first time) by the likes of Bill Moyers, Dan Rather, and Marilyn Berger. During this period, Hellman was also interviewed by Dick Cavett; that tape was, unfortunately, unavailable for transcription.

Typically, Moyers' 1974 interview begins with Hellman elaborating on her trip to the front with the Russian army in 1945 and on her friendships with Hemingway and Dorothy Parker, continues with discussions of such personal matters as her temper, her fear of confrontation, the bases of her relationship with Hammett, and her suspicion of "the words of love," and concerns itself as well with such familiar subjects as the McCarthy era, women's liberation, and why Hellman stopped writing plays. Only very briefly does he ask her anything about the plays themselves. Again, Moyers' title—"Lillian Hellman: The Great Playwright Candidly Reflects on a Long, Rich Life"—suggests his focus, as do the titles of other late interviews: "Lillian Hellman on Lillian Hellman" and "Lillian Hellman: She Never Turns down an Adventure."

Moyers' piece also demonstrates what is gained in these later interviews at the expense of concern with Hellman as playwright—they become far more personal. Perhaps by telling so much about herself and her life in the memoirs, Hellman seemed to interviewers to be tacitly agreeing to be questioned on a much more intimate level. The ultimate extreme of this is reached in Marilyn Berger's fascinating and highly revealing five-part Public Television interview in which Hellman as a playwright never comes up as a topic. What we get instead are in-depth portraits of the woman behind the plays. Here or elsewhere in the later interviews, Hellman speaks of her feelings about growing up as a Jew in the South, of her years in therapy, of her fears, of her habit of talking out loud to an alter-ego figure named "Nursie," of her abortions and ambivalent feelings about never having had children, and of her anger and frustration in the face of steadily advancing and debilitating old age. We are a long way here from the superficiality of Hellman's opinions on the American theatre.

But, in another sense, we are not very far at all; because this division of the interviews into three stages is at best a convenient means of describing them and at worst misleading. Through all three stages, the same toughness and direct honesty which are Lillian Hellman's hallmarks dominate. Above all, these conversations confirm Jane Fonda's sense of Hellman as "very complex and very full of the most miraculous kind of contradictions." As many times as she has a pointed and ready reply to a question, almost as often she says she doesn't know. As tough and as forthright as she frequently appears, she can become equally as sentimental, especially when speaking of her relationship with Hammett. As oblivious as she sometimes seems of her femininity, there are ample glimpses as well of the woman Fonda calls "flirtatious and feminine and sensual." The same person whose life experiences certainly made her the epitome of worldly sophistication admits sheepishly that it never occurred to her that her name would be used in the film version of *Julia*. If her favoring of Beckett over other contemporary dramatists is not surprising, surely her praise of Thomas Pynchon in a 1981 interview is unexpected.

At least two interviewers, upon meeting Hellman for the first time, comment on how she is shorter than they had anticipated—as if someone who has the reputation of being so formidable must be large of stature. This is but one of the more superficial surprises she held for those who engaged her in conversation. Through the half-century covered in this collection she never ceases to be provocative; her observations more often than not seem on target; and, above all, she exhibits the strong moral sense and commitment which underlay both her life and creative work. For that reason, the gradual shift in these interviews from concern with Hellman's works to a focus on her life and opinions is actually not an alteration at all. Hellman's writings and her life were based on the same qualities, qualities abundantly evident in all these interviews. Whether she is talking about *The Little Foxes* or her childhood in New Orleans, about *The Children's Hour* or her appearance before the Un-American Activities Committee, about *Watch on the Rhine* or her famous secret mission on behalf of her childhood friend Julia, the characteristics on display are the same—loyalty, honesty, dislike of sham and pretension, a search for the truth, an outrage at those who refuse to stand up for what they believe. The title of the final interview in this collection—and surely one of the last she gave—is appropriate: "Lillian Hellman as Herself." From first to last, she was herself; and if this volume can give some glimpses into that self, it has succeeded.

As with the other books in the Literary Conversations series, the interviews are reprinted uncut, except where reprint rights could only be secured if a minor cut was made (that instance is indicated in the headnote). In newspaper interviews, paragraph breaks have been omitted. In all texts, titles of plays have been regularized into italics. Where transcriptions have been provided, they have not been edited; where transcriptions have been prepared especially for this collection, they have been rendered as faithfully as possible and have only been edited for the sake of intelligibility. The result is that there is a certain amount of repetition; inevitably, Hellman was asked the same questions in several interviews, and she just as inevitably told and retold the same stories to different interviewers. But no two interviews are exactly alike; each one adds significantly to the portrait of this remarkable and intriguing artist. Hellman's plays have been unduly neglected by scholars and critics; her life has dominated the discussion for the past two decades. Her place in modern American literary history has yet to be satisfactorily explored and defined. It is hoped that this volume by providing a generous sampling of her conversation, will help stimulate that exploration.

For significant assistance in preparing this collection, I wish to thank Ruth M. Alvarez, who helped locate and photocopy many of the interviews, prepared all the original transcriptions, and compiled the index. Beatriz Dailey typed the final drafts of several transcriptions. William Abrahams helped smooth out the transcriptions and provided authoritative information about Hellman's life. Mark W. Estrin, Traugott Lawler, George Monteiro, and Kenneth D. Craven helped me identify and get copies of pieces for the volume. I am also grateful to the various interviewers, editors, publishers, and agents who granted me permission to use material over which they have jurisdiction.

This book is for my friends Sam and Marilyn Schoenbaum, who thoughtfully and generously gave me the opportunity to have my own memorable conversation with Lillian Hellman.

JRB
November 1985

Chronology

1905   Lillian Florence Hellman born in New Orleans on 20 June, only child of Julia Newhouse and Max Bernard Hellman.

1911   Hellmans move to New York City; but LH still spends six months of each year in New Orleans and attends schools in both cities.

1922–24   LH attends New York University, but leaves before her senior year.

1925   LH works as a manuscript reader for New York publisher Horace Liveright. On 31 December, she marries Arthur Kober, press agent for producer Jed Harris and later a successful playwright *(Having Wonderful Time)* and screenwriter.

1926–29   LH lives in Paris for the first four months of 1926 and publishes two short stories in *The Paris Comet,* a magazine edited by Kober. After she returns to New York, she reads play scripts for producers Harry Moses, Leo Bulgakov, and Anne Nichols, writes book reviews for the *New York Herald Tribune,* and takes classes at Columbia University. In the spring of 1929, she spends four months doing publicity for the Cukor-Kondolph stock company in Rochester, NY. In the summer of 1929, she travels alone in Europe, spending most of her time in Germany.

1930–31   In the fall of 1930, LH and Kober move to Hollywood, where Kober works as a scriptwriter for Paramount and LH as a manuscript reader for Metro-Goldwyn-Mayer. In

Hollywood in November 1930, she meets Dashiell Hammett.

1932–34   LH moves back to New York in March 1931. She
            divorces Arthur Kober, and she and Hammett live at the
            Sutton Hotel, managed by Nathanael West. Hammett
            writes *The Thin Man,* basing Nora Charles on LH. LH
            publishes two "short-short" stories in *The American
            Spectator* ("I Call Her Mama Now," September 1933;
            "Perberty in Los Angeles," January 1934) and collabo-
            rates with Louis Kronenberger on a play, *Dear Queen*
            (copyrighted December 30, 1932, but never produced).
            LH meets Dorothy Parker and becomes reacquainted
            with producer Herman Shumlin; in the fall of 1933, she
            takes a job as a play reader for Shumlin. In January
            1934, *The Thin Man* is published by Alfred A. Knopf,
            with the dedication "To Lillian." On 20 November 1934,
            The Children's Hour opens at the Maxine Elliott Theatre
            and runs for 691 performances.

1935   LH returns to Hollywood as a screenwriter for Metro-
            Goldwyn-Mayer at $2,500 a week. Julia Newhouse
            Hellman dies. *Dark Angel,* adapted for the screen by LH
            from a novel by Guy Bolton, opens in September.

1936   In March, LH's sanitized screen adaptation of *The Chil-
            dren's Hour, These Three,* opens. She moves back to
            New York in the spring. In November, *The Children's
            Hour* is performed privately at London's Gate Theatre,
            having been banned from public performance by the
            Lord Chamberlain. Her second play, *Days to Come,*
            opens on 15 December at the Vanderbilt Theatre and
            closes after only seven performances.

1937   LH returns to Hollywood in February to work on a film
            adaptation of Sidney Kingsley's *Dead End,* which opens
            in August. While in Hollywood, she joins with John Dos
            Passos, Archibald MacLeish, and Ernest Hemingway to

form Contemporary Historians, Inc., and produces *The Spanish Earth,* a documentary about the Spanish Civil War by Joris Ivens. In late August, she sails for Europe with Dorothy Parker and her husband, Alan Campbell. After spending time in Paris with, among others, Hemingway and Gerald and Sara Murphy, she leaves, ostensibly for Moscow to attend a theatre festival. On the way, she secretly stops in Berlin and delivers $50,000 which she has smuggled across the border to her childhood friend "Julia" who is working for the anti-fascist underground. After attending the theatre festival in Moscow, she returns to Paris; and in October, she goes to Spain to observe the Civil War at firsthand. In November, she returns to New York.

1938–39   During 1938, LH works on ideas for two plays, one later to become *Watch on the Rhine* and the other *The Little Foxes. The Little Foxes* opens on 15 February 1939 at the National Theatre and runs for 410 performances. In May 1939, LH buys a 130-acre farm in Pleasantville, Westchester County, NY, which she calls "Hardscrabble Farm."

1940–41   LH covers the Republican convention in Philadelphia in June 1940 for *PM,* a New York newspaper. Her film adaptation of *The Little Foxes* opens in August 1941. *Watch on the Rhine* opens on 1 April 1941, at the Martin Beck Theatre and runs for 378 performances; and it wins for LH the New York Drama Critics' Circle Award as the best American play of the year. In June 1941, she is awarded an honorary M.A. degree by Tufts University. She moves into a house at 5 East 83rd Street in New York and retains the Pleasantville farm as well.

1942   On 25 January, *Watch on the Rhine* is given a special "command performance" at Washington's National Theatre in connection with Franklin D. Roosevelt's Diamond Jubilee Birthday Celebration, with F.D.R. in attendance.

Watch on the Rhine opens in London in April, directed by Emlyn Williams; and *The Little Foxes* receives its first stage production in London in October. In the spring, Random House publishes LH's first *Four Plays,* with an introduction by the author. In the summer, although 48 years old, Hammett enlists in the army as a private and is stationed at Fort Monmouth, N.J. After a plan to collaborate with director William Wyler on a documentary film about the war in Russia falls through, LH agrees to work with Lewis Milestone on a semidocumentary.

1943   LH buys a New York townhouse at 63 East 82nd Street. Hammett's film version of *Watch on the Rhine* opens in August and is selected as the best movie of the year by the New York Film Critics, who also name Paul Lukas as best actor (he later wins the Academy Award for his performance). A highly emasculated version of LH's screen collaboration with Milestone, *North Star,* opens in October; and she is so angry that she buys back her contract with Samuel Goldwyn for $30,000.

1944–45   *The Searching Wind* opens on 12 April 1944 at the Fulton Theatre and runs for 326 performances. In September, LH leaves for Russia, via Fairbanks, Alaska, on a cultural mission. In Moscow, she spends time with Sergei Eisenstein and attends rehearsals of Russian productions of *The Little Foxes* and *Watch on the Rhine.* In late December 1944 and early 1945, she spends two weeks at the front with the Russian army but refuses their general's invitation to accompany them into Warsaw and Berlin, returning to New York in February 1945.

1946–48   LH is inducted into the National Institute of Arts and Letters in May 1946. Her film adaptation of *The Searching Wind* opens in June 1946. *Another Part of the Forest* opens at the Fulton Theatre on 20 November 1946 and runs for 182 performances, with LH directing her own play for the first time. In August 1947, she participates in a UNESCO conference in Paris. A film version of *Another Part of the Forest,* adapted by Vladimir Posner, opens in May 1948. She teaches a one-week writing course in Indiana University's Writer's Conference in the summer of 1948; and in the fall, she supports Henry Wallace's Progressive Party candidacy for President. In October, she flies to Europe, where she interviews Marshall Tito in Belgrade, visits the vice-premier of Czechoslovakia in Prague, and in Paris sees a performance of Emmanuel Roblès' play *Montserrat,* which she decides to adapt for the Broadway stage. Max Bernard Hellman dies.

1949–50   In the spring of 1949, LH, along with Albert Einstein, Arthur Miller, Norman Mailer, Dorothy Parker, and others, attends the Cultural and Scientific Conference for World Peace, sponsored by the National Council of the Arts, Sciences and Professions, and is labeled pro-Communist by the American press. Her adaptation of *Montserrat* opens at the Fulton Theatre on 29 October 1949 and runs for 65 performances, directed by LH. *Regina,* an opera by Marc Blitzstein based on *The Little Foxes,* opens at the Forty-Sixth Street Theatre on 31 October 1949 and runs for 56 performances. In December 1950, *The Children's Hour,* still banned from the public stage in England, receives another private production in London, at New Boltons, a club theatre.

1951   *The Autumn Garden* opens on 7 March at the Coronet Theatre and runs for 101 performances. In April, Federal Judge Sylvester Ryan sentences Hammett to six months in jail for refusing to name persons who had contributed to the bail-bond fund of the Civil Rights Congress, thought to be a pro-Communist organization; he is released in December.

1952   On 21 May, LH testifies before the House Un-American Activities Committee after having written the committee, in response to their subpoena, that she would talk about her own views and activities but would refuse to speak about other people. She acts accordingly during her appearance, and this action enforces her black-listing in Hollywood, which had begun in 1948. Dunned by the Internal Revenue Service for back taxes, she is forced to sell Hardscrabble Farm in the spring. On 18 December, a revival of *The Children's Hour,* directed by LH who also made minor revisions in the script, opens at the Coronet Theatre and runs for 189 performances.

1953–54   On 26 March 1953, Hammett testifies before Senator Joseph McCarthy's Committee on Government Operations, denies his involvement in espionage or sabotage, and takes the Fifth Amendment in response to other questions. During the summer of 1953, LH goes to Rome to work on a movie for Alexander Korda at one-fifth of her preblacklisting salary; but she is forced to abandon that project when Korda has financial problems. Upon her return to the United States, money is so scarce that, for a brief time, she works at a department store under an assumed name. *The Children's Hour* receives its first stage production in Chicago in November 1953, after having been banned for nineteen years. LH's aunt dies and leaves her a modest inheritance.

1955   LH's edition of *The Selected Letters of Anton Chekhov* is published by Farrar, Straus and Cudahy. She buys a house on Martha's Vineyard. Her adaptation of Anouilh's *L'Alouette, The Lark,* opens on 17 November at the Longacre Theatre and runs for 229 performances.

1956–59   *The Children's Hour* is given another private production at London's Arts Theatre Club in October 1956. *Candide,* with book by LH, score by Leonard Bernstein, and lyrics by Richard Wilbur, John Latouche, and Dorothy Parker, opens on 1 December 1956 at the Martin Beck Theatre and runs for 73 performances. Late in 1957, LH forms a producing partnership with Lester Osterman, Jr., gives

Saul Bellow an advance on *The Last Analysis,* acquires rights to Camus' adaptation of Dostoevsky's *The Possessed,* and options a new play by Roger Vailland; but no plays are ever produced by the partnership.

1960   *Toys in the Attic* opens at the Hudson Theatre on 25 February and runs for 556 performances. In May, it wins the New York Drama Critics' Circle Award as best American play of the year. In the same month, LH is elected a fellow of the American Academy of Arts and Sciences. Random House publishes *Six Plays* by LH in a Modern Library edition. LH goes to London to supervise a production of *Toys in the Attic,* which opens in November.

1961   Dashiell Hammett dies on 10 January. LH is a Visiting Lecturer for the spring term at Harvard. In May, she is named one of six recipients of achievement awards from the Women's Division of the Albert Einstein College of Medicine of Yeshiva University; and in June, she is awarded the Brandeis University Creative Arts Award and receives an honorary Litt.D. from Wheaton College (Norton, MA).

1962   The second film version of *The Children's Hour* (adapted by John Michael Hayes) opens in February; it is released in England under the title *The Loudest Whisper.* Also in February, LH is elected vice-president of the National Institute of Arts and Letters. In the summer, she builds and moves into a new house on Martha's Vineyard. In December, *The Little Foxes* opens in Paris, adapted into French by Simone Signoret who plays Regina in the production.

1963   *My Mother, My Father and Me,* adapted for the stage by LH from Burt Blechman's novel *How Much?,* opens on 23 March at the Plymouth Theatre and runs for only 17 performances. In May, LH is inducted as a member of the

American Academy of Arts and Letters; and in June, she
is awarded an honorary Litt.D. by Douglass College of
Rutgers University. The film version of *Toys in the Attic*
(adapted by James Poe) opens in the summer, and LH
attends the Edinburgh Festival and concurrent sessions of
the International Drama Conference. In August, she
covers the Civil Rights March on Washington.

1964–65   LH goes to Israel to cover Pope Paul's visit. In May 1964,
she receives the Gold Medal for Drama from the National
Institute for Arts and Letters; and in June 1965, she is
awarded an honorary Doctor of Humane Letters degree
by Brandeis University.

1966–67   In February 1966, LH teaches an intensive one-week
Freshman Seminar on literature and writing at Yale; and
in the same month, *The Chase,* her screen adaptation of
Horton Foote's novel, opens. Her edition of Hammett's
fiction, *The Big Knockover* (published in England as *The
Dashiell Hammett Story Omnibus*), is published, with an
introduction by LH. In the fall of 1966, she is awarded an
honorary Doctor of Fine Arts degree by Mt. Holyoke
College. In October 1966, she goes to Moscow, on to
London and Paris in April 1967, Budapest, and back to
Moscow in May 1967, to attend the Fourth National
Congress of the Union of Writers. She returns to the
United States in May, and Dorothy Parker dies on 7 June
1967, naming LH her executrix. In October, she visits
Moscow, London, and Paris. On 26 October 1967, a
revival of *The Little Foxes,* directed by Mike Nichols,
opens at Lincoln Center's Vivian Beaumont Theatre and
runs for 100 performances.

1968   During the spring, LH teaches at both Harvard and M.I.T.
In April, she receives the first Award of Distinction from
Jackson College of Tufts University. In December, she
joins "100 Notables" as participants in a seminar at

Princeton on "The United States, Its Problems, Impact and Image in the World."

1969   *An Unfinished Woman,* a book of memoirs, is published on 26 June.

1970–71   On 4 March 1970, LH is awarded the National Book Award for *An Unfinished Woman.* She sells her house on 82nd Street and moves into a Park Avenue apartment in the spring of 1970. In November, she helps organize and serves on the executive council of the Committee for Public Justice, "an organization of private citizens concerned that the nation has entered . . . a 'period of political repression.' " She teaches one-month seminars at both M.I.T. and the University of California-Berkeley in the spring of 1971.

1972   LH's *Collected Plays* is published by Little, Brown, containing texts of her eight original plays and four adaptations, with LH's revisions and emendations. In the fall, she is appointed Distinguished Professor of Romance Languages at the City University of New York's Hunter College.

1973   On 25 September, *Pentimento,* another volume of memoirs, is published. LH is named to the Theater Hall of Fame in November. In December, she is awarded the first Women of the Year Award by the New York University Alumnae Club.

1974   LH receives honorary degrees from Smith, Yale, and New York University.

1975   LH is appointed to the editorial board of the *American Scholar.* In April, she is named one of *Ladies Home Journal*'s Women of the Year; and in November, she is honored at a celebration at the Circle in the Square to benefit the Committee for Public Justice.

1976   On 26 April, *Scoundrel Time,* the third of LH's memoirs,
            is published. In May, she is awarded an honorary Doctor
            of Letters degree by Columbia. She receives the Edward
            MacDowell Medal in August; and in October, the Paul
            Robeson Award of Actors' Equity.

1977   In October, *Julia,* a film based on one of the chapters in
            Pentimento, opens; and in November, LH wins the Lord
            and Taylor Rose Award, given annually to "an outstand-
            ing individual whose creative mind has brought new
            beauty and deeper understanding into our lives."

1978–81   In April 1978, LH participates in a conference at Rutgers
            University on "Women and the Arts in the 1920's in Paris
            and New York." A one-volume collection of LH's three
            books of memoirs is published on 24 May 1979, as
            Three, with an introduction by Richard Poirier. In Febru-
            ary 1980, LH files a defamation suit against Mary
            McCarthy and Dick Cavett for remarks McCarthy made
            about her on Cavett's TV show. *Maybe: A Story* is
            published on 24 May 1980. On 7 May 1981, after a sold-
            out run in Washington, a revival of *The Little Foxes,*
            starring Elizabeth Taylor, opens at the Martin Beck The-
            atre and runs for 126 performances. It then goes on to
            very successful engagements in Los Angeles and London.

1982–83   LH is seriously ill and is in and out of hospitals. She
            spends time working with Peter Feibleman on *Eating
            Together: Recollections & Recipes,* which is not published
            until 13 November 1984.

1984   LH dies at Martha's Vineyard Hospital on 30 June.

Conversations with Lillian Hellman

An Adult's Hour
Is Miss Hellman's Next Effort

Lucius Beebe/1936

From the *New York Herald Tribune,* 13 December 1936,
sec. 7, 2.

It is not getting an idea for a play that drives playwrights mad so
much as the business of having the idea still recognizable, even to its
author, at the completion of the script, according to Lillian Hellman,
whose first Broadway show since *The Children's Hour* will come to
town Tuesday evening. It is called *Days to Come,* and opens at the
Vanderbilt, and Miss Hellman is concerned to see if any of the ideas
are visible in its texture that she intended should be when she
undertook writing it several years since. In Miss Hellman's mind *Days
to Come* antedated *The Children's Hour* by a substantial period.

"You have no notion of how hard it is to retain an editorial point of
view or an idea that you want to put across all through the business
of writing a play," Miss Hellman says. "You may have a clearly
defined point of view and something, as we say with a titter, vital on
your mind when you sit down to those nice new pencils and that nice
fresh copy paper. But when you get all through and write 'curtain' for
the last time, only faintly penciling in cries of 'author, author' in a
moment of unjustified optimism, where are those fine ideas? Like
pale hands above the Shalimar; like Villon's 'nieges d'antan,' like last
week's royalty check—they just aren't there. Something happens to
them, and when the lights go on you had better send for Hercule
Poirot. Nobody but a competent detective can find them."

Miss Hellman was in her flat in Seventy-fifth Street, just off Fifth
Avenue, petting a sort of buffalo-robe color French poodle the size of
a fortnight calf. The dog is stenciled in curious arabesques and
clipped like an old box hedge. It answers to the slightly tacky name of
Jummy, having been named originally Jumbo by Mrs. Sherman

Hoyt, who raised it on the slender provocation that one of its brothers had been bought by Billy Rose. You can see at a glance that this being in the theater has its complex side.

There were other dogs on the premises—two lovely china ones on either side of the mantle, also a china porcelain horse, several cut glass and silver decanters; tall windows with dark blue hangings, a number of books along the wall and a copy of the *New Republic,* like Cataline in the senate, resting quite alone on a long blue sofa.

"And if you can't transfer your ideas into lines and action on the stage, what excuse is there writing for the legitimate theater?" Miss Hellman asked, presumably rhetorically. "One doesn't use the speaking stage any more as a medium of pure amusement or as a scene for spectacle. The films are vastly superior in both those fields. Technically the theater hasn't a ghost of a show against the screen any more than it has as a source of revenue, but it has one great warrant for its being, one excuse for its continued existence—the theater can survive as a place for the expression and exchange of ideas.

"You can say what you like in the theater within any reasonable bounds. You have a liberty of speech and editorial expression you can't find in any other dramatic medium. And you can present an idea for the consideration of intelligent audiences, which, of course, is completely outside the gaudiest opium dreams of possibility in Hollywood. They wouldn't know an idea if they saw it on the Coast, and if by any chance they should recognize it the film people would be frightened right out of their suede shoes. I'm not patronizing in my attitude toward the films, just realistic. And I say again that the presentation of something besides mere entertainment and spectacle is the great function of the legitimate theater of the world today."

It was tea time, and Miss Hellman was sipping a pale sherry. She wore a gray dress fastened up the front with a zipper but open at the throat, with a black silk scarf criscrossed in front like a soldier's and secured with a crystal clasp. She had a slender gold wrist watch and black pumps.

"What sort of a play is *Days to Come?*" she continued. "Well, it's about life in a small Ohio town, say about 5,000 people, where the dominant industry is a brush factory, the owners of which are the first family of the community. They're reasonably well off folk who have grown up with the town and everybody knows everybody else. There's never been any hard feeling between the owners and the workers, you see, until hard times came along, and there is a strike. It's the family I'm interested in principally; the strike and social manifestations are just backgrounds. It's a story of innocent people on both sides who are drawn into conflict and events far beyond their comprehension. It's the saga of a man who started something he cannot stop, a parallel among adults to what I did with children in *The Children's Hour*."

The urge to write *Days to Come* has been on Miss Hellman for five or six years, but when she really got around to writing it she was only about eight months at the job itself. The setting is a small university town a few miles outside of Cleveland, where she passed a few days last year during an "atmosphere" tour of small Ohio communities which lasted three or four weeks. As a matter of fact, she says, she didn't get a great deal she hadn't known before out of her voyage of discovery between Cleveland and Cincinnati, but it served as a sort of sop to her professional conscience to visit the scene she was writing of, just to see what the people looked like and how they spoke.

Miss Hellman's services and loyalties are divided about fifty-fifty between New York and Hollywood, the latter of which localities she unhesitatingly says gives her the gripes. However, according to her contract with Sam Goldwyn, she must pass sufficient time on the Coast to complete two original film scripts a year, and she looks forward to her impending safari among the curiosae of Sunset Boulevard with no bright anticipation.

"Except," she says, "the place isn't as bad if you're working there. Of course, it's unbearable to any civilized person as a mere visitor, but with something to do it's no worse than being in jail and working all day in the jute mill. It keeps your mind off things.

"It still stands as the most preposterous civilization of all time, however, and in a way that's fascinating. I mean, things like the elaborate and pretentious dinner parties the film people give. You find yourself twelve at table with twelve footmen and two major domos, and then food that you'd throw right back at the counterman in a dairy lunch is set before you with fancy gestures and on gold plate. I've had tired old chicken put in front of me by powdered flunkies out there that they wouldn't serve at a public lunch for 5,000 people in New York.

"Was *Days Without End* designed with an eye to the films? By no means. If it were a howling Broadway success, they might poke at it tentatively on that basis alone; but if it is just a moderate success, they will avoid it like the plague."

Stage Asides: Miss Hellman Talks of Her Latest Play, *The Little Foxes*

Lucius Beebe/1939

From the *New York Herald Tribune*, 12 March 1939, sec. 6, 1, 2.

More than anything else, Miss Lillian Hellman is anxious to disperse, subdue and, in a word, totally abate the belief that she is a misanthrope or inclines to view the human comedy with anything more than the average leaven of tolerant cynicism. Her first Broadway success, *The Children's Hour,* centered about the ruin and devastation caused by as offensive a little brat as the theater had seen in decades, with various low instincts and character deficiencies distributed among the rest of the cast, while her current sell-out, called *The Little Foxes,* concerns itself with the evils of avarice and exploitation in a Southern family, neither the public policy nor the private lives of which serve as any paradigm of morality.

It is from this brace of not altogether cheery 'scripts that the rumor springs that Miss Hellman thinks something less than highly of the human race.

"I assure you, however, that both *The Children's Hour* and *The Little Foxes* were designed as dramas of morality first and last and that any one who reads too much cynicism into them is being misled," Miss Hellman says. "In the particular case of *The Little Foxes* I wanted especially to write about people's beginnings, to deal with the material which in most play construction is antecedent to the action, to show how characters more frequently shown in the maturity of their careers get that way. I like to think there is a moral in the play because I believe there is a certain amount of morality, of propaganda if you prefer, but propaganda in the proper use of the word, in all good writing, and I like to imagine my plays are good writing. That is, of course, open to debate.

"It seemed to me, in *The Little Foxes* an essay in dramatic technique as well as an interesting business to depict a family just as it was on the way to the achievements which were to bring it wealth or failure, fame or obliquy. At the final curtain the Hubbards are just starting to get on in the world in a big way, but their various futures, individually and collectively, I like to think I leave to the imagination of the audience. I meant to be neither misanthropic nor cynical, merely truthful and realistic."

Certainly, there is very little about Miss Hellman's person to suggest a cynical philosophy. She is quartered this year in the stately precincts of the Plaza just a floor above Clara Bell Walsh and her world is apparently as well ordered and tranquil as the worlds of her dramatic fashioning are filled with tumult and disaster. Miss Hellman is an early riser, usually along 8 o'clock, and she received the reporter one morning last week at an hour when most professional folk are still snoozing prettily between their sheets. She wore a greenish blue tweed skirt and a bold plaid jacket to match and was absorbing, at the moment, a dish of tea, which she vastly prefers in the morning.

"The selection of the South as a setting for *The Little Foxes* was purely incidental and fortuitous," she says in reply to people who want to read into the play a slur on her native section. "I merely wanted, in essence, to say: 'Here I am representing for you the sort of person who ruins the world for us.'

"That it was set in the milling district of the South stems from the circumstance that I wanted to set the time scheme of the play at about the turn of the century and that it was in the cotton states that these years witnessed the sort of exploitation I wanted to write about. If the time of the action had been in the 1860's the scene would have been laid in Lawrence or Lowell in Massachusetts or Manchester, N.H. A few years later it would have been in the industrial regions of Ohio or Indiana. I merely chose the South because it fitted the period I wanted for dramatic purposes and because it is a part of the world whose atmosphere I personally am familiar with as a Southerner. I also wanted a certain naive or innocent quality in some of my characters which I could find in the South but which would have been quite out of place in any other American setting."

The casting of Miss Tallulah Bankhead and the success she achieved in the role of Regina Giddens Miss Hellman credits entirely to Herman Shumlin, although she is willing to admit that after she first saw Miss Bankhead in rehearsal she was sold on her for the part.

"I'm not good at casting," Miss Hellman says. "If I've known the actor in question before, I invariably associate them with some previous part or else with their proper offstage selves and can't for the life of me visualize them in anything new and untried." Miss Bankhead's family and that of Miss Hellman's mother, incidentally, originally lived in the same county.

Miss Hellman is returning to the coast shortly for a fortnight, but doesn't expect to do any writing at this time. She has, in fact, no screen script in view, but is scheduled for a series of conferences with Samuel Goldwyn since the long-distance telephone has been found unsatisfactory as a medium for discussion of the renewal of her Hollywood contract. For her next legitimate play, however, she is anxious to undertake an adaptation of Zola's *Germinal* (1885), a drama about a coal strike in northern France, although she is waiting for a translation to be prepared for her, since the technical terminology used in the text is beyond the idiom of ordinary literary French.

"*Germinal,* when, if and as I get around to it, will be a much more abruptly social play than anything I have done," says she. "I think it is the most powerful social novel I know of.

"Do I believe that all literature must have social or economic implications? No, I don't, but I do feel that all good writing must, either implicitly or explicitly, be propaganda for something. Propaganda, of course, has come to be a much corrupted word. Just the way 'vice' has come to mean almost exclusively sexual vice, so propaganda has come to mean almost exclusively economic or political propaganda. It really has much broader implications than that, and unless you are a pathological escapist there must be some sort of propaganda in everything you write.

"Some sort of truth, profound or trivial, but the truth must be the main objective of any one who seeks a form of literary expression, excepting of course the pure music of lyrical poetry and a few allied forms. If a person doesn't want to involve himself with the truth he has no business trying to write at all."

Only one minor irritation arises from Miss Hellman's success as the one of the two most talked-of lady playwrights of the momentary

Broadway stage and that is comparison with Clare Boothe, author of
Kiss the Boys Goodbye, and a comparison which she feels must be
as distasteful to Miss Boothe as to herself.

"Miss Boothe and I don't write about the same things," she says.
"We don't write the same way and we aren't interested in the same
ends. There is no possible basis for comparison except that we are
women dramatists with successes to our credit. I'm sure that com-
parisons are as odious to Miss Boothe as they seem silly to me. They
are simply products of the facile imaginations of reviewers and
reporters who will go to any length to achieve an easy and meaningless generality."

Of Lillian Hellman: Being a Conversation with the Author of *Watch on the Rhine*

Robert Van Gelder/1941

From the *New York Times*, 20 April 1941, sec. 9, 1, 3. Copyright © 1941 by The New York Times Company. Reprinted by permission.

Lillian Hellman is small, looks as though she didn't eat much, drinks strong coffee, New Orleans style. She does not talk easily about herself. "I had a rather bad experience with an interviewer once. Perhaps I should have warned you that I'm difficult—that I can't think good quotes." She answers questions with the air of one who wants to do her best, and to be truthful. But she seems unable to clear her imagination of how rubbishy her words may look when they have been milled through the mind and the typewriter of some one else.

Perhaps she relieves this tension by frequently bringing in the names of other people. "Dotty Parker gave me the name for *The Little Foxes*." "Did you know that Louis Kronenberger is writing a book? Yes, on the eighteenth century. He writes so well of the eighteenth century. Herman Shumlin threatened to stop rehearsals unless I'd put a title on the play. When Dick Maney heard the title he started singing the song. He knows all the words. I'm told that people of his generation learned the song in school. They dropped it during the last war, of course."

The search for a title went on until the play was nearly ready to open. *Watch on the Rhine* is a compromise. Miss Hellman wanted to use the German phrase. Mr. Shumlin, who has had trouble before with one of her titles—*The Children's Hour,* which a lot of people connected with Longfellow rather than lesbianism—demanded at the very least an English rendering. "He said that so many people would be afraid they were mispronouncing the German that they would hesitate either to order tickets or talk about the play after they had seen it." On an end table was a copy of the poems and sermons of

11

John Donne. "Yes, I was hunting through it for something better. No luck. Donne has supplied a lot of titles, you know. Hemingway isn't the only one to use him. I've read Donne since he came back into fashion in the Nineteen Twenties."

The two rooms and kitchenette on the third floor of the Henry Clews house—one of New York's most stately mansions—in spite of the massive, attractive, rented furnishings, seemed swept very bare as though a new tenant would be along any minute, and the trunks were packed. What is it like to write a play that in all likelihood, judging on your past performance, will bring you in a couple of hundred thousand dollars? Eager hands out for the script, expectancy everywhere, people sending you handwritten advertisements on penny postcards: "Dear Miss Hellman: I hear great things about the new play. Do you want to buy a mink coat? Sam." No one knows yet who Sam is. Sam will appear in due time—after the reviews are published. The reviews kicked one of Miss Hellman's plays, *Days to Come,* right out of the theatre. The other two, *The Children's Hour* and *The Little Foxes,* were smash hits.

"The evolution of *Watch on the Rhine,*" said Miss Hellman, "is quite involved and, I'm afraid, not very interesting. When I was working on *The Little Foxes* I hit on the idea—well, there's a small, Midwestern American town, average or perhaps a little more isolated than average, and into that town Europe walks in the form of a titled couple—a pair of titled Europeans—pausing on their way to the West Coast. I was quite excited, thought of shelving the foxes to work on it. But when I did get to it I couldn't get it moving. It started all right—and then stuck.

"Later I had another idea. What would be the reactions of some sensitive people who had spent much of their lives starving in Europe and found themselves as house guests in the home of some very wealthy Americans? What would they make out of all the furious rushing around, the sleeping tablets taken when there is no time to sleep them off, the wonderful dinners ordered and never eaten, and so on and so on? The contrasts of the two worlds, the ways of life.

"That play didn't work, either. I kept worrying at it, and the earlier people, the titled couple, returned continually. It would take all afternoon and probably a lot of tomorrow to trail all the steps that made those two plays into *Watch on the Rhine.* The titled couple are still in, but as minor characters. The Americans are nice people, and so on. It all is changed, but the new play grew out of the other two."

When a play is complete and the reviewers and the public have made their decision upon it, Miss Hellman usually roams around for a while, hunting a new idea. She writes for the movies—working for Samuel Goldwyn—but never stays very long in Hollywood. In Westchester she owns a big house and 130 acres. Returning there with an idea, she gathers together a collection of books and starts to read, making copious notes.

"I made digests of twenty-five books before I started writing *Watch on the Rhine*. Political argument, memoirs, recent German history. My notebooks for the play run to well over 100,000 words and, do you know, I used material from the notes for only two speeches. Sometimes I wonder—you can't help wondering—if there is any sense in all that research. But I seem to have to do it before I can be sure that I know what I'm talking about.

"Also, the reading helps keep my mind on the job that I've chosen; keeps, I suppose you might put it, the aim in view, the points to be made, straightens out kinks, not directly but indirectly. I guess that if you played bridge or pinochle when you were trying to think out a play, after a while the cards would mean more than the play; or if you just went on living ordinarily, hanging around with your friends, the play would be pushed from your mind.

"By giving so much time to reading the object of the search stays always with me. My friends come to stay and amuse themselves any way they want to—most of them read. We meet at meals. When I write I still leave myself plenty of time around the meal hours; work three hours or so in the morning, two or three hours in the afternoon, and start again at 10 and work until 1 or 2 in the morning. Yes, I rewrite a lot—nine complete drafts on one play, four or five on the others. I've tried all the methods—making a very careful plan before starting is one. I didn't stick to it. Then another time I just started writing, with no plan, simply with something to say, and let it run. Both plays kept me at work more than a year, so it doesn't seem to matter how I go about it.

"Once I decided that by working very slowly in longhand I might be able to make each sentence count and save in the rewriting time the time that I'd spend brooding and choosing and selecting the exact right word, the precise and revelatory action. I fitted myself all out for this effort, planning to write in bed as Proust did, and Mark Twain, complete with drawing board and pencils and fountain pens. I had to give it up. Writing in bed was much too uncomfortable, and my hand went much too slowly. I go wrong a lot on the typewriter, but it is the best way for me."

Born in New Orleans, Miss Hellman was brought North when a very small child, but for the first sixteen years of her life spent about six months each year visiting in the South. She was graduated from New York University in 1925, immediately pouncing upon a job with Boni-Liveright, "a very menial position—a little advertising work, a little publicity and a lot of manuscript reading."

This was in the days when Liveright had the great list—perhaps the greatest list of authors that any American publisher had assembled, Hemingway, Anderson, Dreiser, O'Neill among them—"but I didn't get their books; I got the stuff that no one else wanted to read." She married Arthur Kober (marriage dissolved some years later) and went with him to Hollywood. It was a change of skies only. "I read manuscripts for motion-picture companies." Back in New York she read play-scripts for Anne Nichols and then for Leo Bulgakov and Harry Moses. "I found one good thing, *Grand Hotel*. My husband tried to raise money with which to put it on, but couldn't get any one interested. Every once in a while I'd quit reading, and if I had any money I'd go to Europe. I never could stay long, because there never was much money. Then I'd come back here and try writing; my short stories didn't sell. So back to reading and book reviewing, that perhaps paid a little worse. About ten years ago I wrote a play with Louis Kronenberger. *My Dear Queen* we called it, and we thought it had much the funniest lines—we'd write a few minutes and then lean back and laugh. No one else ever cracked a smile."

After that she became a reader for Herman Shumlin, and it was while at this job that she started work on an idea drawn from one of William Roughead's reports of old Scottish trials. It seemed that around 1830 a little Indian girl had succeeded in disrupting a British school. Her first success, *The Children's Hour*, was based on this situation.

The clock on the mantel showed noon. "Won't you have a drink?" said Miss Hellman, with only a trace of the rather forced enthusiasm with which one hospitably offers a stranger a drink at noon. "It's late enough in the day." At the outer door of the apartment, another penny postcard from Sam: "Best wishes for the play. I hope it runs all Summer." Going down in the elevator a memory of a newspaper piece Miss Hellman wrote in 1939:

"It is very difficult to explain that one goes through a play with elation, depression, hope. That is the exact order. Hope sets in toward nightfall. That's when you tell yourself that you're going to be better the next time, so help you God. I am not special in this: I don't believe there ever was a writer who wanted to be a decent writer who was satisfied with what he had done and who wasn't willing to kid himself he'd be a Dostoyevsky the very next time."

Miss Hellman
and Her First Screen Venture
Irving Drutman/1943

From the *New York Herald Tribune,* 21 February 1943,
sec. 6, 3.

Interrupted from time to time by calls from Hollywood, Lillian
Hellman could still find an hour one afternoon last week to talk about
the script she has just completed for Samuel Goldwyn. Called *The
North Star,* after the name of the Soviet village in which the action
takes place, the story will tell of the effect of the German invasion of
Russia on a group of Russian children. It will be, advance reports
indicate, "a picture about average Russians for average Americans."

This is Miss Hellman's first original screen play (*These Three, The
Little Foxes* and the forthcoming *Watch on the Rhine* have been
adaptations of her stage successes), and she found the going com-
paratively rough.

"The whole thing started about eight months ago," she said,
"when it was suggested to Goldwyn by what they call 'Washington'
that he make a picture dealing with some phase of the United
Nations' war effort. Goldwyn spoke to me about it and I got the idea
of going to Russia with William Wyler to get photographic background and story material. I had been on a 'grand tour' of Russia in
1937, but I hadn't covered the Ukraine, where I thought the story
should take place. Then Wyler got an Army commission, and that
was the end of that plan."

"Before he signed any contracts, Goldwyn naturally enough
wanted to see an outline of the story. That's something I have never
done before. Usually I start work with a general idea of what I want
to do and then gradually details begin to come in. Actually, I have
great difficulty writing. I think of things in terms of novels, then I have
to transpose my ideas into play form. That seems to be the best
medium for me. I did once start work on a novel, but I gave it up
when I found I didn't like the way it was going.

"Once the outline had been finished and approved, I wrote the first complete draft on the cuff, you might say. I was cheerful when I began and assured Goldwyn that it would take me only three months. Actually it took six. That's some sort of speed record for me—*The Children's Hour* took me a year and a half to finish, *The Little Foxes* a year and *Watch on the Rhine* eight months."

Before she gets down to writing, Miss Hellman first makes sure that she is thoroughly familiar with her subject. For *The North Star* she and Lelia Alexander, head of the Goldwyn research department, passed seven weeks digging up background material.

Even if much of the material collected may never be used, she says it is helpful to her in absorbing the atmosphere of the life of which she is writing. Thus, although the completed script calls for only one brief schoolroom scene, the twenty or so pages in her notebook devoted to "Education" cover all phases of Russian schooling. From the section subheaded "Literature" one may learn that required supplementary reading for the elementary grades in Soviet schools includes such books as Hans Christian Andersen's *Fairy Tales, Grimm's Tales,* selected stories from Victor Hugo, Daniel Defoe's *Robinson Crusoe,* Rudyard Kipling's *Rikki-Tikki-Tavi* and the "Mowgli" stories, Jack London's *The Wolf* and Mark Twain's *Tom Sawyer* and *Huckleberry Finn* (prime favorites in the Soviet Union, published in editions of 500,000 and never enough to supply the demand). There is even a story by Ouida on the list.

While her material was being collected, and even after she had started work on the story, Miss Hellman went through an intensive six-month course of rereading Russian novels, in an attempt to soak in as much atmosphere as possible. Each night before she went to bed she would pick up a volume of Pushkin or Tolstoy and read for twenty minutes. "In that way," she says, "I found myself actually living in Russia."

She deliberately refrained from reading contemporary books on Russia, so that she would not be tempted to make use of some other author's material. She did, however, have a month and a half's editions of *Pravda,* the official Soviet newspaper, translated so she could keep up with the Russian viewpoint on current events.

"Two of the scenes in the story," she says, "were suggested by actual news events. One told about the Germans taking blood transfusions from undernourished children and then leaving them without medical care. This was done extensively in both Poland and Russia, and thousands of deaths resulted.

"Another was a story about Russian aviators who dived their planes straight into lines of enemy tanks. I found out later that there had been many of those.

"My trip to Russia in 1937 also turned out to be valuable. For one thing, the action of *The North Star* takes place in a farming community, and I had once been taken through a collective farm near Moscow. I found it helpful to have a mental picture of that for use now. Then little things kept coming back to me—the way a dining-room table was laid, the faces of village people as they walked along the road or shopped in the village store, and snatches of their conversation. The script sounds authentic, I suppose, because Russian motion-picture people to whom I've shown it said it read like a Russian script, which pleased me very much.

"Goldwyn must have liked it too, because every time I would try to cut out a scene or some bits of dialogue he would shout at me, 'You're a vandal!' "

Miss Hellman Discusses Directors

Murray Schumach/1949

From the *New York Times*, 23 October 1949, sec. 2, 1, 3.
Copyright © 1949 by the New York Times Company. Reprinted
by permission.

Princeton—Lillian Hellman was trying to explain the other day, between rehearsals of *Montserrat,* why she now stages her scripts. "Directing," she decided, "is no great feat." Not that Miss Hellman considers herself a top-flight director. She just figures she's good enough to get by and that most directors have become expert mainly at camouflaging ignorance with technical jargon.

"The greatest sin in the theatre today," said Miss Hellman, "is to admit you don't know something." Whereupon the author of seven plays, who has adapted the work of Emmanuel Robles for this Saturday night's opening, pleaded guilty on many counts to violation of the principle of directorial omniscience.

Then, a trifle defensively, she outlined the case in favor of theatre-wise playwrights doubling as directors. She confessed to sadness at being forced to realize fifteen years had passed since she started accumulating theatre lore by writing *The Children's Hour.* Wryly, she regarded Princeton's ageless Gothic buildings, gulped black coffee and began sifting directorial pretension from accomplishment.

"The only directors who count," Miss Hellman said, "are those who make creative contributions and there are very few of those. Elia Kazan, Jed Harris, Herman Shumlin and maybe one or two others. And even for those creative directors the play must be there to begin with."

She then considered the contention that without the seeing-eye director the purblind playwright goes astray in his wilderness of words. Experienced playwrights, she said, should have little difficulty knowing where to cut speeches or how to smooth out entrances and exits of actors. First drafts of her own plays, Miss Hellman pointed out, run about thirty pages shorter than most finished scripts. Her

speeches are short and she writes careful and detailed stage directions. Directing under those conditions, she implied, required
something less than genius.

Directing "techniques" were next on the Hellman agenda. "There
shouldn't be any rules in the theatre" is her answer to those who
claim actors should study lines for a certain time before being allowed
to move across a stage. She does not care how actors learn parts and
has an aversion for those who talk about "handling" performers.
"There is no such thing as handling people," she declared. "That's
kind of playing God in the wrong way."

Miss Hellman's own approach to directing has remained un-
changed since she first tried it in 1946, staging her *Another Part of the
Forest.* At that time she told her cast at the first rehearsal: "I'm going
to fumble." She still follows the fumble method. "I never think I'm
doing anything well."

At this point, Kermit Bloomgarden, co-producer of *Montserrat,*
who had been sitting near by munching a cigar, made his only
conversational contribution. He nodded his head vigorously, grunted
confirmation and added: "She never wanted to be a director. I had to
talk her into it."

Previously, the writer had leaned on Mr. Shumlin to stage all her
plays, including successes such as *The Little Foxes* and *Watch on the
Rhine.* That the writer-director is still somewhat cowed by her new
duties is indicated by her refusal to direct a big-budget movie. "I'd
like to start on something less important," she observed.

But no matter how undecided she may be as a director, Miss
Hellman is convinced that as a playwright she has the advantage of
understanding her characters better than any director. Furthermore,
she is suspicious of directors who resolve a play to a basic theme and
operate on the theory that the author worked from that premise.

"I don't believe in so-called thematic writing," says Miss Hellman.
"You know the people in the play and those people have to say and
do what they have to say and do. Not even *Watch on the Rhine* was
thematic."

This freedom of decision on the part of her literary progeny has led
the playwright to make considerable changes in adapting *Montserrat,*
though she retained the basic plot and added only one character. "If
you're a creative writer," she says, "you just can't do what is merely a

glorified translation. You have to adapt. I didn't do it deliberately and if I had known how much work it would mean I don't think I'd have started it."

Now that Miss Hellman is both writer and director she may some day test a pet theory—that the length of a play does not matter. "If a play is good," she asserted, "the public does not care if it runs one hour or eight hours." Producer Bloomgarden snorted and puffed noisily on his cigar.

Miss Hellman first ran across *Montserrat* in Paris a year ago, when she saw one act. With the help of a translation and exchange of letters with M. Robles, the adaptor was able to work without the considerable research that usually precedes her own plays.

Montserrat is built around the relationship between a Spanish colonel in search of Bolivar and a subordinate who is helping the revolutionary to hide. Though the play deals with revolt against the Spanish oppression, Miss Hellman says she did not consciously seek to draw parallels with contemporary life in her free adaptation.

Only once to Miss Hellman's knowledge has one of her plays been adapted. Many years ago Henri Bernstein adapted her *The Children's Hour.* When the American learned that the French playwright had defined translation as a rewrite of her third act she had the show closed within a week. That situation, she is convinced, will not arise in her adaptation of *Montserrat.*

Garden Pleases Miss Hellman

Ward Morehouse/1951

From the *New York World-Telegram and Sun,* 3 March 1951, 7.
Reprinted by permission of the Publication Systems Division,
Bell & Howell Company.

Philadelphia—"This new play," said Lillian Hellman, after she'd
ordered martinis at the Vesper Club, "is No. 8. That's not wonderful;
I'm just getting old. If you live long enough you can do eight plays. I
don't think my opinion matters much, but *Autumn Garden* is, to me,
my most satisfying play—certainly it was in the writing.

"It's about a group of people who go in the summertime to a guest
house on the Gulf, run by a woman they grew up with. These people
are in their forties and some of them struggle to turn around and go
another way. . . . I'm no judge, but I'm pleased with the play. I think
a lot happens in the lives of my people, although I don't know
whether it's traditional 'action' or not. . . . But I'm not crazy about
plays in which nothing happens. I think writing is story-telling."

Miss Hellman wore a black crepe blouse and a checked blue and
white skirt as she sat at dinner with me last night in the Vesper Club,
a tastefully decorated retreat in South Sydenham St. She is not given
to flourishes of speech when she is talking for an interview; just quiet
and unhurried conversation, and always speaking her mind.

In such fashion as this:

"I never think of titles; my play could be called play No. 8 for all I
care. I fooled around; I think I got *The Autumn Garden* out of
desperation. We were well along with *The Little Foxes* before
Dorothy Parker gave me the title. . . . I still want to write a novel, but
I haven't the nerve. You and I will grow old, Mr. M., with my saying
that to you."

And about the present state, the hit-or-miss status, of the American
theater:

"There just shouldn't be a business in which money competition
matters so much; the ugliest part of the theater is the idea of

22

competition. The idea that you succeed, or that you fail, is offensive. Many good plays have closed. Many bad plays have collected fortunes. We'll have to do $17,000 to $18,000 weekly with *The Autumn Garden* (Coronet Theater, next Wednesday night) to live. If we do it, fine, but if we don't that doesn't mean that *Autumn Garden* is any less of a play. I do care, of course, about the box office, but at least, when I'm writing, it doesn't enter my head. I'm concerned as anybody by the success or failure of a play of mine, but I don't like being concerned. . . . God knows, I have no complaints with the theater's treatment of my plays. I've made a lot of money."

Miss Hellman took a sip of her wine, and we got back to *The Autumn Garden* and the writing of it.

"It took me nine or 10 months, and I did a great deal of it at Peggy Webster's place at Martha's Vineyard—a tiny, pleasant house. It's a serious play, sure, but it started as a comedy; the locale is the Gulf Coast between New Orleans and Mobile, and we're almost on top of Tennessee Williams and *The Rose Tattoo*. There is no central character in my play; it really is about 10 people of almost equal importance.

"I haven't been conscious of trying to do anything different. You change and what you do changes with it. I've always done what I was doing at the moment. Perhaps, in the play, I've wanted to say that if you've had something to stand on inwardly when you reach the middle years you have a chance of being all right; if you haven't you just live out your life."

Miss Hellman has no immediate plans after March 7; she might go to Europe. She will catch up on her playgoing. She has great respect for the writings of Tennessee Williams and Arthur Miller and she says:

"Now that Mr. Shaw is dead, nobody is next to O'Casey for my money."

She will be showing up at the Coronet for the opening of *The Autumn Garden* because she feels that making an appearance is all a part of an author's job.

"Sure," she said, "I'll go to the first night, probably somewhere in the back. I usually smoke until an usher tells me to put my cigaret out."

The Bigger the Lie

Harry Gilroy/1952

From the *New York Times,* 14 December 1952, sec. 2, 3, 4.
Copyright © 1952 by the New York Times Company. Reprinted
by permission.

The play which turned a nice quiet young woman named Lillian
Hellman into one of the best-known modern playwrights—*The
Children's Hour*--again comes to life in all its tragic fascination
Thursday night at the Coronet. Most people interested in the theatre
probably know this is a drama about a girl in a boarding school who
spreads the story that two women teachers have an abnormal
attachment for one another. Theatregoers may know also that it was
a great success—it ran 691 performances starting in November,
1934—but few can realize the controversies it created behind the
scenes.

Miss Hellman recounted these doings a few days ago in a whisper.
The sotto voce effect was not to keep eavesdroppers from hearing,
since she was alone with the interviewer in the spacious, fire-
brightened drawing room of her Manhattan apartment. It was simply
that she had weakened her voice when she began to direct the
company which will present the play and, after several weeks of
rehearsals conducted by microphone, her vocal cords had gone on
strike.

Among the things she confided in her whisper, was that it had
been impossible to get any of Broadway's leading ladies to take roles
in the original production. Alice Brady and other actresses were afraid
police would close the play. But it scored a critical success and then,
Miss Hellman recalled, there was talk that it had a chance for the
Pulitzer prize. "However, the rumor was that Professor William Lyon
Phelps of Yale refused to attend the play," Miss Hellman said, "and
he was the Pulitzer play committee in those days." (The award went
to a drama by Zoe Akins, called *The Old Maid,* based on a story by
Edith Wharton.)

24

Apart from the excitement stirred by *The Children's Hour,* it was a remarkable performance for a young writer. "I'd had a couple of little stories published," Miss Hellman said. "I was married to Arthur Kober at that time and these stories appeared in a magazine of which he was an editor. Not, of course, that that was the reason for their publication. And I'd written, with Louis Kronenberger, a comedy about a royal family who wanted to be middle-class people—that play was always being bought but never produced. Then I read the book which gave rise to *The Children's Hour.*"

The book was William Roughead's *Bad Companions,* which was published in Scotland in 1930. In one chapter entitled "Closed Doors, or The Great Drumsheugh Case," there is the story of a scandal in Edinburgh in 1809, caused by a malicious child who said that the two headmistresses at her school had "an inordinate affection" for each other.

Lillian Hellman, 26 years old, a writer of no considerable experience, took this theme and made it into a play which has been widely praised for dramatic intensity and psychological insight. Reflecting on how she had achieved such a result, Miss Hellman said: "One thing that has struck me about *The Children's Hour* is that anyone young ordinarily writes autobiographically. Yet I picked on a story that I could treat with complete impersonality. I hadn't even been to boarding school—I went to school here in New York.

"Here's another observation I make about the play today as I work over it. On the stage a person is twice as villainous as, say, in a novel. When I read that story I thought of the child as neurotic, sly, but not the utterly malignant creature which playgoers see in her. I never see characters as monstrously as the audiences do—in her case I saw her as a bad character but never outside life. It's the results of her lie that make her so dreadful—this is really not a play about lesbianism, but about a lie. The bigger the lie the better, as always."

The author had a maid bring in coffee to sluice over the rasping vocal cords. "That's a little better," she said. "Perhaps I got this affliction because I was uneasy about working on the play before I began. Kermit Bloomgarden, the producer, wanted it revived. Of course I did, too—no one likes money more than I do—and beyond that you don't like to see a work die. A writer must want money and want people to like what he writes—but the important thing is wanting but not writing for it, if you know what I mean. Anyhow, when I got into the work, I felt this was a good play to be doing again because it isn't about a time or a movement. It's a story."

What work has Miss Hellman done on her play? "Oh, some lines seemed slightly literary, and I've changed them. Then I had a great temptation to rewrite it. In a sense I had to stand by the play. What you did some years ago, you did that day. Eighteen years later you are a different person with a whole different series of emotions. I was afraid that I'd be weepy, but I wasn't sorry about the lapse of time—I found I'm glad it's past."

The playwright touched her graying hair and smiled as a kind of philosophical comment on her words. "Well, now we have a fine cast playing *The Children's Hour*. I believe that people who have seen the play before will find that this is in many ways a different interpretation."

Miss Hellman phrased the next query for herself, "But what am I going to tackle after the play opens?" She tried to dredge up the answer under the hypnotic influence of the crackling fire. "You may know that I've been editing the Chekhov letters for that 'Great Letters' series that Louis Kronenberger is bringing out as the over-all editor. Now that job is finished, too, so I'm really free to write a play. I do have two or three characters rattling around."

Then she volunteered—"Have I mentioned to you that I thought of doing more about the people of *The Little Foxes?* I've always thought about that story as requiring a trilogy to finish it." She would not say where, in the matter of time, she visualized the third play fitting into the series with *Another Part of the Forest* and *The Little Foxes*.

"All I can say is that I'm a little baffled about the characters I now have in my mind because in the past the characters which rattle around there—as I say—have always been the ones for the play beyond the one I was writing. But at the present I'm not writing one. I don't know whether that's a bad sign or not. In any case, I must get to work. Work engenders work. And at my age I believe it is time that I began to get in a hurry." Miss Hellman gulped another cup of coffee. "It's a miracle," she whispered, "that my voice lasted through this talk."

An Interview with Lillian Hellman

Richard G. Stern/1958

This is a transcript of an interview conducted in Chicago on 21 May 1958 by Richard G. Stern. An edited version appeared as "Lillian Hellman on Her Plays," *Contact #3* (1959), 113–19. Transcribed by Ruth M. Alvarez from a taped recording of the interview. Reprinted by permission of Richard G. Stern and the Estate of Lillian Hellman.

Richard Stern: You said the other day that you're writing a play now about a man, that you've never written about a man before. I said that's funny because there are men in all your plays. And you don't think of a play having a point of view as you do a novel, a piece of fiction. What do you think about this question of point of view in a play? Or what did you mean when you said you were writing a play about a man for the first time and never had before?

Lillian Hellman: Well, I've written a great many men before, of course, more men than I've probably written women; but for the first time a play revolves around a man, only around a man. He's the main character.

RS: How about *Watch on the Rhine?*

LH: Well, he was the hero. I'm not sure that the importance wasn't rather evenly divided. He forced the action, and he made the action, but. . . . This man is probably less important to the play in one sense, but his nature, what he is, is what makes the play. It's probably not true that that's the reason I'm being stopped. It's just that I've thought this up. There's probably something more wrong than that.

RS: Do you have any idea what it is?

LH: It may be that the idea for the play is almost too good. It sounds whacky to say, but somewhere it's a little too neat. This might be the reason. I've never had neat ideas before.

RS: Neat idea, you mean you have a complicated plot?

LH: No, a very complicated plot, but a very. . . . This is the first play I've ever tried to write where I could, if I wanted to, sum it up in four or five sentences, the idea. And that may be what's wrong.

RS: You haven't written about ideas, you haven't had an idea to begin with usually?

LH: No, and I didn't have here either. This evolved out of the people. I didn't start this way. If I had an idea to begin with, I'd be very worried. Idea plays don't seem to me good as a rule.

RS: Well, now the other day you were talking about *The Autumn Garden,* and you summed up that play very briefly in one sense. At least, you said something technical about it. You said you wanted to write a novel in theater form, and then you talked about the subject matter of the play. It isn't *that* kind of idea then, is it?

LH: No, no, and also that was something that isn't so much an idea as it is a technique.

RS: Technique?

LH: I'm referring to *Autumn Garden.*

RS: Yeah. You want to say what this idea is?

LH: Sure, if you'd like me to. At this minute I don't think it's going . . . that what's going to be . . . but at this minute it's about two very nice, hard-working, middle-class, maiden ladies who live in New Orleans around 1912 or '14, who have a large house, whose family long ago lost all their money, and they have raised and loved a much younger brother who, by the time the play opens, has been married a year to an heiress of about nineteen. He's about thirty. And they have moved away, the brother and his wife, to Chicago. And as the play opens at this minute, the sisters haven't . . . one sister has heard from him and the other sister knows that she's heard from him, but doesn't know what she's heard. The one who's heard from him is mystified too. But they are getting ready to take a long-planned trip to Europe on a little money they've saved. They haven't had to support him for a year for the first time, and so they've saved a little money. They've a couple of thousand dollars, and this trip has been planned for many, many years. They're going. They have no spec-ified date of going, but they're going now. Both of them are intelligent women. They have a sense that if they don't go now, they won't ever go. One's about forty-eight, and one's about forty. And at the point of their expectations and their worry about why they haven't heard from Julian, Julian appears with the young wife, very happy. He's come home very happy, and they're puzzled by this because it's obvious he's lost—he says he's lost—all his wife's money. His wife's mother is a very rich lady who's given them ten thousand dollars for a wedding present, and he's lost the ten thousand dollars in a shoe factory in Chicago, and he's pleased. He's not concerned about it, and they're very puzzled by this. They're also puzzled by the fact that this young girl, the wife, who simply seemed to them a rather strange, pretty young girl a year ago, is a little odder and queerer than she was. It turns out very shortly that he has lost the wife's money, it's perfectly true, but he's taken a wild gamble on something which is too complicated here to go into, a piece of real estate, and he's won the gamble, and he's got potentially and really, a lot of money, a hundred thousand dollars. And he's come home. This trip home has been as a surprise to them because he's brought them everything he always wanted to buy them. He's bought them two fur coats, and he's bought them passage on the fanciest boat to Europe, and he's bought up the mortgage on this house they've always hated and pretended to him that they liked and always intended to get rid of. He's bought them very fancy clothes, that, of course, are not right for them, and they could never wear. And the rest of the play is their violent disappointment and the wife's violent fear. They are disappointed, the sisters. The wife is fearful that if he has money he will leave her. She's terribly in love with him. All three, the two sisters and the wife, find that this man whom they thought they wanted to do fine and be independent . . . they haven't wanted that way at all. They all loved him for being this kind of schlemiel that they brought him up to be. The wife had married him for this reason. The sisters had raised him for this reason, and they don't like the independence. So they proceed to take the money away from him. The plot is too . . . not only too complicated, but I don't know it.

RS: Is that what's holding you up? The plot or is. . . ?

LH: Partly. I'm making too much fuss about the plot though. It's not really the plot, because the plot could go any way, and it doesn't matter what.

RS: You mean how to get the money away from him?

LH: How they take it away from him.

RS: Yeah.

LH: I'm making too much fuss about it. Which is also a bad sign really.

RS: You mean a bad personal sign?

LH: Yes.

RS: That you're not interested in the play or you don't feel like writing or something like that?

LH: No, I wouldn't say not interested, I don't feel like writing. I feel like writing it very much. I've written half of it. It's a bad sign that something's gone wrong when you're using technical problems for excuses. It's a bad sign for me, I mean.

RS: Where did you stop in the play?

LH: About halfway in the second act.

RS: And what has been revealed? How much of what you said? Is that the way it proceeds, a series of revelations all through the play?

LH: Well, a friend of mine whom I have great trust in, Dashiell Hammett, who read it said, I think quite rightly, that he was absolutely bewildered by why I wouldn't get down to the play. That I . . . up till half of the play I haven't let anything happen.

RS: Do you have the sisters talking in the first act? And then the return?

LH: Yes, the most I've let happen—and then I did it the second round, I didn't even do it in the first writing—is to at least let him announce that he had the money. But for some reason that I don't know about, which is what makes me so nervous that this may not be the right play for me, is I just won't get down to it. I had a fine time with it. Everybody comes out kind of interesting, except him. He just kind of remains lifeless. I don't know why.

RS: You want him to be a very intelligent man?

LH: No, I don't want him to be . . . I want him just to be a sort of nice slob. Well, slob's not the right word. Pleasant, semi-intelligent, good-natured, kindly, nothing one way or the other. But bewildered by the end of the play. He's done everything they've told him to do, and it doesn't please anybody.

RS: It's hard to think that he's the man about whom the play revolves.

LH: Yes, that's the trouble, of course. That's the trouble because he can't be one thing or the other. If he's too intelligent, he would have seen through it too long ago.

RS: Yet he has to be intelligent enough to work out the deals.

LH: Yes, intelligent enough to leave them which I think he's going to do in the end of the play. I'm not sure. He just should be one of many people.

RS: How are the sisters different or is it important that they're different? How did you make them different, if they are, from each other?

LH: One is very intelligent, and one is not very intelligent, and what I started out to do was two seemingly quite nice women who have been devoted to each other and devoted to their brother and peaceful and relatively happy and try to show by the end of the play that neither . . . that the one hasn't liked the other and the bright one has been very bored by the not so bright one, and they've been in competition for the brother's affection for many years under a very polite guise, that neither has ever told the truth about anything, not that they've lied, but they've just never seen the truth about anything. One has a beau whom she's never married and never married because she's been in love with her brother all her life. They come out, I think, quite well so far.

RS: How are they, are they. . . ?

LH: It's Betty that doesn't come out too well.

RS: Have you decided how you're going to get them to reveal the antipathy which they felt for each other? Is it going to be an argument between them, or is it going to be something which one of them . . . both of them do, one of them does or both of them do, something violent?

LH: I don't know yet. I don't know yet. I've gone through a number of phases of what they do to it. Once, for a little while, I had the wife kill him.

RS: The wife kill him?

LH: Uh-huh; at this minute she just injures him. She suspects that the information about the gamble, the winning gamble, has come from a woman, and, in a fit of jealousy, she cripples him, shoots him. But I'm not sure that's right either.

RS: Doesn't that blur what you mean? It makes seem jealousy what you want to be her love of his dependence entirely.

LH: Yes, it could blur it, which is one of the reasons it worries me. It could also not blur it.

RS: It makes it something different.

LH: Yes, truth is I don't know.

RS: How about the wife and the sisters? Have you worked out how they feel about each other and does that change and so on?

LH: No. They don't feel very . . . the wife has a mother. I've left out the second most important character. Probably because I didn't want to talk to her, talk about her. The wife has a mother who almost dominates the play now. And is going to have to stop dominating or the play's not going to be done. She's a very rich lady who has . . . one of the reasons she's given them a big wedding present and comes around with another check is that she's wanted to get rid of this girl. The girl's made her uncomfortable and bored her for the whole nineteen years she had her. So the marriage has just delighted her, and she's the only one who really feels sort of sorry for this poor bastard, and she would like to see him keep the money and keep the girl for that matter, too. She's very nice to the girl, surfacely, very polite to her, but the girl has always known the mother didn't like her.

RS: She's come down with the couple?

LH: No, she lives . . . the mother?

RS: Yes.

LH: She lives in New Orleans.

RS: I see.

LH: She has a colored chauffeur who is the only person she's ever really liked in her life, on whom she's very dependent. She's the only one who really has any sympathy for Julian.

RS: How does she dominate the play?

LH: I got too interested in her.

RS: What is she doing now? She's on stage and she's. . . .

LH: She's trying at this minute not to listen to the girl who's rambling on about her Chicago experiences and how she's frightened to lose . . . of losing Julian, and she's just trying not to listen to her, as she's tried not to listen to her all her life. The girl is kind of, I hope if she comes out right, kind of sadly whacky, not crazy, but fey, and disjointed, and sweet, and lost, and the mother will try to stop them all from taking the money away from him. She doesn't like him or dislike him, but he's better off with money in her eyes than he is without it.

RS: It doesn't sound like there should be or certainly need be any other issues, but are there any other things in the play, things I mean that people talk about? Class distinctions or loss of money, North-South?

LH: No, no I don't think so; I don't think so.

RS: Do you have any comic people in the play, I mean strictly comical?

LH: No.

RS: No servants?

LH: No, no. The negro chauffeur is a very wise, rather quiet fellow.

RS: Good.

LH: He doesn't talk much through the play and doesn't like the woman he works for very much, but is well paid, and she interests him. He stayed with her for years because she interested him.

RS: Do you shift from house to house? The mother's house and the sisters' house or is it all in the sisters' house?

LH: At this minute it's all in the sisters' house but I don't think this play's going to be written this way, and I think almost the proof it isn't going to be is that it's the first time in my life I've ever been able to talk about a play, and I'm scared to death of this sign. I would never have done what we're doing now about any other play.

RS: Have you talked a lot about it? Is this the first time you've talked about it or have you been talking a lot about it?

LH: No, I haven't talked a lot about it, but people ask me what it's about and for the first time in my life I sometimes tell them. This is a very bad sign. It's as if I intended to fribble it away.

RS: No.

LH: I've never talked about writing. I have a horror of telling anybody what anything is about, and the fear that it will all get lost.

RS: No, this is not uncommon.

LH: No, of course it isn't.

RS: But . . . I don't know why, but it shouldn't . . . it should help you to clarify some of the things.

LH: I don't think it does anything. The only person it ever helps to clarify is somebody who knows you so well and how you write so well that you don't even have to finish the sentence. You know then you're not talking and that's valuable, I think.

RS: Well, maybe we better get off the play.

LH: Oh, it'll come now one way or the other. I'll tear it up in the next month if it doesn't because it's been six months now.

RS: Have you ever thrown away a play?

LH: Yes. I haven't thrown away a whole play, no.

RS: What have you thrown away?

LH: Well, I threw away the first version of *Watch on the Rhine* which was totally different. It took place in Ohio in a college.

RS: What was the matter with it?

LH: It just didn't seem to me right, so I . . . what did I do instead? I did another play instead.

RS: You wanted something dangerous?

LH: I did *Little Foxes* instead actually! I started *Watch on the Rhine* before I started *Little Foxes*.

RS: Oh, that's interesting.

LH: And then put it up and threw it away. I've forgotten it. I guess it's been thrown away. And went and did *Little Foxes*. I've often done that, getting an idea and starting it and then putting it up for something else and coming back to it in two or three years. I don't get many ideas. I'm the only writer living I think doesn't.

RS: Then you'd be a philosopher, if you did.

LH: No, everybody else seems to have. I'm always reading interviews where people have.

RS: Ideas?

LH: Fifteen and twenty ideas or two hundred. Don't you, don't you read about these people?

RS: Let's say a little bit about what you said the other day about . . . you were kind of surprised when you had finished *The Little Foxes* and noticed that Regina wasn't very nice. You hadn't thought about this, you just were writing about it. Does this happen to you only in your better plays, those you consider your better plays?

LH: No, I think it happens to everybody all the time. That you . . . you, as I said the other day, you don't know what you do, and you have no right to know what you do. You have no right to think of people as good or bad, or comic or uncomic, or villainesses or heroes or. . . .

RS: Well, let's put on also that you originally wanted Regina to be played by somebody strong and not unattractive but let's say masculine and powerful. And then Shumlin persuaded you it should be played by someone flamboyantly attractive.

LH: Yes, yes.

RS: How do you think that changed the play? For the better I think you said, but how do you think it did?

LH: I don't think it changed the play, because even though Bankhead is a beautiful woman or was, the quality that was Regina was there, the aggressiveness and the pretend femininity and the strength and the power of the brothers.

RS: But the pretense could be much greater this way and the hypocrisy and whatever.

LH: Yes, because she was such a handsome woman. No, I think that was a fine idea.

RS: When you're doing Regina you get, not angry in a sense, but a kind of imitation anger when you're writing a part like that or do you find I suppose you can't register the emotions you have when you're writing because you don't have time to do anything but write?

LH: No. I never was angry with Regina. I think Regina's kind of funny. If anything, I was amused with her.

RS: What's amusing about her?

LH: I think the teasing of the brothers is funny.

RS: Yeah, that's. . . .

LH: I think the brothers are funny. The brothers amuse me.

RS: The brothers are certainly funny, particularly Oscar.

LH: The only one I think I had any such emotion as you're describing about is the girl. I felt very strongly that the girl had to leave, and I think I felt sentimental about the girl too.

RS: How about Birdie? Were you sentimental about her?

LH: No, I just thought Birdie was silly. I was also amazed to wake up and find that Birdie was this great. . . .

RS: Touching.

LH: Touching character, because I just think she's kind of silly.

RS: No.

LH: She is touching, as a great many silly people are touching, but I didn't mean it. I just meant her to be, you know, a lost drunk. I was amazed to find that. I was amazed to find much about *The Little*

Foxes, though I had meant the aristocracy as against the middle class and. . . .

RS: It's nice we've had the two parts because what you're saying about the people after the play you've written . . . you are talking about them in terms of their sympathy or lack of sympathy or your interest, whereas in the first play you didn't. I don't think you said anything about any of the characters being nice or moving or touching or anything like that. You just talked about their relationships, how they felt about one another, what they were going to do and so on.

LH: You mean *Little Foxes* and *Another Part of the Forest?*

RS: No, I'm talking about the play that you are now doing.

LH: Oh, I see. Well, that's because one has been done and one hasn't been done.

RS: Yeah, and you're not thinking about doing it in terms of how can I make X really seem nice to the audience here or anything like that, which is kind of. . . .

LH: That's awful dangerous going-on.

RS: I think so but a lot of critics. . . .

LH: It's a very sound way to be popular, particularly now when niceness has such a premium on it.

RS: Well, you certainly simplify your drama when you do that, don't you?

LH: You simplify it; you sure do, and you consciously or unconsciously play for the sympathy of the audience and the sympathy of the critic. And it's very simple to do; it isn't very hard to do, particularly in the theater.

RS: We were talking about the miscalculations audiences and critics make about such characters, say, as Archie in *The Entertainer,* calling him vicious and immoral and so on. I think both of us disagree he was something else.

LH: Well, this has amazed me in people for a long time, and I think happens more in the theater than it ever does with books, and what its reason is I don't know. People who have themselves led very full lives and must be conscious of their own lives and what's happened in them will suddenly get highly fake moral about what they see on the stage, such as Archie in *The Entertainer,* as an example.

RS: Is it the tradition of talking? I mean you have to say something about people and the easiest thing to say about them is that they're nice or not nice or something like that.

LH: I've never decided what it is except if it's the hypocrisy of all of us, or if that's given a greater play in a public place where you are more embarrassed, or you're more embarrassed because a human being is playing it.

RS: Well, it's so hard to detach, to recreate the theatrical experience—namely that people in the play exist as a function of the whole play, and you're not thinking of them in parts.

LH: Yes, yes.

RS: Just as you don't take a piece out of a vase and say oh this is made out of such and such a stone or it's treated in such and such a way. When you're looking at the vase, if you like the vase, you see it as a whole.

LH: Yes. Well it also, I suppose, depends upon when the play comes along. I'm hipped on this subject as you know because I talked about it the other day. In what period it comes. We've been through a period of self-deception, I think. Sort of childish self-deception which we . . . I think we wanted to think of ourselves as the best and kindest and most generous and most moral and most middle-class and most split-level and most wall-to-wall carpeting people that ever existed, and anything that intruded on that. . . . I had an example. May I tell you an example of that which has amused me for a long time?

RS: Please.

LH: I have some friends who have a sixteen-year-old daughter, and these friends invested in *Candide,* a musical as you know.

RS: Are they still friends?

LH: Yes, we're still friends, and at the time they did I'd met the daughter but I didn't really know her. And they'd been telling me about her for a long time, telling me what a rebel she was. They're quite rich people, and they live in a quite fancy house and have two or three cars and three servants. And she was in rebellion against this life, and every time they told me of her rebellion I would say what I thought which was that the young should rebel. And I thought well maybe there's going to be all this business all over again of the rich child wishing to go back to the worker and you know all that we all went through in the Thirties. And that seemed to me very interesting. It's the first sign I'd ever heard of it. Until *Candide* opened, and she told her mother and father that she was absolutely shocked that they would invest in this show, shocked that they would have anything to do with Voltaire's book. And than I said well then I've misunderstood you all these months. What is she rebelling about? I don't understand this. And they said very puzzled, oh, we thought we'd explained. She doesn't want to live in our house. She wants a split-level house. She doesn't mind a car. She doesn't want a Cadillac; she wants a Ford. She doesn't want three servants; she wants a half-day maid, which has always seemed to me the kind of summation of what we've all been going through for ten years. Maybe it's the first revolt of the upper middle class to the lower middle class.

RS: Well, Orwell tried that but he. . . .

LH: The what?

RS: When Orwell decided to change his class, it wasn't to the split-level house.

LH: No, exactly. I don't think it's ever been before, has it?

RS: Not that I can think of.

LH: Royalty, I suppose, has always wanted. . . .

RS: It's kind of like playing dolls, going back to *The Doll House* in a way.

LH: And not playing with very pretty dolls.

RS: No.

LH: It's usually been the opposite way; you wanted your doll dressed in ermine.

RS: I don't think sixteen-year-olds should count really as thermometers.

LH: But I don't know. She and her friends evidently all share this. They will count in two or three years.

RS: Well then are they balanced by the motorcyclists and the leather jackets?

LH: Well, I'm not sure that's not what they want too.

RS: You think they're after the split-level house? I think they're after the split-level skull.

LH: Split-level skull, I suppose.

RS: Well, you said the other day that this feeling of tranquility and this lack of exploration on the part of this generation is responsible either for or it's part of the general atmosphere which has depressed the theater among other things, depressed the arts in general and that the things that have interested you most in the theater have come out of the European experience in the last ten years. Last night you saw an example of one of these products. Do you feel that that has distinctions which nothing in the American theater in the last ten years has? The piece we better say was Beckett's *End Game, Fin de Partie*. Or is its peculiarity so special that it is just an untraditional . . . it's just off the beaten path, off anything that can be followed or it's off anything that can be really enjoyed for very long? You enjoy it because of its oddity and its occasional invention, but does it have anything really to do with what you and I probably know as theater, as plays in the theater?

LH: It's too odd for me, but I do think it has certain qualities which we are sorely in need of and which is a good thing for us.

RS: What are they?

LH: It's sharp and hard-hitting and funny and basically gay in spite of its outlook on life. As a play, it's slightly too strange for my taste. There's too much I didn't really understand in it, but . . . you know, it is nice to see somebody come into the theater without all the mush-headedness that's been true of us for so long.

RS: It isn't that it is. . . .

LH: Not to see somebody be truly funny.

RS: Yes, yes that was . . . wasn't that the nicest part of it? That redeemed everything in it.

LH: Yes, truly satiric, truly biting.

RS: Of course, that comes from a temperament rather than a tradition or an atmosphere.

LH: Yes.

RS: And Beckett's always been an odd ball, to use one of the terms which this generation has made up to cover anybody who's. . . .

LH: Well, we could stand some more of them I think. We don't have to admire the I think too great oddness of the play, but we sure could stand some of the real looking at life that such a man does. We've looked at it in most cases I think so untruthfully and sentimentally in the theater for so long.

RS: Yes, it isn't just the past ten years, is it? Has any American ever been as bleak and bleakly funny as Beckett?

LH: No, I don't think it's our temperament to be. Although I think there have been a few people who have been. I suppose Twain was in his way, wasn't he? I don't mean in method.

RS: I suppose so.

LH: But in outlook? I suppose Bierce was to a large extent. We've lost it though.

RS: Well, I don't think we've lost it in fiction. I do think Flannery O'Connor has much of what Beckett has—a grotesque, fantastic, gothic humor.

LH: Well, so is Carson McCullers. There've been a lot of people who've had it, but I think in general we don't make fun of ourselves the way we did. You know that kind of good healthy humor that. . . .

RS: Of course, I don't think Beckett is.

LH: No, he's not making fun.

RS: Fun, no; but the people who don't care. . . .

LH: He's making fun of a civilization, of a life though, isn't he?

RS: I suppose so, yeah. The play is kind of a . . . it's just kind of variations on a theme as we were saying last night. It takes part of life that everybody goes through and says well let's just explore.

LH: Let's just see that as all of life.

RS: Yes. Let's see what this is and as if it were everything, make a kind of nightmare exploration out of it.

LH: I think he's a quite charming writer. I'm sorry that the play is so long, but *Godot* was a charming play. It's hard to take it very seriously; I mean it's hard to take its meaning too seriously, I think. But it's got enormous charm and humor.

RS: When you go to a play like that, do you get any ideas about it for your own work? Or have you ever gone to a play and gotten ideas which you felt that you'd like to put into practice, that you'd like to change, that you'd like to do something, that you've learned something from?

LH: Well, as I told you last night, that is one of the reasons I don't go to the theater a great deal, that there are times and thank God for them when I've gone to the theater and wanted to go home and write. This is the best feeling in the world, of course. But it doesn't happen very often and usually the opposite takes place, and I try if

I'm writing not to go very often to the theater for just this reason because I get depressed, and I have a sense that this is the way it is, and this is the way it's going to be, and I'm tired and bored with it. But once in a while, then I think the theater offers something that almost no other form of art offers, which is that you're terribly close to it and excited by it, and it's immediately communicable.

RS: But you yourself have not yet gone to a play or read a play and said well, why don't I do this or why have I been dragging things out so or why do I do things?

LH: Oh, many times, many times. Yes that's what I meant that when I. . . .

RS: Can you recall . . . ?

LH: Well, not many times but a fair number of times.

RS: Any play or playwright?

LH: Yes; *Richard the Third*, the few times I've ever seen it, has always done it for me. The other night when I saw *The Visit*, the Lunt and Fontanne play, I had a sense of excitement and wanting to go back to work.

RS: Nothing specific, just that?

LH: Oh, you meant did I have some particular idea, no. I don't think I've ever had any . . . you meant—can I use this situation?

RS: Yes, shall I not bring in the characters, shall I quit writing about people who come back after long visits, shall I have people come back after visits? Start something explosive that way?

LH: No, I don't think so. I don't think so. If so, I'm not conscious of it. We all steal, but I don't think many of us would be brave enough to admit we had.

RS: Well, what actually started you writing plays, to ask you a question that must have been asked a million times. I know you were writing fiction, and you were in Herman Shumlin's office more or less. Did you write plays because you were there in the theatrical atmosphere? We're not talking about making money or something like that.

LH: I don't know. I really don't know. Louis Kronenberger and I had written a farce together before *The Children's Hour*. We thought it was very funny. Nobody else seems to have thought so; but I don't know, I don't know why I did. I had worked in the theater, but then I had worked for a publisher also.

RS: What had you done in the theater?

LH: Oh, I had done press work. I had done a little bit of everything. I worked in a stock company, not as an actress. All kinds of grimy, crummy jobs.

RS: When did you get interested in the theater so that you did go to work . . . when you went to ask for a job you asked around the theater?

LH: That was the accident of marrying somebody who was in the theater. When the Depression came, I needed a job. So it was obviously easier to get one with people he knew.

RS: I see.

LH: I had worked for a publishing house.

RS: So you didn't write or read a lot of plays when you were . . . ?

LH: No.

RS: Sixteen, seventeen?

LH: No, I didn't. I had very little interest in the theater actually. It was a sheer accident. It had been the other way around. I had great interest in books, and when I got out of school I went for work for Boni and Liveright. I did book reviews for years when the *Herald Tribune* first started.

RS: Did you go to the theater in those days when you were married and so on?

LH: Yes, I suppose I went more than I had ever gone because Arthur Kober worked in the theater.

RS: Do you remember plays that you liked particularly then? Are they vivid to you?

LH: I remember liking Sidney Howard's plays very much. I went to the theater as a kid. I went almost every Saturday afternoon.

RS: In New York or New Orleans?

LH: In New York. But I just went to see anything. It didn't matter what it was. I really don't think I have any distinct date or reason for being interested in the theater. I'm not sure I was. At least, if I was, I never thought about it very much. I must have been because that's where I turned when. . . .

RS: Was there a period when you liked, as you now seem to dislike, the life which surrounds the theater, the penumbra of the theater?

LH: No, but then I've never liked any life where there was one group of people. I didn't like the life I grew up with for the same reasons. I don't like lives which included just one profession. I'm not talking English, but do you know what I mean?

RS: Sure. When you were mixed up with politics a lot, did you have the same feeling?

LH: Oh, yes, oh, yes. I couldn't stand seeing all those people.

RS: But the causes were important, you know.

LH: Yes, they were.

RS: Just as writing plays was important. I guess in other ways your family was.

LH: It's not that I had any dislike of the individual people, it's just that I. . . .

RS: You needed variety.

LH: I don't like groups of shop talk.

RS: Well, let's cut off this shop talk.

LH: All right.

Q: Miss Hellman, What's Wrong with Broadway?
A: It's a Bore.

Thomas Meehan/1962

From *Esquire*, 58 (December 1962), 140, 142, 235–36. Reprinted with permission from *Esquire* (December 1962). Copyright © 1962 by Esquire Associates.

Since the sensational Broadway success of her first play, *The Children's Hour,* in 1934, Lillian Hellman has generally been recognized as America's leading woman playwright. Reviewers welcomed her most recent production, *Toys in the Attic,* as a tonic to the dull 1959–60 season, and it won the New York Drama Critics Circle Award as best American drama of that year. Other of Miss Hellman's work includes *The Little Foxes, Watch on the Rhine, The Searching Wind, Another Part of the Forest,* and *The Autumn Garden.* Most of these plays explore the problems of evil, political and moral; they are known for great theatrical power and for a remarkable incisiveness in language and characterization. The creator of this muscular body of work is herself a soft-spoken, brown-eyed lady of gentle manner and tough conviction. Some samples of the latter follow.

LH: I don't know why it's a bore, but there's very little that's any fun. By fun I mean something you're interested in, enjoy the way you might enjoy a good book, maybe not a great book, just a good book. The theatre has grown so middle-class, even when it's *avant-garde.* I don't mean in subject matter—there's no such thing as a middle-class subject. I mean in its way of looking at things.

   TM: Do you mean the theatre used to be better? The Twenties, for instance, were certainly an unboring time.

   LH: Yes, I think so. There was a group of extraordinarily talented writers in the Twenties and the theatre had its share. Most remarkable

44

people—Eugene O'Neill, George Kelly, Sidney Howard, George Kaufman, Elmer Rice, whatever one thinks of them now, whatever their final work has come to—were breaking new ground, going new ways and having something to say.

TM: In the Twenties there were sixty or seventy productions a year. Now we have about half that many.

LH: In the late Twenties, when I first knew the theatre, six and seven shows used to open in a night.

TM: And weren't there a lot more comedies in the Twenties and Thirties?

LH: Yes, I guess the Twenties laughed more than we do. We don't get many good comedies anymore. We get homey little comedies now, homey little middle-class comedies in which *everybody* talks as if they'd gone through four years of college and read the latest best-seller. Even musicals used to have more bite and point. As many advances as the musical theatre has taken, I don't think it's ever again come near the kind of bold funniness of *Pal Joey*.

TM: What do you think accounts for this loss in, well, bite?

LH: The theatre, in every country, is a fairly accurate gauge of popular desire. Books and music and architecture will often go their own way, but the theatre is so concerned with money that it has to make good guesses about what is wanted, and what is wanted now is not bite or boldness. I don't think we want to be flattered—we did, but we've passed through that—but we do want to be tickled. A little glimpse of homosexuality, a mite of dopesters, Mr. Genet's romantic peeps at an underworld and, above all—the surest buck of all—something about "aloneness." Big deal. You're alone. When the play goes into rehearsal, the hero ends alone. Round about the first week on the road, nobody thinks that's nice, so he finds love. Not alone anymore. Or, more skillfully, half-alone. God knows love is a great theme but we're sure busy making it mingy.

TM: There's a song in which the line keeps repeating: *Love is the answer. . . .*

LH: The great answer of our time. The idiot word nobody bothers to define. "Love"—and "aloneness." I have great respect for psycho-analysis, but I think our preoccupation with "love" and "aloneness" comes straight out of ten-cent-store Freud. Love is a *very* large theme and unless writers can do it big, they should leave it alone. And the discovery that all of us are, finally, alone must have been made by the first ape as he stood up to look over his shoulder.

TM: Who in your opinion is making the taste in the theatre? In a way I think you've indicated that it's the audience.

LH: It's a combination, of course. It's what the writer, the producer, the director think the audience wants and what the audience lets them know they do want.

TM: Then what do you think has gone wrong? There are more educated people in this country today than there ever were before.

LH: Are there? You mean more people who go to college? Well, maybe. Maybe that's what it is, the theatre doesn't offer the educated what they're looking for. The young people I know, and by young I mean twenty to thirty, have little interest in the theatre. One of them told me the other night that his generation was far more interested in movies than in plays, that he didn't like to get theatre tickets two or three weeks ahead of time, and that the tickets cost too much. He said even if he could afford to go, there was little that would interest him. I knew what he meant—the theatre doesn't interest me much anymore.

TM: Do you feel this might have something to do with the shortage of good new writers?

LH: Yes, I think so. There are not many young people in the theatre who are good writers. Certainly fewer than there were in the Twenties and possibly fewer than there were in the Thirties. Maybe things go in a circle. The plays aren't very good and so the good young writer turns to some other form. But the theatre will have a renascence and the good writer will come toward it again.

TM: Do you see very many plays?

LH: No. If I'm writing, I have the superstitious belief that you'd better keep the unborn child away from what might harm it. If I go to see bad theatre—and by bad theatre I mean theatre that bores me— I'm scared that I'll have a tough time writing or that I won't write well. If I go to good theatre, I feel exhilarated and pleased, and I want to write better and more. But I'm real scared of going near junk or half-junk. Half-junk is very dangerous.

TM: Do you think the critics have some responsibility for killing off the interesting things? Are they too severe?

LH: No, I think they're frequently too easy, especially on musical shows. I suppose that comes from being bored so often that you're glad to have pretty girls and a nice song. And it's true, of course, that within the last ten years the musical show has been more serious and more interesting than has the straight play.

TM: Comparing *Leave It to Jane* with *West Side Story,* it's easy to see the progress in musicals. You don't think there's been that kind of advance in the straight play?

LH: I guess not. Although I don't know much about advances or retreats. I dislike such words. There's a tendency in the theatre—the brilliant Kenneth Tynan shares it, too bad—to think that an advance in technique and an *avant-garde* idea make a good play. Of course it's fine that people should be breaking rules and throwing things about and being adventurous, but writing's got to be more than that, and the aim higher and surer.

TM: Would you consider Jack Gelber's *The Connection* an example of this kind of writing?

LH: Yes, and I enjoyed it. It's a good show, but it's not a good play—like a fine time at the circus.

TM: How did you feel about *Rhinoceros?*

LH: Fun for a while, not much more than that.

TM: Why?

LH: One joke. It was brilliantly acted, brilliantly directed, and that's what I found interesting. Ionesco is a charming writer and that would be enough if the pretend-depth wasn't in the way.

TM: Since we're talking about specific writers now, which ones impress you?

LH: I think the only writer of importance to come along in the theatre in the last ten or twelve years is Beckett. For my money he's the only man who should be taken seriously. I don't think he's written great plays, but they're very good.

TM: Which play in particular? *Waiting for Godot?*

LH: *Godot* was a charming play, a funny play. *Krapp's Last Tape* is a really moving play. He's good, is Mr. Beckett.

TM: Who do you feel is good among American playwrights?

LH: Williams is good. Or was, and will be again. He's a natural dramatist, knows what he is doing by instinct, and sometimes knows too much. I think he worries about success and failure, understandably; we all do, but he pushes too hard because of it, or is pushed by other people. It takes a long time for all of us to learn that the theatre is a world of fashion, and fashions turn, and I guess you just pray you'll live long enough to see them turn back again. Your job is to pay no attention to them.

TM: Which do you think is his best play?

LH: *A Streetcar Named Desire.* And I very much liked *27 Wagons Full of Cotton.*

TM: The latter was made into the movie, *Baby Doll,* wasn't it?

LH: Yes. I didn't like the movie. All decorated and not as funny.

TM: What about Arthur Miller?

LH: Miller is good and I think will be even better as the years go on. He has force and spirit. Too much newspaper stuff and too much writing about writing. But it doesn't matter—he's good.

TM: How about specific plays of his? *Death of a Salesman?*

LH: I liked it. A remarkable play. I didn't like *The Crucible*—I don't like theme plays—but I thought *A View from the Bridge* was a very good play when I read the script.

TM: Didn't you like the production?

LH: Not much. It was self-conscious. It *told* us what it was about—large theme, Greek columns, and so on. Writers should not *see* their work. Do you know what I'm awkwardly trying to say? Writers shouldn't have anything to do with words like betrayal or courage or bigness or smallness or sex or Greek or new or old. You write it down but you mustn't stand back and see it. You do it and go to bed and leave the big words for other people. I'm not saying any of this very well. But it just isn't your business to tell people what you're doing or wanted to do.

TM: Miller hasn't written a play since *A View from the Bridge,* has he?

LH: No, but that's not necessarily bad. Too often playwrights think if Mr. Smith has a play this year, then they must have a play next year or people will forget them. Competitiveness is an easy disease to catch.

TM: Williams clips off one a year, though.

LH: That's not bad either. You write when you're ready to write. But success should buy the right to take your time.

TM: How do you feel about William Inge?

LH: He's a skillful man. The plays aren't up my alley.

TM: Do you put Paddy Chayefsky in the same group?

LH: The comedy in *The Tenth Man* was very funny. I wish the whole play had been a comedy.

TM: We've talked about Jack Gelber a little. There are a few other young playwrights—Arthur Kopit, Richardson, Albee. Not very many more; this is one of the problems.

LH: Albee is a promising man. I haven't seen Richardson. *Poor Dad* is sometimes brilliant and doesn't come out anywhere. But, you see, Beckett's my candidate.

TM: What do you think about Brecht?

LH: Oh, well, now you're in the big league. Wonderful most of the time. I think *The Threepenny Opera* and *Mother Courage* are the great plays of our time.

TM: What about material for the dramatist? In the Thirties and Forties, for instance, there were a lot of political and social-comment plays that don't seem to get written anymore.

LH: Like Clifford Odets' *Waiting for Lefty.* I liked it. Dashiell Hammett and I went to see *Awake and Sing* and we had a fight because I liked it and he didn't. He said it wasn't enough for a writer to have wanted a bicycle when he was young. Maybe he's turned out right. I don't believe in theme plays. I liked Odets best when he wasn't being political.

TM: Your own play, *Watch on the Rhine,* was in the political tradition, wasn't it?

LH: I don't know. I don't think so. I guess I don't think there's any such thing as a really good political play. Good writers have a look at the world around them and then they write it down. That's all.

TM: We've been talking about playwrights up to now. What do you think about the performers today?

LH: I think they're good. There's a very high level of acting now, higher than it used to be.

TM: Do you think that's partially due to the Actors Studio?

LH: I don't know. Maybe. They did good. They also did harm.

TM: It's true, though, that there aren't many people who draw you in just by their names.

LH: There are not as many stage personalities now. Star person-alities are rare and nothing substitutes for that mysterious ability to take over a stage. One misses whatever it is that made a W. C. Fields or Fanny Brice or Laurette Taylor.

TM: Ethel Merman still has star quality.

LH: And Kim Stanley and Maureen Stapleton and Nichols and May.

TM: How about Marlon Brando?

LH: Yes. He has it, too. I wish he'd cut out the high jinks and get down to work. There's too little personality on the stage now. But there's too little personality anywhere. The only eccentrics we have have invented themselves and that's no good. We're all so anxious to be charming. Everybody has to be loved by everybody else. We're all so smooth to the touch.

TM: Sometimes you feel that directors want the audience to "like" the play more than anything else. In that connection, I believe directors are having more and more influence on the way a play finally appears before the public. In a sense the director seems to be taking over some of the playwright's duties. Is that true?

LH: Oh, yes. It's common practice now. Writing by democratic-majority vote with the director, producer, friends, cast and all relatives as the Board of Directors. The only time I listened to an army of people—during *Candide*—I went to pieces.

TM: There's a kind of hit psychology behind all that.

LH: Oh, sure, sure. You start to feel that it's all your fault, all that money put up by all those kind strangers. The play opens out of town and you're the guilty one if it gets bad notices and you begin to listen to everybody and then you patch and patch and sometimes it works, but usually it's just a mess. The play possibly started out to say there is no solution for the poor bastards I am writing about, or if there is one I don't know it, but around Boston it is clearly seen that doesn't give what is called audience satisfaction, and so you fix it. That's a very dangerous game to play. Fix it once for the Board of Directors, and you'll possibly do it forever.

TM: Before we leave the subject of direction, what about [Elia] Kazan? He's had quite a bit of influence on the Broadway theatre in the past ten or so years.

LH: He's very wise about the theatre—maybe too wise.

TM: You mentioned once you thought Tyrone Guthrie was good.

TM: Oh, yes, very, very good. He knows how to do so many things. And he doesn't do things for money. He does what he likes, and sometimes what he likes isn't very good, but that is the penalty you pay for independence and honesty. I admire him very much.

TM: Now we're getting into the financial aspect of Broadway. Big shows, big producers, theatre parties, big names, big advance sales—sometimes a show is a financial success before it even opens. Aren't these things perpetuating all the troubles of the theatre, putting too high a value on commercial success?

LH: It's not good enough to say that the theatre party is doing harm or the advance sale is doing harm. Maybe they are, but it's only minor harm. The troubles go much deeper.

TM: How would you feel about state aid to the theatre?

LH: I used to think it was the solution. There should be state aid, of course, but I've grown frightened of people who hold the money. Bureaucrats are dangerous in any art, in any land. It would be fine if government would put up the money and then go mind its business. But it won't.

TM: The off-Broadway movement originally was supposed to be a solution to all Broadway's problems.

LH: Some of off-Broadway's good. Most of it isn't. But it's nice that it's there—a good sign.

TM: Can you envision a day when there might not be a Broadway theatre?

LH: I think the day may come when there won't be a serious Broadway theatre. We're almost there now. I said before that I think many serious people have lost the habit of going to the theatre. When I was a kid it was fun; I went all the time. The theatre should be, has to be, attractive to the young. It should be better fun, more interesting, than going to see a movie, but I guess it isn't any more.

TM: Do you think a new playwright today faces problems that didn't exist when you began to write?

LH: Any play now faces serious money-production problems. When I started in the theatre, you knew that you only had a fair chance with a serious play—not a very good chance even then—but a fair chance was good enough, and a run of six or eight months was fine. But now a play couldn't earn back its investment in six months. You have, usually, to be an immediate hit or close. No serious work should be—can be—under such pressure. Bad for everybody and bound to influence everybody.

TM: What do you think would happen if you were a new playwright today and arrived in New York with *The Children's Hour,* just as you did in 1934?

LH: I didn't arrive in New York. We had moved from New Orleans many years before. I was here and young and broke and not minding that much. I don't like cutting up old touches, the past was better than the present, and so on, but there were certain differences. You took for granted then that if you wanted to be a writer, you took your chance, and chance meant that you wouldn't be rich, and maybe not happy, and certainly not secure. You didn't think about jobs, you didn't teach at colleges—maybe because nobody asked you—you just hoped that the novel or story or play would sell and you'd have enough to live on for a few months. You didn't think of yourself in competition with stockbrokers and you rather looked down on people who knew about next week's whiskey. Yes, I think *The Children's Hour* would still get produced. But I'm not so sure the atmosphere wouldn't be clouded now with worry about production costs and failure. I don't think success or failure meant much to me then and, when success came, I gave it four days of fun and then ran away fast, frightened that it would become a way of life. Writers are wacks, aren't they?

The Art of the Theater I:
Lillian Hellman—An Interview

John Phillips and Anne Hollander/1964

From *Paris Review*, 33 (Winter-Spring 1965), 64–95. Interview with Lillian Hellman reprinted in *Writers at Work: The Paris Review Interviews, Third Series*, ed. George Plimpton. Copyright © 1967 by The Paris Review, Inc. Reprinted by permission of Viking Penguin Inc.

Miss Hellman spends her summers in a comfortable white house, at the bottom of a sandbank in the town of Vineyard Haven, Massachusetts, on the island of Martha's Vineyard. There is none of old Cape Cod about it; a modern house, newly built with lots of big windows and a wooden deck facing on the harbour. Miss Hellman observes the ferries of Woods Hole-Martha's Vineyard-Nantucket Steamship Authority, weighted down with passengers and automobiles, push through the harbour on their midsummer schedule and disgorge ever more visitors upon this teeming, heterogenous resort. It is a measure of Miss Hellman's dedication to her work that she achieves so much in her exposed situation, not half a mile from the ferry dock. Here she stays with her maid, and a big barking poodle that discourages few of the peak-of-the-season visitors who troop through her parlour.

Behind this new house and out of view on top of the sandbank is the old one, which Miss Hellman sold after Dashiell Hammett died. A frame house with yellow painted shingles and climbing roses, plainer and more regional in its architecture, like a Yankee farmhouse of the last century, it had a complex of boxlike rooms where Miss Hellman's guests thronged. Removed from these, on the far east wing of the house, stood a tower formed by the shell of an old Cape Cod windmill. Up in this windmill-tower was the room where Dashiell Hammett lived; he always escaped there when company came. He had been an invalid since the war; he became a recluse and at the end of his life talked to almost nobody. Hammett was

53

a thin, finely built man and not tall—although when he
was seen walking in delicate silence, in the cruel wasting
of his illness, down a crowded sidewalk on his way to the
library, unrecognized, unknown, forgotten, the proudness
of his bearing set him off from the summer people.

Very occasionally a stranger would come in the house
uninvited and catch Dashiell Hammett off guard. He
might be reading in an easy chair. Miss Hellman would
introduce him, and he elegantly rise and shake hands.
Like many a famous writer who detests being disturbed in
his private self, a million miles from any social confrontation, he had learned to scare off the intruder with his
smile. Here he was luckier than most; for rather than
looking pained and fraudulent, rather than a predictable
Sam Spade/Humphrey Bogart hard-guy leer, the smile
Dashiell Hammett produced on his clear-eyed, lean, aristocratic face was so nearly beatific that it disarmed the
intruder long enough for Dashiell Hammett, with no
more than a how-do-you-do, to vanish from the room.
The arm chair or the book gave his only evidence. Even
the invited dinner guest coming punctually into the room
would know the same ectoplasmic presence, when Miss
Hellman, the laughter mingled in her greeting, would
immediately explain what Dash had said—what his joking
exit line had been on, it seemed, the instant of your
entrance. He was elusive but never aloof. Through the
medium of Miss Hellman it was possible to carry on a
running extrasensory conversation. A question to him,
put through to her, on one evening (as how to clean a
meerschaum pipe) or a request for an opinion (on somebody's writing, on something President Eisenhower did)
was sure to be answered on another. And five years ago a
request was put in writing for an interview to be included
in this series. He was by then at the end of his tether,
often too weak to take his meals at the table. An answer
came: *Sorry. Don't think it would work. Lilly will explain.*
Which she does, though neither by design nor coinci-
dence, in this interview. On a table in the parlour where
she talked was a framed snapshot of Dashiell Hammett as
he looked in World War II as a corporal in the Army
Service Forces. He is lighting his cigarette on a PX-Zippo
lighter and looking every inch a soldier in his impeccably
creased suntans and overseas cap tilted toward the right
of his head of white hair.

Miss Hellman's voice has a quality, not to be captured

on the page, of being at once angry, funny, slyly feminine, sad, affectionate and harsh. While talking here she
often allowed her laughter, like an antidote to bitterness,
to break into her thoughts and give a more generous
dimension to her comments which, in print, may seem at
first glance merely captious. These pages are compiled
from three afternoon conversations in the more than
usually harrying conditions of the Labor Day weekend on
Martha's Vineyard, while Miss Hellman was driving herself to finish a movie script for Sam Spiegel. There were
many interruptions, telephone calls and people coming
and going in the room. Such circumstances cannot excuse but may in part explain some of the interviewers'
unrehearsed and too eagerly "literary" questions.

Interviewer: Before you wrote plays, did you write anything else?

Hellman: Yes, short stories, a few poems. A couple of the stories
were printed in a long dead magazine called *The Paris Comet* for
which Arthur Kober worked. Arthur and I were married and living in
Paris. Let's see, about 1928, 1929, somewhere in there. They were
very lady-writer stories. I re-read them a few years ago. The kind of
stories where the man puts his fork down and the woman knows it's
all over. You know.

I: Was it Dashiell Hammett who encouraged you to write plays?

H: No. He disliked the theater. He always wanted me to write a
novel. I wrote a play before *The Children's Hour* with Louis Kronenberger called *The Dear Queen* . . . It was about a royal family. A
royal family who wanted to be bourgeois. They kept running away to
be middle class, and Dash used to say the play was no good because
Louis would laugh only at his lines and I would laugh only at mine.

I: Which of your plays do you like best?

H: I don't like that question. You always like best the last thing
you did. You like to think that you got better with time. But you know
it isn't always true. I very seldom re-read the plays. The few times I
have, I have been pleasantly surprised by things that were better than
I had remembered and horrified by other things I had thought were
good. But I suppose *Autumn Garden*. I suppose I think it is the best
play, if that is what you mean by "like."

I: Somebody who saw you watch the opening night in Paris of Simone Signoret's adaptation of *The Little Foxes* said that through the performance you kept leaving your seat and pacing the vestibule.

H: I jump up and down through most performances. But that particular night I was shaken by what I was seeing. I like *Little Foxes*, but I'm tired of it. I don't think many writers like best their best known piece of work, particularly when it was written a long time ago.

I: What prompted you to go back to the theme and the characters of *The Little Foxes*? Only seven years later you wrote *Another Part of The Forest*.

H: I always intended to do *The Little Foxes* as a trilogy. Regina in *The Little Foxes* is about thirty-eight years old, and the year is 1900. I had meant to take up with her again in about 1920 or 1925, in Europe. And her daughter, Alexandra, was to have become maybe a spinsterish social worker, disappointed, a rather angry woman.

I: In the third act of *The Little Foxes* is a speech which carries the burden of the play. It says there are people who eat the earth and all the people on it, like the locusts in the Bible. And there are the people who let them do it. "Sometimes I think it ain't right to stand by and watch them do it." At the end of this play Alexandra decides that she is not going to be one of those passive people. She is going to leave her mother.

H: Yes, I meant her to leave. But to my great surprise, the ending of the play was taken to be a statement of faith in Alexandra, in her denial of her family. I never meant it that way. She did have courage enough to leave, but she would never have the force or vigor of her mother's family. That's what I meant. Or maybe I made it up afterwards.

I: These wheelers and dealers in your plays—the gouging, avaricious Hubbards. Had you known many people like that?

H: Lots of people thought it was my mother's family.

I: Might you ever write that third play?

H: I'm tired of the people in *The Little Foxes*.

I: In *Regina*, the opera Marc Blitzstein based on *The Little Foxes*, the badness of Regina is most emphatic.

H: Marc and I were close friends but we never collaborated. I had nothing to do with the opera. I never saw Regina that way. You have no right to see your characters as good or bad. Such words have nothing to do with people you write about. Other people see them that way.

I: You say in your introduction that *The Children's Hour* is about goodness and badness.

H: Goodness and badness is different from good and bad people, isn't it? *The Children's Hour*—I was pleased with the results—was a kind of exercise. I didn't know how to write a play and I was teaching myself. I chose, or Dashiell Hammett chose for me, an actual law case, on the theory that I would do better with something that was there, had a foundation in fact. I didn't want to write about myself at the age of twenty-six. The play was based on a law case in a book by William Roughead . . . I changed it, of course, completely, by the time I finished. The case took place in Edinburgh in the nineteenth century, and was about two old-maid school teachers who ran a sort of second-rate private school. A little Indian girl, an India Indian, had been enrolled by her grandmother in the school. She brought charges of lesbianism against the two teachers. The two poor middle-aged ladies spent the rest of their lives suing, sometimes losing, sometimes winning, until they no longer had any money and no school.

I: As a rule does the germ of a play come to you abstractly? Do you work from a general conception?

H: No, I've never done that . . . I used to say that I saw a play only in terms of the people in it. I used to say that because I believed that is the way you do the best work. I have come now to think that it is people *and* ideas.

I: Have characters invented themselves before you write them?

H: I don't think characters turn out the way you think they are going to turn out. They don't always go your way. At least they don't go my way. If I wanted to start writing about you, by page ten I probably wouldn't be. I don't think you start with a person. I think you start with the parts of many people. Drama has to do with conflict in people, with denials . . . But I don't really know much about the process of creation and I don't like talking about it.

I: Is there something mysterious in what a play evokes as art and the craft of writing it?

H: Sure. That is really the only mystery because theories may work for one person and not for another. It's very hard, at least for me, to have theories about writing.

I: But you had to begin with a clear idea of what the action of the play would be?

H: Not always. Not as I got older. It was bright of Hammett to see that somebody starting to write should have a solid foundation to build on. It made the wheels go easier. When I first started to write I used to do two or three page outlines. Afterwards, I didn't.

I: Do you think the kind of play you do—the well made play, one which runs the honest risk of melodrama for a purpose—is going to survive?

H: I don't know what survives and what doesn't. Like everybody else, I hope I will survive. But survival won't have anything to do with well-made or not well-made, or words like melodrama. I don't like labels and isms. They are for people who raise or lower skirts because that's the thing you do for this year. You write as you write, in your time, as you see your world. One form is as good as another. There are a thousand ways to write, and each is as good as the other if it fits you, if you are any good. If you can break into a new pattern along the way, and it opens things up, and allows you more freedom, that's something. But not everything, maybe even not much. Take any form, and if you're good—

I: Do you have to do with the casting of your plays?

H: Yes.

I: Do you feel you were well served always?

H: Sometimes, sometimes not. *Candide, My Mother, My Father And Me* were botched, and I helped to do the botching. You never know with failures who has done the harm. *Days To Come* was botched. The whole production was botched, including my botching. It was an absolute horror of a failure. I mean the curtain wasn't up ten minutes and catastrophe set in. It was just an awful failure. Mr. William Randolph Hearst caused a little excitement by getting up in the middle of the first act and leaving with his party of ten. I vomited in the back aisle. I did. I had to go home and change my clothes. I was drunk.

I: Have you enjoyed the adaptations you have done of European plays?

H: Sometimes, not always. I didn't like Anouilh's *The Lark* very much. But I didn't discover I didn't like it until I was half-way through . . . I liked *Montserrat*. I don't seem to have good luck with adaptations. I got nothing but pain out of *Candide*. That's a long story . . . No, I had a good time on *Candide* when I was working alone. I am not a collaborator. It was a stormy collaboration. But I had a good time alone.

I: *Candide* was a box office failure, but obviously it was a success. The record is very popular.

H: It has become a cult show. It happens. I'm glad.

I: Do you think *My Mother, My Father and Me* was a cult show?

H: It opened during the newspaper strike, and that was fatal. Yes, I guess we were a cult show. Oddly enough, mostly with jazz musicians. The last week the audience was filled with jazz musicians. Stan Getz had come to see it and liked it, and he must have told his friends about it. I hope it will be revived because I like it. Off Broadway. I had wanted it done off-Broadway in the beginning.

I: Can you comment on your contemporaries—Arthur Miller?

H: I like *Death of A Salesman*. I have reservations about it, but I thought it was an effective play. I like best *View From The Bridge*.

I: *After The Fall?*

H: So you put on a stage your ex-wife who is dead from suicide and you dress her up so nobody can mistake her. Her name is Marilyn Monroe, good at any box office, so you cash in on her, and cash in on yourself, which is maybe even worse.

I: In an important sub-plot of this play a man who was once briefly a Communist names a close friend before a congressional committee.

H: I couldn't understand all that. Miller felt differently once upon a time, although I never much liked his House Un-American Committee testimony: a little breast-beating and a little apology. And recently I went back to reread it and liked it even less. I suppose, in the play, he was being tolerant: those who betrayed their friends had a point, those who didn't also had a point. Two sides to every question and all that rot.

I: And Tennessee Williams?

H: I think he is a natural playwright. He writes by sanded fingertips. I don't always like his plays—the last three or four seem to me to have gone off, kind of way out in a conventional way. He is throwing his talent around.

I: Mary McCarthy wrote in a review that you get the feeling that no matter what happens Mr. Williams will be rich and famous.

H: I have the same feeling about Miss McCarthy.

I: She has accused you, among other things, of a certain "lubricity," of an overfacility in answering complex questions. Being too facile, relying on contrivance.

H: I don't like to defend myself against Miss McCarthy's opinions, or anybody else's. I think Miss McCarthy is often brilliant and sometimes even sound. But, in fiction, she is a lady writer, a lady magazine writer. Of course, that doesn't mean that she isn't right about me. But if I thought she was, I'd quit. I would like critics to like my plays because that is what makes plays successful. But a few people I respect are the only ones whose opinions I've worried about in the end.

I: There is a special element in your plays—of tension rising into violence. In *Days To Come* and *Watch On The Rhine* there are killings directly on stage. Was there possibly, from your association with Dashiell Hammett and his work, some sort of influence, probably indirect, on you?

H: I don't think so, I don't think so. Dash and I thought differently and were totally different writers. He frequently objected to my use of violence. He often felt that I was far too held up by how to do things, by the technique. I guess he was right. But he wasn't writing for the theater and I was.

I: You have written a lot of movies?

H: Let's see. I wrote a picture called *The Dark Angel* when I first started. I did the adaptation of *Dead End*. I did the adaptation of *The Little Foxes*. Right now I'm doing a picture called *The Chase*.

I: Did you ever worry about Hollywood being a dead end for a serious writer?

H: Never. I wouldn't have written movies if I'd thought that. When I first went out to Hollywood one heard talk from writers about whoring. But you are not tempted to whore unless you want to be a whore.

I: The other night when we listened to Peter Seeger sing his folk songs you seemed nostalgic.

H: I was moved by seeing a man of conviction again.

I: We aren't making them like that any more?

H: Not too many. Seeger's naivete and the sweetness, the hard work, the depth of belief I found touching. He reminded me of very different times and people. There were always x number of clowns, x number of simple-minded fools, x number of fashionables who just went along with what was being said and done, but there were also remarkable people, people of belief, people willing to live by their beliefs. Roosevelt gave you a feeling that you had something to do with your government, something to do with better conditions for yourself and for other people. With all its foolishness the thirties were a good time and I often have regrets for it. Many people of my age make fun of that period, and are bitter about it. A few do so out of a genuine regret for foolish things said or foolish things done—but many do so because belief is unfashionable now and fear comes with middle-age.

I: Do people still mention your statement before the House Un-American Activities Committee, "I can't cut my conscience to fit this year's fashions"?

H: Yes.

I: Did that put you in contempt of Congress?

H: No, I never was in contempt. They brought no contempt charges at the end of that day. My lawyer, Joseph Rauh, was so proud and pleased. He was afraid I would be harmed because I might have waived my rights under the Fifth Amendment.

I: You took the stand that you would tell the Committee all they wanted to know about you, but you weren't going to bring bad trouble upon innocent people no matter if they had been fooled?

H: We sent a letter saying that I would come and testify about myself as long as I wasn't asked questions about other people. But the Committee wasn't interested in that. I think they knew I was innocent, but they were interested in other people. It was very common in those days, not only to talk about other people, but to make the talk as interesting as possible. Friendly witnesses, so called, would often make their past more colorful than ever was the case. Otherwise you might turn out to be dull. I thought mine was a good position to take—I still think so.

I: Was it something of a custom among theater people in those days, when they were going to name some old acquaintance to a committee, to call him beforehand and let him know? Just to be fair and square, as it were?

H: Yes. They would telephone around among their friends. In several cases the to-be-injured people actually gave their permission. They understood the motive of their friends' betrayal—money, injury to a career. Oh, yes, there was a great deal of telephoning around. Kind of worse than testifying, isn't it?—the fraternity of the betrayers and the betrayed. There was a man in California who had been barred from pictures because he had been a Communist. After a while he was broke, this Mr. Smith, and his mother-in-law who was getting bored with him—and anybody would have been bored with him—said that he could have a little piece of land. So he started to build a two-room house, and he borrowed the tools from his closest friend, his old college room-mate, Mr. Jones. He had been working on his house for about seven or eight months and almost had it finished when Mr. Jones arrived to say that he had to have the tools back because, he, Mr. Jones, was being called before the Committee the next day and was going to name Mr. Smith and thought it was rather unethical for Mr. Smith to have his tools while he was naming him. I don't know whether the house ever got finished. . . . Clowns, they were.

I: A little known aspect of Lillian Hellman is that she was the inspiration for Dashiell Hammett's Nora Charles, the loyal wife of Nick Charles, the detective-hero of *The Thin Man*. That marriage is beautifully evoked in the book and was played by William Powell and Myrna Loy in the movies.

H: Yes.

I: Didn't it give you some gratification?

H: It did, indeed.

I: When Myrna Loy turned into her, then she became the perfect wife.

H: Yes. I liked that. But Nora is often a foolish lady. She goes around trying to get Nick into trouble.

I: And that was about you both?

H: Well, Hammett and I had a good time together. Most of it, not all of it. We were amused by each other.

I: Was it because of that book that Gertrude Stein invited you to dinner?

H: Miss Stein arrived in America and said that there were two people that she wanted to meet. They were both in California at that minute—Chaplin and Dash. And we were invited to dinner at the house of a friend of Miss Stein; Charlie Chaplin, Dash and myself, Paulette Goddard, Miss Toklas, our host and hostess and another man. There was this magnificent china and lace tablecloth. Chaplin turned over his coffee cup, nowhere near Stein, just all over this beautiful cloth, and the first thing Miss Stein said was, "Don't worry, it didn't get on me." She was miles away from him. She said it perfectly seriously. Then she told Dash he was the only American writer who wrote well about women. He was very pleased.

I: Did he give you any credit for that?

H: He pointed to me, but she didn't pay any attention. She wasn't having any part of me. I was just a girl around the table. I talked to Miss Toklas. We talked about food. It was very pleasant.

I: Did you know Nathanael West?

H: He managed a hotel, the Sutton Hotel. We all lived there half-free, sometimes all-free. Dash wrote *The Thin Man* at the Sutton Hotel. Pep West's uncle or cousin owned it, I think. He gave Pep a job out of kindness. There couldn't have been any other reason. Pep liked opening letters addressed to the guests. He was writing, you know, and he was curious about everything and everybody. He would steam open envelopes, and I would help him. He wanted to know about everybody.

Dash had the Royal Suite—three very small rooms. And we had to eat there most of the time because we didn't have enough money to eat any place else. It was awful food, almost spoiled. I think Pep bought it extra cheap. But it was the depressioin and I couldn't get a job. I remember reading the manuscript of *Balso Snell* in the hotel. And I think he was also writing *Lonelyhearts* at that time. Dash was writing *The Thin Man*. The hotel had started out very fancy—it had a swimming pool. I spent a good deal of time in the swimming pool . . . I had nothing else to do with myself.

Then the Perelmans [S. J. Perelman, West's brother-in-law] bought a house in Bucks County. We all went down to see it. There was a dead fish in a closet. I don't know why I remember that fish. Later we would all go down for weekends, to hunt. I have a snapshot of the Perelmans and Dash and me and Pep and Bob Coates.

Even in a fuzzy snapshot you can see that we were all drunk. We used to go hunting. My memory of those hunting trips is of trying to be the last to climb the fence, with the other guns in front of me, just in case. Pep was a good shot. He used to hunt with Faulkner. So was Dash.

I: Did Faulkner come around a lot in those days?

H: Faulkner and Dash liked each other. Dash's short stories were selling, the movies were selling. So we had a lot of money, and he gave it away and we lived fine. Always, he gave it away—to the end of his life when there wasn't much, anymore. We met every night at some point for months on end, during one of Faulkner's New York visits. We had literary discussions. A constant argument about Thomas Mann. This must have taken up weeks of time.

I: Was Faulkner quiet?

H: He was a gallant man, very southern. He used to call me Miss Lillian. I never was to see him much after that period, until a few years ago when I saw him a couple of times. We remembered the days with Dash, and he said what a good time in his life that was and what a good time we had had together.

I: Was any play easy to write?

H: *Autumn Garden* was easier than any other.

I: At the very end of the play, the retired general, Griggs, makes one of the rare speeches in your plays that is of a remotely "philosophic" nature.

H: Dash wrote that speech. I worked on it over and over again but it never came right. One night he said, "Go to bed and let me try." Dash comes into this interview very often, doesn't he?

I: "That big hour of decision, the turning point in your life, the someday you've counted on when you'd suddenly wipe out your past mistakes, do the work you'd never done, think the way you'd never thought, have what you'd never had, it just doesn't come suddenly. You trained yourself for it while you waited—or you've let it all run past you and frittered yourself away."

H: Yes, the basic idea was his. Dash was hipped on the subject. I think I believe that speech . . . I know I do . . . Dash worked at it far harder than I ever have, as his death proved. He wasn't prepared for death, but he was prepared for the trouble and the sickness he had, and was able to bear it, I think because of this belief, with enormous courage, and quietness.

I: What is the sensation the writer has when he hears his own words from the mouth of somebody else? Of even the most gifted actor?

H: Sometimes you're pleased and the words take on meanings they didn't have before, larger meanings. But sometimes it is the opposite. There is no rule. I don't have to tell you that speech on the stage is not the speech of life, not even the written speech.

I: But do you hear dialogue spoken when you are writing it?

H: I guess I do. Anyway, I read it to myself. I usually know in the first few days of rehearsals what I have made actors stumble over, and what can or cannot be cured.

I: Do you have disputes with actors who want their lines changed?

H: Not too many. I took a stubborn stand on the first play and now I have a reputation for stubborness.

I: Is that because you have written always to be read, even more than to be acted?

H: Partly. But I had learned early that in the theater, good or bad, you'd better stand on what you did. In *Candide* I was persuaded to do what I didn't believe in, and I am no good at all at that game. It wasn't that the other people were necessarily wrong, I just couldn't do what they wanted. With age, I guess, I began to want to be agreeable.

I: Would you mind if your plays were never produced ever again but only read?

H: I wouldn't like it. Plays are there to be acted. I want both.

I: The famous Hemingway dialogue, the best of it, turns to parody when actors speak it verbatim in adaptations of his work.

H: That's right. It shows up, it shows up. That's just what I meant by listening to the actor. Writing for the theater is a totally different form. But then, if you want to be good and hope people will also read the plays, then it becomes a question of making sure the two forms come together. Very often in the printed form, you must recast a sentence. I do it—when I'm not too lazy—for the published version.

But in minor ways, like changing the place of a verb, or punctuation. I over-punctuate for theater scripts.

I: Do you think the political message in some of your plays is more important than the characters and the development?

H: I've never been interested in political messages, so it is hard for me to believe I wrote them. Like every other writer I use myself and the time I live in. The nearest thing to a political play was *The Searching Wind,* which is probably why I don't like it much any more. But even there I meant only to write about nice, well born people who, with good intentions, helped to sell out a world.

I: Maybe this was one play in which you were more concerned with a situation of crisis than with your characters?

H: Yes. But I didn't know that when I was writing it. I felt very strongly that people had gotten us into a bad situation—gotten us into a war that could have been avoided if Fascism had been recognized early enough.

I: What were you doing in those war years?

H: In 1944 I was invited by the Russians to come on a kind of cultural mission. Maybe because they were producing *Watch on The Rhine* and *The Little Foxes* in Moscow.

I: What were those productions like?

H: *The Little Foxes* was an excellent production. *Watch on The Rhine* was very bad. I had thought it would be the other way around. I would go to rehearsals of *Watch on The Rhine* with Serge Eisenstein and when I made faces or noises, he would say, "Never mind, never mind. It's a good play. Don't pay any attention to what they are doing. They can't ruin it." I saw a great deal of Eisenstein. I was very fond of him.

I: When did you discover that you could no longer earn money by writing for the movies?

H: I learned about the blacklisting by accident in 1948. Wyler and I were going to do *Sister Carrie.* Somebody, I think Mr. Balaban, told Wyler that I couldn't be hired. That unwritten, unofficial, powerful blacklist stayed in effect until two or three years ago.

I: Weren't you offered clearance if you would sign something? If you made an appropriate act of contrition?

H: Later. Shortly after the first blacklisting I was offered a contract by Columbia Pictures—a contract that I had always wanted—to direct, produce and write, all three or any. And a great, great deal of money. But it came at the time of the famous movie conference of top Hollywood producers . . . They met to face the attacks of the Red-baiters and to appease them down. A new clause went into movie contracts. I no longer remember the legal phrases, but it was a lulu. I didn't sign the contract.

I: What did you think about what was happening?

H: I was so unprepared for it all, so surprised McCarthy was happening in America. So few people fought, so few people spoke out. I think I was more surprised by that than I was by McCarthy.

I: People in the theater or pictures?

H: Yes and literary people and liberals. Still painful to me, still puzzling. Recently I was asked to sign a protest about Polish writers. I signed it, it was a good protest, I thought, and went out to mail it. But I tore it up when I realized not one of the people protesting had ever protested about any of us.

I: What did you think was going to happen?

H: I thought McCarthy would last longer than he did. I thought the whole period would be worse and longer than it was. You know, I was very worried about Dash. He was a sick man and I was scared that he might go back to prison and get sicker—I lived for a long time in fear that he would go back and not get good medical treatment and be alone and—But jail hadn't worried him much or he pretended it hadn't. It amused him to act as if jail was like college. He talked about going to jail the way people talk about going to college. He used to make me angry. . .

I: *The Maltese Falcon* was taken off the shelves of the USIS libraries when Roy Cohn and David Shine were riding high. Dashiell Hammett was called before Senator McCarthy's committee.

H: Yes. It was on television and I watched it. They called Dash, and Dash was a handsome man, a remarkably handsome man, and he looked nice. One of the Senators, I think McCarthy, said to him, "Mr. Hammett, if you were in our position, would you allow your books in USIS libraries?" And he said, "If I were you, Senator, I would not allow any libraries." A good remark. McCarthy laughed. Nobody else did, but McCarthy did. . . . Dash had an extremely irritating habit of shrugging his shoulders. For years I would say, "Please don't shrug your shoulders." I don't know why it worried me, but it did. He was shrugging his shoulders like mad at the committee. He'd give an answer, and he'd shrug his shoulders with it. And when he was finished and got to the airport he rang me up and said, "Hey, how did you like it? I was shrugging my shoulders just for you."

I: Did that period—and its effect on people—appeal to you as a subject?

H: I've never known how to do it. It was really a clownish period. It was full of clowns talking their heads off, apologizing, inventing sins to apologize for. And other clowns, liberals, who just took to the hills. Ugly clowning is a hard thing to write about. Few people acted large enough for drama and not pleasant enough for comedy.

I: Then you went to England to do a movie?

H: I used to try to explain that it wasn't as bad as they thought it was. And it wasn't. They were exaggerating it because they don't always like us very much. So much talk about fascism here and how many people were in jail. The only time I ever met Richard Crossman, he didn't know I knew Hammett. Hammett was in jail, and Crossman said what a disgrace that was. "What's the matter with all of you, you don't lift a finger for this man? It couldn't happen here, we'd have raised a row." I told him I had lifted a finger.

I: Did you ever think of living abroad as other Americans were doing?

H: I was tempted to stay in England, but I couldn't. I like this country. This is where I belong. Anyway, I don't much like exiles. But I used to try to persuade Dash to go away, just to save his life. He had emphysema. He caught tuberculosis in the First World War and emphysema in the Second. He had never been to Europe. He used to laugh when I suggested his leaving here. He had a provincial dislike of foreigners, and an amused contempt for Russian bureaucracy. He didn't understand all of our trotting around Europe. Thought it was a waste of time.

I: Did he laugh at the idea that they admired him over there?

H: No. He liked it but it didn't interest him much. When I told him that Andre Gide admired him, he made a joke which you can't print in this family magazine.

I: Let's be bold.

H: All right. He said, "I wish that fag would take me out of his mouth."

I: Who did he want to admire his work?

H: Like most writers he wanted to be admired by good writers. He had started off as a pulp writer, you know, and had a wide audience—He wrote a lot for a pulp mystery magazine, *The Black Mask.* But I believe Dash took himself very seriously as a writer from the beginning.

I: He helped you with your work. Did you help him with his?

H: No, No.

I: Did he show you his novels while he was writing them?

H: *The Thin Man* and some stories, and a novel unfinished at his death. The other novels were written before I met him.

I: But he worked very painstakingly with you, on your work.

H: Oh yes, and was very critical of me. The rules didn't apply the other way. I had many problems writing *The Little Foxes.* When I thought I had got it right, I wanted Dash to read it. It was five o'clock in the morning. I was pleased with this sixth version, and I put the manuscript near his door with a note, "I hope *this* satisfies you." When I got up, the manuscript was outside my door with a note saying, "Things are going pretty well if you will just cut out the liberal blackamoor chit-chat."

I: He meant the Negro servants talking?

H: Yes. No other praise, just that.

I: So you knew you were all right?

H: No, I wrote it all over again . . . He was generous with anybody who asked for help. He felt that you didn't lie about writing and anybody who couldn't take hard words was about to be shrugged off, anyway. He was a dedicated man about writing. Tough and generous.

I: Was he always reasonably successful?

H: Oh, no. He earned a kind of living at first, but pulp magazines didn't pay much. He was not really discovered until shortly before I met him, in 1930. He had been writing for a long time.

I: He read constantly?

H: Enormously. He had little formal education. He quit school at thirteen to work. He was the most widely read person I ever knew. He read anything, just anything. All kinds of science books, farm books, books on making turtle traps, tying knots, novels—He spent almost a year on the retina of the eye. I got very tired of retinas. And there was a period of poisonous plants and Icelandic sagas and how to take the muddy taste from lake bass. I finally made a rule that I would not listen to any more retina of the eye talk or knot talk or baseball talk or football talk.

I: Do you consider yourself to be closely tied to the theater and to "theater people"?

H: In the early days I didn't think it out, but I stayed away from them. I was frightened of competing. I felt that the further I stayed away, the better chance I had. No, I don't know too many theater people.

I: A man, who has known both breeds, said that on the whole writers are even more narcissistic and nastier and more competitive than people in show biz.

H: Hard to know the more or less. But people in the theater are usually generous with money and often with good-will. Maybe the old troopers world—having to live together and sharing. Writers are interesting people, but often mean and petty. Competing with each other and ungenerous about each other. Hemingway was very ungenerous about other writers. Most writers are. Writers can be the stinkers of all time, can't they?

I: The playwright knows dangers that are different from those the novelists know?

H: Yes, because failure is faster in the theater. It is necessary that you not become frightened of failure. Failure in the theater is more dramatic and uglier than in any other form of writing. It costs so much, you feel so guilty. In the production of *Candide,* for the first time in my life, I guess, I was worried by all this. It was bad for me.

I: Writing about the Lincoln Center Repertory in *The New York Review of Books,* Elizabeth Hardwick said that the trouble with the present theater is that it is all professionalism and is divorced from literature.

H: Yes, of course she was right. There shouldn't be any difference between writing for the theater and writing for anything else. Only that one has to know the theater. Know it. To publish a novel or a poem one doesn't have to know print types or the publishing world. But to do a play, no matter how much one wishes to stay away from it, one has to *know* the theater. Playwrights have tried to stay away, including Shaw and Chekov, but in the end, they were involved.

Chekov used to send letters of instructions and angry notes. A play is
not only on paper. It is there to share with actors, directors, scene
designers, electricians.

I: Do you believe there are many talented writers working at
present?

H: Yes, but nothing like the period when I was very young, in the
twenties. That was a wonderfully talented generation, the one before
mine. But, you know, I think there's talent around now. Maybe not
great talent, but how often does that occur anyway? It is good that we
have this much. And there are signs now of cutting up. They are not
always to my taste, but that doesn't matter. Cutting up is a form of
belief, a negative expression of it, but belief.

I: The hard professionalism in writers of that generation, like Ring
Lardner, Dashiell Hammett or Dorothy Parker, seems very unfashionable now. Young writers take themselves very seriously as
highbrows and artists.

H: The writer's intention hasn't anything to do with what he
achieves. The intent to earn money or the intent to be famous or the
intent to be great doesn't matter in the end. Just what comes out. It is
a present fashion to believe that the best writing comes out of a
hophead's dream. You pitch it around and paste it up. So sentimental.

I: Sentimental or romantic?

H: Romantic and sentimental. I am surprised, for example, at the
sentimentality in much of Genet, and surprised that people are
romantic enough not to see its sentimentality. I mean a sentimental
way of looking at life, at sex, at love, at the way you live or the way
you think. It is interesting that the "way-out" is not the sharpness of a
point of view or the toughness, but just tough words and tough
actions, masking the romantic. Violence, in space, is a romantic
notion. Anti-bourgeois in an old fashioned sense.

I: Philip Rahv said the old idea of *epatisme* is dead. You can no
longer scandalize the bourgeois. He may be vicious about defending
his property; but as to morality, he is wide open to any and all
nihilistic ideas.

H: Yes, indeed. He has caught up. That is what words like "the
sexual revolution" mean, I guess—the bourgeois sexual revolution. I

agree with Philip. Epataying is just a sticking out of the tongue now, isn't it? The tongue or other organs.

I: You have seen a lot of the contemporary theater in Europe. How does it compare with ours?

H: The British have more talented young men and women than we have here, but I doubt if they are major talents. Genet and Ionesco are interesting men, but they are not to my taste in the theater. Beckett is the only possibly first-rate talent in the world theater. But he must grow larger, the scale's too small. We don't know much about the Russian theater. Obviously, it hasn't produced good playwrights. Certainly, not when I was there. But Russian production, directing and acting are often wonderful. But that's a dead end. When the major talents are directors, actors and scene designers—that's dead end theater. Fine to see, but it ain't going nowhere. You have to turn out good new writers.

I: What about the revival of Brecht?

H: Brecht was the truest talent of the last forty or fifty years. But a great deal of nonsense has been written about Brecht. Brecht himself talked a great deal of nonsense. Deliberately, I think. He was a showman and it is showmanlike in the theater to have theories. But that doesn't matter. What a wonderful play *Galileo* is. Writers talk too much.

I: What do you want to do next?

H: I am going to edit that anthology. I had a struggle with myself because Dash would not have wanted it. He didn't want the short stories printed again. But I decided that I was going to have to forget what he wanted. Someday even the second copyrights will expire and the stories will be in public domain. I don't really know why he didn't want them reprinted—maybe because he was too sick to care. It will be a hard job. I have already started the introduction and I find it very difficult to write about so complex a man, and even I knew so little of what he was. I am not sure I can do it in the end, but I am going to have a try. But I don't know his reasons. Probably when you're sick enough you don't care much. He went through a bad time.

A Playwright Looks at the Theater Today

Robert Murray and Gary Waldhorn/1966

From *Yale Reports*, No. 402 (5 June 1966), 1–8.

Announcer—Good evening, ladies and gentlemen, and welcome to the 402nd edition of *Yale Reports*. Tonight is the last in a series of programs on the American Theater—"A Playwright Looks at the Theater Today."

It is clear that despite the expansion of Community Theater in this country, there is a continued dearth of young successful playwrights. Lillian Hellman, an enormously gifted playwright and author of such classics as *The Little Foxes,* and *The Children's Hour* is here with us this evening. She will discuss some of the problems confronting the young American playwright and the conditions necessary for the revival of meaningful original work in the theater today.

Joining Miss Hellman, will be Mr. Robert Murray, author of *The Good Lieutenant* produced earlier this year at Yale University and Mr. Gary Waldhorn, a young English actor studying at the Yale Drama School.

Here to begin tonight's discussion is Mr. Murray:

Murray: In discussing with Howard Taubman of the *New York Times* the sudden flowering of at least a platoon of distinguished young British playwrights, we raised the question as to why there was a continuing dearth of young and distinguished American playwrights? Why hasn't there been the equivalent renaissance in this country?

Hellman: I don't think it necessarily has anything to do with playwrights. There's been a renaissance in England—the post-war break-through of classes, the overthrow, to some extent, of the class system in England—I mean in the sense that the intellectual is no longer always coming from the middle and upper classes. It's also coming from the lower classes. But I'm not so sure the renaissance

73

can be explained that simply. Immediately after the war of course it looked as if Italy had it, and in many ways Italy did have it. Now, I don't think it looks as hopeful as far as the arts go in Italy. I don't think we had it in this country. We skipped it. Why we skipped it I don't know. We've had almost go good new playwrights since the war, very few at any rate. I'm not sure that the best writers aren't still men in their sixties and fifties, which is not really post-war. I don't think there are any easy answers to it. It probably requires a sociological study and then I even might doubt the conclusions.

Waldhorn: Do you think the reason might be that in England at the moment, there is more theater to write for, there is not a great commercial interest in the repertory theaters, they don't have to break even, they are subsidized by the British government. The acting is better, generally speaking, the directing is better, there is more theater to write a play for, consequently there are more playwrights interested and therefore playwrighting flourishes.

Hellman: I think that certainly contributes to it. It contributes to better acting, however, much more than it would contribute to playwrighting, because then you'd have to explain why the West German theater, which is a highly subsidized theater—probably dollar for dollar way above England—has turned out only one or two interesting playwrights, while England has turned out far more than that. England has subsidy but it's not a giant subsidy and it comes in various forms. Subsidized theater is probably better for the actor and although it's good for the playwright it doesn't necessarily make the playwright. Certainly it can be said that the playwright in England has more places to go than he has here. What you say is partly true, but I always suspect large conclusions about the theater.

Waldhorn: Would you recommend subsidized theater in this country?

Hellman: Yes. I don't like the word subsidized, but everybody wants as many theaters as possible, and everybody knows the theater cannot be privately financed any longer. This is clearly one of the reasons it's dying. There is no possibility of privately financed theater, except for purely commercial theater. It's an old dream which was over a long, long time ago, except for isolated cases which don't really affect the whole culture.

Murray: It's been pointed out that the better American writers have avoided or shied away from the theater simply because it seemed either that they were too refined for what they felt was the midway atmosphere of the American theater, or because they had no genuine interest in writing for the theater. In certain movements now there is an effort being made to try and lure men of refined literary tastes into the theater. Do you think this is going to work, or do you think this is a hollow experiment?

Hellman: I hope it's going to work; in any case it's worth trying. It's perfectly true that particularly in America, the first-rate writer in any other field, such as poetry, or novel, has not wished to write for the theater. Any attempt to see that it happened would be worthwhile. I myself arranged subsidies, for at least ten novelists during the last 20 or 25 years—and not one play turned out well. Maybe I picked the wrong novelists, but I'm afraid—and I'm most reluctant to say it—that I think writing for the theater requires some kind of instinct for the theater. I didn't think this once, but I do think it now. What is is, I don't know. I don't necessarily admire it or not admire it. But I think perhaps it's the way some kind of musical instinct is necessary for a musician. It's a special form of writing and obviously cannot be taught as easily as I once thought.

Waldhorn: Well, there are people like Robert Lowell, an American poet, who has written successfully for the theater. Even Jules Feiffer has written some plays, and American Place Theater, for example, has a studio for such people.

Hellman: You're picking two people. One, Feiffer, has written for the theater, but I don't think he's written very well. Two, Lowell, has written for the theater, but he's based his plays on material of other people, which isn't quite the same although the plays were very good indeed. But two people are a very small number. Consider the novelists and the poets who have wanted to write for the theater. This doesn't mean I don't think it's worth trying. I think millions should be spent trying it.

Murray: Last week Mr. Taubman placed a great deal of blame on the lack of support for serious drama, on the audience. This seems, perhaps, to be putting the blame where it belongs, but what are you going to do about it? Do you agree with that point of view, and if you do, Miss Hellman, what is there about the American audience that they don't want to support serious drama? Is it because the serious drama is not serious enough—it's only serious in intent but not in production—or is it because there's something that they want to avoid or evade that reflects on them in serious drama?

Hellman: I think Mr. Taubman is right, and it's one of the reasons, I suppose, that the theater has to be subsidized—so that the audience can be forgotten about. Mr. Taubman is talking about a New York audience, and there's no question—there hasn't been any question for many, many years—that it's an expense account audience, and it is not going to allow, except for an occasional stylish success which it can't help but support because it must be informed about certain artistic matters for its own survival, the kind of play that flourished as recently, say, as 25 years ago. It has little interest in the serious play, and the play can no longer survive financially on the amount of audience it used to survive on. So that it becomes a circle with a dangerous hollow in it. My first play, *The Children's Hour,* which was a large success, playing in a small, quite beautiful theater which doesn't exist any more. It never had as large an audience as a giant musical. I no longer really remember accurately, but I think it did very large business for six or eight months, then fell off, which is perfectly understandable because there are only X number of people for serious plays. Nevertheless, we were able to play for way over two years, because there was a profit shown with as little as nine and ten thousand dollars a week coming into the box office. And when there wasn't a profit, it didn't matter very much. The producer wasn't losing a great deal. Now this would be an absolute impossibility. It's true that that nine or ten thousand would probably now be equal to twenty-three or twenty-four thousand, but it wouldn't be allowed to stay in a theater, doing that much business. It would close imme-diately. The real estate owner would need the theater for something more profitable. A small audience cannot sustain a play any longer, which is one of the reasons that the theater must move out of New York.

Murray: Do you think if it does move, that there will be an audience receptive to serious drama outside of New York?

Hellman: I don't have this great belief of the receptivity of culture outside of New York. It will have a smaller receptive audience outside of New York. I don't see any signs that it will have the size audience it should have. I think when you get good theaters like the Arena in

Washington you get a small audience. That has value enough but I don't believe Washington has any greater culture than New York, or Minneapolis either, which has a subsidized theater with a subscription list.

Waldhorn: I gather from your remarks before, that it would be the best advice for a young performing artist to go, perhaps to England, in his early formative years.

Hellman: It might be. It's a hard thing to do, because most people don't have money enough to go to England or any country to live. Conditions would be very difficult in a foreign country where you have to be able to support yourself while studying.

Murray: It seems unique indeed to have a woman succeed as well in the American Theater as you have. Most of the playwrights that one puts in the Hall of Fame are men. Why is it, do you think, that playwrighting has primarily been a man's profession although women have succeeded, particularly as actresses, for any number of years?

Hellman: I don't know, I've asked myself that question many times. I just don't know. There have been a few women playwrights, none of them very good—except me, of course—. I don't know, since women make quite good writers in other fields and certainly write a great deal in other fields. There's certainly no barrier to women in the theater, and as you say the acting profession was almost a woman's field, for a long time. I haven't the slightest idea. I think it's just one of those historical accidents. Why haven't more women been composers? There have been successful lady composers. Yet there have been a great many fine lady instrumentalists. There haven't been very many great lady painters, either. I suppose it's the same thing. Maybe we don't do as well as we think we do, maybe that's the answer. I'm sounding grumpy.

Murray: I think one of the distinctions of your plays, Miss Hellman, has been the rather uncompromising glance, or hard look, I should say, at the mendacity, or at least the greed that seems to motivate a number of your characters. And also a very unsentimental streak about your characters. You haven't been harsh or antagonistic toward them all, but you have been unsentimental. This seems to me rather unique in the theater that's supported by people who are accused of being fond of the very things that you've attacked.

Hellman: I haven't always attacked them. I think you're thinking of *Little Foxes* more than any other play, probably. Perhaps *Another Part of the Forest.* Things come along at the right time often and that has something to do with it. Whether if *Little Foxes* had come seven or eight years later, it would have been quite the success it was, I don't know. I have often asked myself that. I hope it would have been, but I don't know. Audiences have a kind of fascination for what attacks them, as they have a kind of fascination for what consoles them, I think as well. I don't think they always know they are being attacked but I didn't mean to attack them. That wasn't my object. I just wrote what I thought I'd write. It turned out to be an attack. I suppose somebody had to tell me about it afterwards, because I really didn't know it.

Murray: *Toys in the Attic* deals with two of the things I mentioned earlier; that too much love can be a rotten thing, and that the effect of sudden affluence on people can be a marvelous catalyst for disaster. It seems to me that in a society, as the United States, this affluence supports what is left of the American theater, and it's lots of fun and daring to illustrate this on stage. Do you think your audience missed that point?

Hellman: No, I don't think they missed it. I meant something, I meant all you have said, and I meant something else by the play which I hope they didn't miss; three ladies loved one man just as long as he was unsuccessful. The minute he dared to do as they had always told him they wanted him to do—to strike out for himself— they all pounced on him to break him in some fashion, and the fashion was money in that sense, of course. I meant money to be the final weapon, really as so often it is. No, I think they understood it. I hope they did.

Waldhorn: I know you've expressed disillusionment with the screen, but I would like to ask nevertheless, is there a future for disgruntled playwrights to express their dramatic instincts through the film media?

Hellman: I was misunderstood; I have no disillusionment with the screen. I like films a great deal. What I said was that I wanted nothing more to do with the regular Hollywood methods of making a picture. I distinctly said that I would like to do another kind of script in another kind of movie world. I love pictures, I think at the moment they are far better than the theater, far more interesting. I just have no possible

interest in ever doing another Hollywood picture because of this last
one called, *The Chase*. I'm just too old for that kind of difficult and
unrewarding experience. But I certainly have no disillusionment with
pictures. And I do think there is a future there. I don't see any reason
that an interesting young writer wouldn't be very taken up with
pictures—if he happens to like them.

Waldhorn: If he doesn't suffer the same thing you did.

Hellman: Well, if he does, he does. I lived through it.

Waldhorn: But why is it that there's this problem even in films?
Many people just sort of shy away from it after one poor experience.
The Cannes Festival reflects this mediocrity. I just read recently that
not one American art film has been accepted.

Hellman: We don't make many to accept. We make very few so-
called art films. We are historically dedicated to Hollywood. It takes a
great deal of courage in this country and a great deal of work to raise
enough money to make any other kind of film. It's a long and difficult
subject but in Europe it isn't that people who have money are so
much more noble than the people who have money here; it is that
the release of a picture is an easier thing in Europe than it is here. It's
a very complicated long business subject.

Murray: It would seem then to me that the problems in both the
theater and the cinema belie some of our so-called American
heritage. If we are indeed the richest country in the world, and a
nation of individualists, then why should the problems be; the
committee method of putting a play on the stage, in that it interferes
with one man's work, and also the constant preoccupation we have
with what things cost rather than any artistic consideration.

Hellman: Of course we do make some good pictures, and we
mustn't assume we don't. We make quite a few good pictures and in
some of the technical fields nobody stands anywhere near us, if that's
any consolation. Probably not more than one or two European
cameramen or electricians or sound people come anywhere near our
people, or even directors, I think, in a technical sense. I don't know
what great good that is if they do rotten pictures. But we do make
some good pictures, despite the fact that movies are in the hands of
big business; bankers who in turn have hired so-called artistic people
to work for them. This is not true in some cases, but it's greatly true.
And it becomes a question of getting your money back and it's a very

difficult way to work. There was a time in Hollywood when mavericks were being turned out. Even those people took chances on themes and on pictures. They do it less and less, I think. The theater is slightly different in this respect because anyone can become a producer tomorrow where a mother or an aunt has enough money to put it up for a show.

Murray: Well the thing that scares me about the future of the American playwright or the American screenwriter is that if he enters into either arena at the present time he is all too well aware of the pressure to make the production succeed that's going to be placed on him.

Hellman: Well, it's never presented to you that way, you see. That's the trap, of course. And if you are any good, you don't think of it that way. And to be any good you have to be a certain kind of silly and naive as well. You believe it for a given minute of time. I honestly went through one solid year believing this picture was going to be a small picture about a Texas town. I don't know what made me believe it but I did, and I have had a great deal of experience in pictures. So, it's not presented to you, as it turns out. Sometimes this is not entirely true. Sometimes a picture comes out exactly as you planned it. Sometimes you yourself have enough power or the director has enough power, or possibly even the star has enough power to insist upon it. There is no hundred percent rule about it.

Waldhorn: What in your estimation, is the value of off, off-Broadway theater?

Hellman: This is a large question. When it's good, it's good. When it's bad, it's bad. I don't think it's been terribly good the last year or two with very few exceptions. It's gotten more and more Broadway rather than off-Broadway but it certainly has done interesting things and maybe it will again. It's a good thing to be doing, it's a healthy thing to be doing. Robert Lowell's play and William Alfred's play were done off Broadway and were both very distinguished things to have done. *Musgrave* is now being done off-Broadway. All these are worth doing.

Waldhorn: I think I was a little misunderstood. I meant off, off-Broadway.

Hellman: What does that mean?

Waldhorn: Well, there are these places that call themselves off off-

Broadway and they do things like "happenings" and "Cafe La Mama."

Hellman: Well, I saw one of them. I don't know. I suppose it's all right. I don't like the theater that much. I don't like the theater at all. I get too restless. But I'm no judge, I've only been a couple of times. I'm not crazy about parlor theater. I'm sure it has some benefits for the young playwright. I'm sure it has some benefits for the young actor. I'm not sure that I'm the right audience for them.

Murray: Miss Hellman, you just said a rather astounding thing; you said you didn't care for the theater. Would you elaborate on that because obviously at one time the theater, was something that was very close to you and something to which you contributed very valuably.

Hellman: Whenever I say that people think I'm joking. It's very understandable to me. I was in Russia in the middle of the war, when I went to a concert one night with Prokofiev. It wasn't really a concert, it was a state dinner with a room off the dinner where a small orchestra played. I sat with Prokofiev and about 20 minutes later he punched me and said, "Let's go have a drink:," and I said "Oh no, I'd like to listen to the music, wouldn't you?" and he said, "No, I hate music" and he got up and left the room. That's a famous old joke but I knew that he had never heard it, it's too American a joke for him ever to have heard. So I followed him out when I could get out of the room without attracting too much attention. And I spent the rest of the evening asking him about that. He was telling the truth. This didn't mean he didn't equally love it. He meant that he just didn't like listening to it. And I feel the same way. I don't like very much to sit in the theater unless I am looking at something that I like very, very much.

Murray: You'd rather do it than see it?

Hellman: I'd rather do something first, of course, anybody would. You know I have a very good time seeing something that I really like very much or interests me very much. The rest of the time, if it's just fairly good, I find I'm restless in the theater. And I want to get out. I don't want to sit in a chair. I'd rather be standing so that I could leave if I wanted to. I know exactly what Prokofiev meant. When he liked something he could sit five or six hours and listen to it. But he didn't like a great deal. And he got nervous and upset and worried about his own work. He couldn't listen to the kind of music that was being played that night. He said it was awful. And I have the same feeling in the theater. I know exactly what he meant. And he meant it quite seriously, it wasn't a joke. I thought at first that it was.

Murray: It seems to me that theater audiences are splitting up into two different groups, similar to what has happened to the American movie audience. You have the mass audience for the world market, and then you have the art theater crowd. It seems to me that the theater is undergoing something like this too. There is a band of people who have become disenchanted with the content of most plays. There is nothing new or nothing astounding or nothing to tickle the intellect about them. But there is now an attempt to create a theater of their own, at least I see certain evidence of this. I think the American Place theater in New York has been perhaps the most remarkable example of this. But if there are many people like yourself who are restless in the theater, can we count on getting a steady audience among that group of so-called intelligent play-goers?

Hellman: Well, I'm not typical of an audience. In the first place I'm a so-called professional. In the second place I'm restless by nature, physically restless. In the third place I've seen a great deal of the theater, I'm not a typical example of an audience. I'm often very interested by things that wouldn't interest another kind of intellectual. I'm often not interested by things that would interest an intellectual. I don't like bad performances of Shakespeare, for example. They would bore me. On the other hand, somebody really studying Shakespeare or very taken up with him would probably enjoy it. I do think you are right that it's already happened that audiences have sharply divided themselves. Much more sharply in pictures, I think. You can almost predict the looks of the audience in so-called art movie houses. It's a much younger group of people than those going to big Broadway houses. It's a totally different age group and dressed group. The same thing is true of off-Broadway and Broadway, I think.

Waldhorn: What would you recommend for the young play-wrights in the face of this unreceptive American audience? What should he be writing and what is the future for him?

Hellman: Go ahead and do what he can do. I don't think the playwright should worry about what the audience is, it's always been trouble. I think he just goes ahead and does the best he can, hopes to get produced, which is all anybody hopes for anyway. It never was as rosy, of course, as it looks now. There's no sense in worrying about audiences, that's a sucker game in any department, just do as well as you can do.

Waldhorn: By the same respect, what would you recommend for the young actor in this country who does not want to suffer the growing pains of young repertory companies around the country?

Hellman: There is no recommendation except suffering the growing pains. You take your chances. The older I get the more convinced I am that if you pick a hard way, you pick it, that's all. And you might get walloped for it,—some people don't, some people do, but you understand at the beginning that's the way you picked.

Interview with Lillian Hellman

Lewis Funke/1968

From *Playwrights Talk About Writing: 12 Interviews With Lewis Funke* (Chicago: Dramatic Publishing Co., 1975), 90–110. Reprinted with special permission from The Dramatic Publishing Co., Inc. All rights reserved. This excerpt may not be reproduced in any way without clearance for royalties. For information contact The Dramatic Publishing Company, P.O. Box 109, Woodstock, IL 60098.

Lillian Hellman emerged from the taxi in front of her house on East 82nd Street in Manhattan, apologized for being a bit late and explained that she had just come from having a tooth extraction. When the suggestion was made that the interview might be postponed she refused vigorously. She would be all right, she insisted, but as it turned out, the sedation which had been administered began wearing off. She was clearly in some pain. Nevertheless, she insisted on going on, typifying the sort of woman she has been all her life—firm, independent, determined. She wears her hair swept back off her forehead, her brow is high, the nose prominent, the lips full, and the face lines indicative of much living— life that encompasses the free-wheeling days of the 20s, the fervent years of the 30s, and the war.

The living room in which we sat looked out on the street and occasional noises drifted through the open window. The afternoon was well along. Still, even in the subdued light, it was clear that the room, uncluttered, was done in simple good taste. Nowhere was there much to indicate that this was the home of a writer, the creative work being done in another room elsewhere in the three-story house which she owns. She also has a house at Martha's Vineyard in Massachusetts where she spends as much time as she can, especially during the summers.

Although her jaw was bothering her, her answers were decisive. She obviously had thought a good deal about her craft. Her insistence that she knew little about how to write was not a false show of modesty. It was instead a token of the humility that comes to many after years of experience. She had no idea of what she might be doing next, though she did say she had been enjoying her seminars deeply, that she liked coming into contact with the youth of our time. She had recently completed her memoir, *An Unfinished Woman,* and was anxious about its reception, an anxiety that proved needless. Although she had eschewed any deep exposure of her private life, her book was an absorbing kaleidoscope of the events she had experienced. Her portrait of her good friend Dorothy Parker and of Dashiell Hammett won praise and the book turned up on the best-seller lists.

F: What do you think is the reason there are so few women playwrights?

H: I don't know. I've asked myself that many times. I really don't think there is any answer to that.

F: Is it possible that women don't like to become involved in the gamble of playwriting as compared to writing novels? We have many women who are novelists.

H: It's possible—and yet it's no greater gamble. It's more painful in the sense that the play closes faster than a book is off a shelf, but I don't think it is any greater gamble in time or money. No, I don't know why.

F: Well, I'll throw out another suggestion. Is it just that, with so few exceptions, women don't write quite with the same vigor that men do? In the newspaper business once in a while you come across a woman writer who, you might say, writes like a man. There's a kind of quality in her writing. I don't like to use the word toughness, but most women do write with a softer quality than most male journalists.

H: I don't know about journalists, but I don't think many women write with the vigor of men, whether they are novelists or playwrights or poets. We would like to think so, but I think the record is fairly clear that with the exception of a few, they don't.

F: One British critic remarked that he felt that women lacked the objectivity that is a dramatist's first prerequisite. Do you think that makes any sense?

H: No. Women lack objectivity, but I'm not sure it's very good for a writer to have objectivity. How many men have had so-called objectivity about writing? Writing is oneself. I don't think it has anything to do with force or vigor or whatever, finally, is the word for great talent. I really don't think it can be broken down or explained. It's just too bad that we all thought that women would be equal and they are not equal. Why and how this is I don't know. Perhaps it's even biological. I mean equal in the arts—they're equal in many other ways. They are very often equal in intelligence. They are very often superior in observation, very often superior emotionally, I think. There's no question, the records show that through the last two hundred years, they have not been equal to men.

F: Creatively.

H: Creatively not equal to men.

F: Lillian, you said a few years ago that you had come to the conclusion that playwriting is a peculiar form and that either you have a feeling for it or you don't. Now what is so peculiar about the form?

H: I'm probably going to end up every question saying, I don't know, which is the way I found I teach. Having started out in the belief in strict definitions, I've come to believe that I don't really think that any of them are any good. I don't believe in sharp definitions any more. I've come out thinking I just don't know the answer to these questions. It differs in some way that is mysterious to me. One has some instinct or talent for it or one doesn't. How that is picked up I don't know. I do know now what I didn't know even fifteen or twenty years ago when I was saying that any good writer could be taught playwriting. I don't believe it. It has nothing to do with being a good writer. A great many novelists are much better than their colleagues in the theatre. What a theatre gift is or a film gift is, I don't know, but it's very different from what I once thought. Maybe it comes by instinct; maybe it comes by something in one's own nature and it's picked up as a child. I don't any longer think that you can make any good writer into a good playwright.

F: We have had this experiment going on for several years at the American Place Theatre that offers an opportunity for poets and novelists and other writers to try their wings as playwrights. There have been a few that have come out like Lowell's *Endecott and The Red Cross* in *The Old Glory* and a few others, but you would still subscribe to the thought that they were successful up to a point because they did have a feel for the theatre.

H: I'll have to put it in another way. Maybe they were playwrights from the beginning. Maybe they learned. I don't know. I wouldn't say that somebody who starts with another form doesn't become a playwright. That isn't at all what I meant. You could be a very good novelist and you could also be a very good playwright. There have been very few of them, but there certainly could be. All I meant was that I don't know how to explain the playwright part. I didn't mean that you couldn't be good at something else and learn it. I don't think you can learn it if it isn't there.

F: I think that's a conclusion that has been reached by other people, too. Writers or playwrights are born. They can't be made.

H: No, I'm afraid not. Whether they're born or not, I don't know. It's a phrase I've never been very sure of, but I don't think they can be made out of somebody who wasn't originally. The most you can do is to take somebody who is, perhaps, and help. I don't think you can take somebody who isn't and do anything.

F: I think the first course in writing that you gave was at Harvard under the persuasion of McGeorge Bundy. Then you went on to Yale and this year you've been at M.I.T. Now I'm curious how you reconciled your point of view . . .

H: Well, you understand none of these courses were ever in drama. I've never taken a drama class.

F: But they do cover a gamut, don't they?

H: They cover English. They are just straight English courses in writing and they included perhaps one play or one movie script if one wants to do it, but they never have had anything to do with drama.

F: Under the circumstances I imagine that the kids do corner you for questions on playwriting.

H: Sometimes they do, sometimes they don't. I tell them whatever I know. Sometimes it's a help. I'm not so sure it's very much.

F: Do you give them any sort of rules, then?

H: No, not any. I don't know any. It would be foolish to give kids rules because the hope is that they won't pay any attention to them.

F: Well, then, what is your approach to the class? What is your procedure, actually?

H: Well, I base the course on other people's work. I suppose the course could be a course on how to steal, which is very hard to teach kids; how to steal and yet make something your own. So I pick out "x" number of things, novels or short stories or poems, or plays, and I draw up a set of ground rules which they have to follow. From that piece of work with the ground rules, they write on their own. Sometimes they write a short play. Twice this season they wrote a play.

F: What are the ground rules?

H: It depends on the piece. I gave them this year Kafka's letter to his father, and the ground rule was that it had to be a gifted young man complaining justly or unjustly and with a great deal of feeling for tenderness toward his father, about the same things that Kafka complained about. The man could be in this century, the 16th century, any place they chose to put him. He had to be young and he had to have a father and a mother.

F: And then it was up to them to develop a plot situation.

H: No, it wasn't a plot piece. It was just a young man writing to his father, just a letter.

F: I read that in one seminar or one of these classes you gave them a story by Graham Greene and you said you could change the woman into a man or vice versa but you always had to remain true to the basic theme. This was a simple person and you couldn't make her a suburban housewife.

H: I think so. I don't remember which story it was of Graham Greene but it sounds right.

F: Young people often go into writing, I think, for the wrong reasons. They go in for reasons of ego. They like to see their name in type, for instance. They go in because they think that there's a great deal of money in writing. They also go in for the sake of what they think will be fame. Now what do you consider the right reasons for becoming a playwright?

H: That you want to do it. There's no other reason.

F: How can a youngster determine that he wants to do it enough or that mixed up somewhere in there is also that ego factor and all the others?

H: Well, he can't any more than any of the rest of us ever could. It's always mixed up with everything, isn't it? I mean if he becomes a football player, the same thing is true, isn't it? There's the noise of people in the stands and there's also the pleasure of the game and how good he is at it. I don't really think it's much different. I don't know how you determine anything as risky as any form of writing except that you take your chances on it. You don't determine to become a stock broker. There it is and somebody offers you the job and you think you can learn it and it's probably going to be a good living. You might be a better one than the next one. You might not be, but that can't ever be true of any form of writing, can it? It has to be whether you think you can do it.

F: What equipment should a young person have in order to become a playwright? If I came to you at age nineteen or twenty and said, "Miss Hellman, I want to be a playwright. What should I do in the way of educating myself to become a playwright?"

H: I'm afraid you're going to find my answers very unsatisfactory, Lewis, because I don't believe in rules. They seem to be no sooner made than they are broken by the next person. I would simply say *read.*

F: Is it necessary to really read widely in all fields?

H: I think so. That's the only necessity. Then see whether the form you are working on is natural to you. Otherwise, I don't see really any way to tell. I had no way of telling. I don't know how anybody else has a way of telling.

F: Would you recommend a very deep course in reading of plays?

H: No, of everything. I don't know of any other way to write except to read. Nobody can teach you to write. That's one thing certain.

F: Did you see the story we had in the *Times* recently that the writers are not reading any more?

H: I did see this and I was very interested in it. I very much doubted the truth of what they were saying or if they'll be writers. They will be writers, I think, for a small amount of time perhaps. Either that or they are not telling the truth, or they think they are telling the truth, but they're not. They are looking at television and movies, but if they are not reading, they can't last very long. People usually say they are not reading. This is a famous form of boasting, you know.

F: In other words, then, you have found among your students in the different courses that you have given that they do do a lot of reading?

H: Not always. They don't do enough, I think, but the very bright ones have read.

F: Would you recommend acquainting oneself with music and other forms of the arts to develop any sort of sensitivity or going out into the world and "living," as we say?

H: Yes, I think the more one knows about everything, the better, but who's to recommend that? Who's to say, "Listen to music." Music either interests you or doesn't interest you. Who's to say, "Live!" Living interests you or it doesn't interest you. I think by the time we meet most kids the decision has been made in some form.

F: The reason I asked that question was because I remember when I was interviewing actors, John Gielgud made the point that he felt that, as an actor, it was necessary to him to steep himself in the various arts and he felt that it deepened his reactions to roles and to plays.

H: Well, acting is quite different. Certainly we would all like to think that of the better educated, the more civilized; the more known, the more delicate. We'd all like to think this and it is very probably true, but I am not at all sure that makes writers. It might just make very cultivated men.

F: I have something here that Walter Kerr wrote recently. He was talking about a play by a young man named Noonan who had written *The Year Boston Won the Pennant*. He said Mr. Noonan is dramatically shrewd yet hasn't learned one of the things that Bernard Malamud knows by instinct; that before the last knock-down, there must be a last successful spurt if we are not to become wearied by the movement of down, down, down. Now, can you cite from your own plays examples of what Walter seems to be talking about? Is this one of the tricks of playwriting?

H: No, I think I know what he means. I think he means that having gone in any direction, you can't continue dramatically down forever. You must come back to some kind of peak, some kind of interest before you can come down again, otherwise the word drama, I suppose, would be out of the window. I would think that's all he meant. I don't quite understand the reference to Bernard Malamud because Malamud is a novelist, but I would think in any art (well, in poetry it probably wouldn't be true) you cannot start high and go straight down in a dramatic sense. You may go down in an emotional sense. You can't go down in a dramatic sense or a comedy sense because you're going to end on the floor. You instinctively have to come back several times before the end to some kind of height.

F: Is this similar to what actors call timing?

H: I don't think so. I think timing has more to do with the way you deliver a line and whether at a second or a second and a quarter. I think this is less to be timed than that. This is over a period of 2½ hours, say, or in a novel over a period of much longer than that, in a short story much less than that.

F: Does this then bring in the consideration of the psychology or mental attitude of the listener, of the audience? Must you learn or have the instinct for sustaining interest because human interest wanes when there isn't a constant up and down of conflict?

H: To an extent. You can go down and seem to come up. I don't think you can have a steady note whether it's a high note or a low note. That hasn't anything to do with theatre.

F: How does a playwright learn that he must do this?

H: I don't know. I don't know how anybody learns anything. I really don't. I come increasingly to believe that I have no idea how. The more I teach, the more convinced I am I don't believe anybody knows how anybody learns anything. You probably start learning at six and by the time you get to college and anybody starts to teach you, you're made up of all those years and all anybody can do is reinforce them or get the use of them or convince you of something else or make something open towards you. The process of education, I think, has been far too much simplified. Everybody has got slogans for it that I don't believe, never did believe in, but believe in less and less and less.

F: Then why do we have such a proliferation of writing courses, playwriting courses, all over the lot?

H: Well, some of them are valuable, I suppose. Some of them are ways for people to earn a living. Some of them are valuable. Some are given by very honest men who, whatever they do or don't do, are deeply interested in their students. It isn't really rules you give students that they pay much attention to. They write them all down busily because that was the way they were brought up to do, but I doubt whether they look at the notebook any more than I look at the ones I took. It's a feeling you give them of some kind of opening up of a world and some kind of vague direction, if you can manage that. You're very lucky if you can. Some kind of, perhaps, delicacy within themselves.

F: This is the prime value of a course if you have the kind of man who can impart this feeling to a class?

H: Plus excitement which you can give about a single work. You hope you can open up the play or the novel to them and sometimes you do.

F: Well, on the basis of what you have said and the gnostic sort of attitude you have taken toward writing, do you ever feel a sense of futility about giving these courses?

H: Very seldom. Whatever futility I have felt has been that I have not been able to reach them. I did feel that a couple of times and I usually got help from one or the other of them.

F: From one of the students?

H: Yes. You sometimes strike a wrong note. You sometimes know that you are talking a private language which I have a very bad habit of doing anyway, as you can tell from this interview. You sometimes know that nobody is understanding you and that you're saying it right, but then it usually clears up.

F: Through the process of the cross-fire of conversation?

H: Yes, and if you don't make it impossible for them to exchange something with you, it clears up as a rule. This time was very lucky. It went well from the beginning, but sometimes it hasn't gone well from the beginning.

F: Do you find yourself bothered by this kind of frustration?

H: When it's happened, very bothered by it. I haven't known what I was doing that was wrong except that I do talk a kind of language very often that nobody understands. I've known this all my life. Kids do want rules as much as your questions want them and I'm very opposed to rules and don't like to make them, don't like to make generalizations about writing. I think I'm a bad person to interview about anything. I've been told this before. I don't know how to define things. There are certain things I know by reading, say. I know if I read a play, it's no good or it's good or it's hopeful, but I don't know how I know it.

F: I couldn't agree with you more because I am supposed to be an editor and one of the problems that I encounter as an editor is the same. I know when a piece is good or when it isn't good, yet I find great difficulty in telling a writer why it isn't good or how to improve it.

H: Whether it's from students or from somebody else. Whether I'm right or I'm wrong, I usually can say for myself what I think is right or wrong. That doesn't mean I'm right. It only means that I think I'm right. I think this is true of most writers. I think it's what makes them the best critics. They sort of can say the second act is wrong or the first part of the piece is fuzzy. I'm sounding vaguer than I mean. I can't make up the rule before I find the piece. I suppose what it really comes down to is, I believe in piano practice. I just believe in sitting down to a piano.

F: In other words, what you are saying is that one has to keep writing.

H: Yes, that's right. While you can make certain rules, it's really best for yourself, as well as for anybody young, possibly not to make them until you see what they can do. Sometimes there's not even any sense in making them. They are never going to have any talent and it's a waste of time to go into why you think certain things. Better to let it ride out. They'll get something else out of the course. I think that's true for yourself. I wrote short stories for years and knew they weren't any good. I don't know why I knew they weren't any good, but they weren't any good. It's probably best not to torture myself with the reasons.

F: I think you agree that a playwright doesn't or shouldn't write for himself, that he must consider the audience. In what sense is this meant? What I'm thinking of is the kind of writing that is going on in the theatre today where it almost seems a self-indulgence. Why do these young people seem to be writing and not caring whether people are listening?

H: It's just another kind of listening. They probably care just as much as we cared. Times change. I cannot believe anybody writes for the theatre without hearing an audience. You can actually hear an audience. There's a big difference between that and trying in a sort of venal way to please an audience which is, of course, death. You have no right in the theatre then. You ought to publish the play and not have it produced, or perhaps even tear it up. There is a symphony of an audience going on in your head. You may guess very wrong, as we have all done, and there's no sound at all from the audience.

F: Do you follow the so-called new theatre at all, Lillian? Do you go to the plays that these young people are writing?

H: Not a great deal any more. I don't go to the theatre regularly any more. It's been a very long time for me now.

F: I know that. I was going to come around to that.

H: I find most of the theatre bores me. I go from time to time and I think some of it is talented, but it has nothing to do with the new theatre or the old theatre. It's just that a great deal of theatre bores me. This has been coming on for a long time now.

F: In your writing, you have been a master of the well-made play and we're not getting the so-called well-made play any more. How do you feel about that?

H: Nothing, nothing. One time does one thing, another time does another thing. I never had any argument to make for the well-made play. I always in turn had a disdain for those who attacked it, which has been entirely my time because I have been very attacked for it all my life. It seemed to me not even worth answering. I don't think it's any more important than what meal you eat. You either eat three courses or you eat a hamburger. What difference does it make if it's some good to you? I don't think the well-made play is fashionable this minute but I'm not sure that it won't be in fashion again, and it doesn't really seem to matter whether it is or it isn't. It's simply a fashion. I can't believe Ibsen is going to be thrown aside in the end by cultivated men or serious men. He certainly was the master of the well-made play. Anything any good is well-made. It's just a different kind of making.

F: In the period that you and I have known, playwrights would generally pay very close attention to a structure. They had either a story to tell or they had a character or ambiance that they were developing. Now this doesn't seem to be happening any more, and what is curious to me is that even those critics who have been fostering the so-called "new theatre" when confronted with, for instance, *The Front Page* or a revisit to Arthur Miller's *The Price*, suddenly say, "My goodness, it's so superior to the other thing." What I'm wondering is whether this new theatre is a passing fancy and the other type of theatre, of playwriting, will return.

H: I don't think it's one thing or the other. I think that part of the new theatre is a very interesting and free form and that's a very great advance over my time. Part of it is junk. Critics' reactions seem to me to mean very little. They're swingers mostly or they are anti-swingers, which is the same as swinging. What's fashionable is fine or what is anti-fashionable is even better with some, but I don't think any of that matters. There are certain forms in the new theatre which seem to me to have opened a whole new world of the theatre and a wonderful world, Mr. Beckett, for example. I don't think many of the rest of them have.

F: We have a lot of imitation and I think this is part of the problem. Beckett in himself is a genius.

H: Yes, he is, in any form. It happens also to be a very well-made form. People are always confusing that term. That somebody finds a new form doesn't mean that they haven't made it very well. I think what they mean by a well-made play in the theatre is a play fashioned in the sense of Ibsen in the 19th century. Of course before Ibsen there was not a 19th century form. There were other forms. I'm sure that when Restoration comedy came in, people were sighing for other kinds of comedy, or one hundred years later, were sighing for Restoration comedy.

F: What exactly led you into playwriting? You didn't start out as a playwright, as I can recall.

H: No, I didn't. I started out as a manuscript reader and then I did book reviews and then I did short stories. I really haven't any idea why I started writing plays. I worked in the theatre. Maybe that was the reason, but that was a kind of accident. Now as I look back upon it, maybe I was, like all young people, trying to find a form in which I could write and found it, having gone to a fair amount of trouble to go through other forms.

F: In other words, you actually never had any training or schooling in playwriting?

H: No, no.

F: But when you started writing plays, had you already read many other playwrights?

H: I read some. I read the usual amount. I don't think I read any large amount. I don't think I read as much as most kids in college today have read. I had read, of course, Shakespeare, which every-

body read, and I had read Ibsen and Strindberg. I had read the
Restoration people and the early Elizabethans, but they were required reading, you know. I don't think I read any more than that.

F: Then you couldn't rightfully say that any one playwright had a
particular influence on you.

H: No, I couldn't say it. I'm sure it's there but I couldn't say it.

F: I understand that *The Children's Hour,* which was the first play
you wrote alone, was based on a famous early 19th century Scottish
law report. How did you happen to read it?

H: I have no memory. I just picked up the book and read it.

F: Were you consciously looking for an idea for a play at that
time?

H: I don't think so. It was Dashiell Hammett's idea that young
people were better off if they rested on something that was already
accomplished and didn't have to rely on their own life history, didn't
have to be autobiographical. They got out of themselves more. They
got away from themselves more, but I have no idea about this story. I
suppose because I knew something about New England I put the
play there and the girls were my age. I changed it. It took me two
years. I think they started out twenty-six and got to be twenty-eight
by the time the play was over. I put the school in a New England
town and changed the whole plot, really.

F: Why did you do that?

H: Well, I could hardly have written about Edinburgh. I suppose I
could have, but it was simply the long way around. I think that's
exactly what he meant. You take from something what you need and
make it your own. Otherwise you're just a copyist. I think I did that
instinctively.

F: What made you feel that there was a dramatic situation here
that could be done as a play?

H: I wish I could remember. I don't remember. I must have
obviously felt it.

F: You once recalled in an interview in connection with *The
Children's Hour* that, in writing the play, you reached back into your
own childhood for material. Is this true of all your work?

H: It's true of everybody's work. I think everybody does exactly
that. You have nothing to reach back to except yourself. Sure, I think
that's writing. This is what I have been trying to tell students for a long

time. There is nothing wrong with taking something from somebody else but it has to be made your own. Otherwise it's just copying. I think it was T. S. Eliot who said good writers steal and bad writers borrow. Somebody did, anyway. Borrowing is terrible. Stealing, you make your own.

F: In terms of *The Little Foxes* or *Toys in the Attic* and *Watch on the Rhine,* can you recall examples where you reached back into memory for particular moments in the play or developing ideas for the play?

H: Well, I don't know that I can give you an example of it because they all were reaching back into either my own memory or what somebody told me, which is the same thing. Now you can't possibly describe anything without reaching back somewhere to yesterday or twenty years ago or what somebody told you. After all, writing is the process of making use of yourself or what you come out with from other people. You mean something definite?

F: Yes, just an example of a situation. It could be any one of the plays.

H: Well, in *Watch on the Rhine,* I suppose it was the hero. I had in some form met the man in Spain. It wasn't at all he, of course, by the time it came out. It never is. The Roumanian I had played poker with once in London—I mean, it wasn't he at all but certainly I stored up the memory of the poker game.

F: In other words, the characters have some germ in reality, lived in the past or experienced.

H: Most of them. But they are so far away from reality.

F: Then what is the process of building a new flesh onto that early skeleton? Does this come purely out of your own imagination?

H: No, I suppose something strikes you about Miss X and you store it for twenty years. About Miss Y you store something else and about Mr. Z you store something else and then, when you sit down to make a character, all three things come together and even are possibly thrown aside and not paid any attention to. You begin to invent from there. I really don't know how to describe it any better than that. I know when people take my fancy as literary characters, but I also know that I have never done them as characters.

F: Does this suggest that you rely on memory, or do you have a notebook?

H: I've done both. Very seldom about people have I ever had a notebook. I remember what I want to remember of people, which is all that matters in writing—what I want to remember. I have usually used a notebook for journeys.

F: Well, that's the diary.

H: Yes. I very seldom take notes on people or events because there I can pretty well trust what I wish to remember. This doesn't at all mean it's the truth about the person. It only means that it has caught my fancy as the truth.

F: Right. What was the genesis of *Watch on the Rhine?* Did it come out of some newspaper story?

H: No. Oddly enough it is one of the few plays I know what the genesis was and it's so far away from what came out that it's almost unbelievable. It started out in an Ohio town and was influenced with my reading of Henry James' *The Europeans,* and that makes absolutely no sense because the play is so far away from it.

F: Except that there is a point of view about Europeans.

H: And Americans, that's right. That's just about all that remained. The play, as you know, takes place in Washington in a totally different atmosphere.

F: What was the propelling motive for writing *Watch on the Rhine?*

H. I suppose, considering when it was done, I felt very strongly anti-Fascist and was moved by the forces of the time it was written.

F: In other words you sat down deliberately to write a play showing the Fascist state of mind.

H: No, I didn't at all. No, no, I'm saying almost the opposite. That's what I've been saying all along. I don't think anybody else sits down to write something with an object in view. Having started one place, I ended in another, I suppose formed by what I felt at that minute of history. I certainly didn't start out to write an anti-Fascist play. I just started out to write a play about some people.

F: They were particular people, weren't they?

H: They were particular people, but I wonder why one asks that question. If somebody sat down to write a play about South America, would one ever say to the man, "Did you sit down to write an anti-American play?" The man is probably not feeling too good about

North Americans this minute but I don't think he sat down to write the play about that. It's what he is.

F: What interests me is that you, contrary to almost any other playwright, seem to be suggesting that one day you thought you wanted to write a play and . . .

H: No, forgive me. Let me correct that. It wasn't that I one day wanted to write a play. I don't know about the first play. That may be true and I was looking for a form to write in. From then on I waited for some idea that interested me or some people that interested me. I haven't really cared about when I wrote a play. I have been quite slow as you know. I had to wait. There was nothing I could do about it.

F: Well, what then would you say was the moment you got that flash and said, "I've got it! This is what I want to do." Do you remember any impelling moment?

H: I remember a lot of impelling minutes but I really don't know what they were. *Watch on the Rhine* happened in a car when I was driving up to the country. I just felt, "Now I know. Now I know how to do it." I don't know. I don't remember many minutes where I thought, that's it.

F: Did *Watch on the Rhine* gestate in any way for you for a long time?

H: Yes, yes, it did. *Watch on the Rhine,* oddly enough, I know better than the rest because I can almost place where the ideas for the people came from.

F: Could you tell me about it?

H: Well, I met probably what I thought was a version of the hero in 1937 and I met what was a version of the villain about 1938. So I suppose it took two or three years. And certainly I didn't start saying, "This is a man I want to use." I don't know. I really don't. I don't mean to be vague, but I mean also to say that I think that anybody who tells you anything much more definite, isn't telling you the truth.

F: Good.

H: You can have definite memories, but I think usually they are the way one wishes to remember them afterwards.

F: Let's say you have got the idea. Then what do you do in terms of filling out the characters? What makes you decide that you're going to have this man married to an American girl who is coming home to her Washington family that has been in diplomacy, and you're going to have a brother like this and a mother like that, and the couple is going to have two children, and they're going to discover that there is a Roumanian in the house?

H: I fool around. That's as much as I can say about it. I think in many plays I fool around too much. I fool around until something falls into place for me, until I have enough people to make for me the kind of play I can write. That doesn't mean that I recommend that to anybody else. It is my kind of writing. I make a first draft and if that doesn't seem right to me, I take some characters out or I put some characters in.

F: When you are in the process of creation, what are the physical surroundings that you seem to require? Do you go for walks in the park?

H: No, no. I don't require very much. I require a room that I like, and it can be very much any kind of room as long as it's not a cluttered room. I prefer the country because I think it's better for work. You're not so disturbed. But I certainly have done a great deal of work in New York.

F: You have been extremely strong in your character development. Do you actually sit down and write reams of notes about your characters?

H: I never wrote reams. I used to write a page or two but I don't any more. As you get more practised you don't need to—or I don't need to.

F: When you've been writing your dialogue, do you talk the dialogue out loud to hear how it sounds?

H: No, but I read it out loud every night and I read it again before I start in the morning.

F: Do you ever read a finished play to friends or some playwright?

H: No, never. I don't like to show people work.

F: What is the reason for that?

H: I have some feeling it dissipates strength. I'm not a performer. I'm a writer, and energy better be conserved for that rather than for performing. I've read plays out loud on the first day of rehearsal once or twice.

F: But not for any group of friends.

H: No, no.

F: Lillian, you have involved yourself in social and political causes from time to time. Have you found this a help or a hindrance in your playwriting?

H: Oh, I don't know. I have found it both a help and a hindrance in my life. Whether that's playwriting or not, I don't know. I really don't know what's a help or a hindrance. You are what you are. You know that certain things have kept you from work and other things have helped you to work, but by the time you know that, they're past.

F: A variety of interpretations have been placed upon *The Little Foxes,* particularly that it is a picture of the evil of the coming of industrialism to the South and the implications that the modern capitalistic world is full of Hubbards. Did you really have this in mind when you wrote the play?

H: I certainly did not. I woke up extremely surprised that anybody thought so.

F: What did you have in mind—simply to tell the story of a Southern family?

H: Yes, I do think a kind of Southerner and a kind of Northerner ravaged the land every place in the world. That certainly was in the back of my head but I didn't mean anything very social in a particular sense by it. I certainly meant something by it in an over-all social sense—that it was a sin to see beautiful land go in a bad way, a bad way for me. I certainly meant no indictment of anything except exactly what I've said.

F: Actually the generating force for that play was your regard over what was happening in the South.

H: No, it wasn't even that. It was just some people. By the time I grew up, of course, it was long, long over. I couldn't have any regrets for it. I'd be insane if I had had any regrets for it. By the time I was growing up, it was long since finished. I just saw some people; some of them I knew.

F: In other words you knew of situations and you knew of people in the South who had done something along the lines that happened in the play.

H: That's right. This doesn't mean that there are not social meanings in the play and that people haven't got a right to see them.

It only means that I, perhaps, didn't even know that they were there. I don't think that what writers intend makes very much difference. It's what comes out.

F: This is a frequent occurrence. Many playwrights don't realize, when they are writing, the levels that the play reaches in terms of an audience. Howard Sackler, for instance, in writing *The Great White Hope,* insists that he did not set out to write a story of a racial confrontation.

H: Well, he probably didn't.

F: And that in actuality he was writing about this man who defied the conventions and mores of the times and how he was forced to pay for it.

H: Well, it's very probable. It doesn't mean that's the way it comes out to you and me, however.

F: It has been noted that, although you have been a radical in politics and outspoken in your approach to social problems, you did not write the sort of political harangues that flowered in the Thirties. How come?

H: I don't believe in political plays. I never did believe in them. I don't think I ever wrote a political play. I'm not that kind of political. I've never liked such plays. I didn't like them here; I didn't like them in the Soviet Union; I don't like them any place.

F: Why is that?

H: They don't seem to me to have anything to do with art. I don't mind them. I don't mind much of anything if somebody wants it. It's the same thing now as being naked on the stage. If somebody wants to be naked, I don't care. It just seems to me to be rather a dull thing to be doing, almost as if one was writing a political play.

F: I have another question somewhere along these lines. Although you have been called a moralist, a playwright examining with a certain anger the world's evil, you have said that you really never were concerned in a literary sense with the world, that playwrights should not write about society. What did you mean by that?

H: I hope I didn't say that. I hope I was misquoted if I did. Everybody is concerned about society. How could you live and not be concerned about it? You would have to be a sort of lap dog, it seems to me, not to be concerned with society and the world you live in. There are many levels of being concerned. Some people are

concerned by the price of potatoes; some people are concerned by
what happens in Washington; some people are concerned by what
happens in many other places plus Washington. I don't see how you
could live and not be concerned with the world around you,
wherever it was. What I meant was that I didn't deliberately set out to
write any propaganda.

F: What was the genesis of *Toys in the Attic?*

H: *Toys in the Attic* came out of an idea of Hammett's which I
couldn't make use of. It interested me very much as an idea, but I
couldn't make use of it so I tore it up.

F: What was the idea?

H: The idea was that a man who has never been successful
becomes successful and honestly believes that that's the way everybody wants it for him in the world. It had nothing to do with sisters or
family, only with discovering that, of course, nobody has wanted it for
him. Nobody wants success for anybody else, basically. I tried this
because it was a very interesting idea, and realized I couldn't do it. It
wasn't my idea and I couldn't do it, but there was the genesis of
something there and the kernel of something. It became to me a man
who had a momentary success, brought up by women who certainly
had never wanted him to have that minute of success. That wasn't
the way they saw him and they ruined it for him. I don't think that is
an uncommon situation.

F. In your memoir, *An Unfinished Woman,* you recalled that both
you and Dashiell Hammett thought that *The Autumn Garden* was
the best play you had ever written. Then you said that during the
rehearsal you saw the life of the play being drained from it. What did
you mean? What happened?

H: Well, it's a complicated business. It was a badly cast play and
for some reason it never came to life and it droned rather than
moved. All the elements of it never coalesced, and I think this can
happen in the theatre.

F: When you realized it was droning rather than moving, wasn't it
possible to recast or throw out the weak actors, bring in a new
director? What happens in the theatre?

H: I think one realizes such things too late and there's too little
time to go in the theatre, and perhaps some part of it was my fault.
There's very little time to turn around in the theatre. Shows have, I

think, been saved but not many—very, very few. There's not enough money to turn around. That's a particular quality which can't be directed because you can't really say somebody who is a good actor is a bad actor. You can only say he is not fulfilling himself and something is lifeless, and then what are you going to do about that? Somebody else might be lifeless, too. Maybe it could have been done. I didn't know how to do it. I think I realized it too late, anyway.

F: In other words, you came up to opening night with no hope for that play at all.

H: Very little. Your newspaper did that play in, and I think it a terrible piece of injustice. Brooks [Atkinson] started out very bad and ended up by saying it was the best play I ever wrote. By the time they got there, of course, everybody had given up the review.

F: Has there been any thought of reviving *The Autumn Garden*?

H.: People have spoken about it. I don't know.

F: For some time now you have been saying in interviews and you said it to me earlier this afternoon and you said it in your book that you have become increasingly alienated from the theatre. How can you explain this? Is it simply a loss of interest or does it go deeper than that? Is there any fear involved?

H: I suppose there is. I don't know. I always knew I was meant for the theatre, but certainly in the last eight or ten years I found myself uncomfortable in it and yet still very attracted by it. I don't at all say I won't do another play. I think I have come to have both an attraction and a great fear of those weeks of rehearsal and the money involved and the possible closing too soon and the sort of over-emphasis, the too-great spotlight on yourself, and then the spotlight removed and the play forgotten. I'm not even sure the theatre was my tempera-ment, as I tried to say in the book. You know, I went through a great many years of it. I hope I haven't come to the end of it; I hope I will write another play. I don't think there is anything wrong with moving from one place to another. I've sold this house after a great many years and I have no idea why. I think it is a piece of foolishness that I did, except that I just have some instinct I should move and I really can't bring myself to think that's wrong or right.

F: That's curious, because I was thinking as I was standing outside, what a smart thing it was to buy a house like this in this area.

H: Well, of course, it was the smart thing and I have lived here a great, great many years of my life. I'm sure I'll have days of regretting it and yet I have some sort of instinct that if I don't do something now, I don't know if I'll ever live to do it. I have done this kind of thing before. I'm not so sure one shouldn't go somewhere else even if it's less comfortable or one is less at home.

F: I find it rather disturbing that you should be drifting away from the theatre or that you have drifted away from the theatre particularly when you said that you have enjoyed writing for the theatre so much. You really enjoyed writing your plays, you have said.

H: Yes, I have. I'll probably write another play.

F: What actually is the joy that you find in writing?

H: I don't know—doing something.

F: It must be something more than that.

H. Creating something, making something out of nothing, I suppose. Worrying about it. Having something that is more to you than anything else is to you. Living with it all the time. So many things, good and bad. It's really so late for me to say! You know I have been writing for so many years of my life. It wouldn't be hard for me to quit. I could quit easily and do nothing for the rest of my life. But there is a great pleasure in making something out of nothing.

F: Yes, yet there is also a great agony, isn't there?

H: Oh, yes, great pain and great worry, you know.

F: You have undoubtedly, like all writers, come up against blocks.

H: Oh, yes.

F: How do you cope with a block? What is your procedure when you have suddenly come up against a scene you know is not working?

H: Usually I start by just tearing up everything I have done and starting again.

F: That takes a tremendous amount of patience and too much fortitude.

H: Well, I'm not sure. Sometimes it's a relief and sometimes it's nice to start again with a clean slate. Certain good things remain, and what you want to use will stay in your head. Twice I put a play aside entirely. I couldn't do anything with it—or I didn't think I could. I don't even know where they are, but I don't need to know where they are because I remember them.

F: Did you encounter blocks in *The Little Foxes*?

H: Not blocks so much. I encountered terrible troubles. I rewrote *Little Foxes* I think, seven, eight times.

F: One has to be able to take that much time.

H: Well, I couldn't afford it but I took it anyway. I certainly could not have afforded it then.

F: What sort of an idea could move you now to write a play?

H: One I liked very much. I don't know anything else that could.

F: As a playwright, aren't ideas constantly kind of percolating in one's head?

H: No. I'm one of the few writers in the world who has few ideas ever. I just have to wait for them to arrive. Other people have countless back ideas they are always using. I have none. I have no idea why this is. I just have to wait for a new one to come.

F: To some writers keeping a notebook is to keep working.

H: I know. Everybody has told me this. I have no idea why it is.

F: What do you think is the most challenging problem that the playwright faces today?

H: The whole damn theatre. The theatre is a mess.

F: In what sense?

H: Nobody can go except rich people.

F: What about off-Broadway?

H: They've got to be pretty rich, too. I paid $10.00 a seat for off-Broadway recently.

F: And yet plays like *The Boys in the Band,* musicals like *Dames at Sea,* which are charging $10.00, are thriving.

H: I know. It's still true, however. Those are the same audiences that go on Broadway. I think the trouble with the theatre is that it now interests only a certain class of people. I very much doubt if it can exist too much longer on a certain class of people. It really has to be for a very large segment of a population for the playwright and the audience and the actor. Kids almost never go to the theatre. They don't know anything about theatre. Nothing. They almost never go. They perform once in a while in colleges, but they have seen almost nothing. This has been true for the ten years I have been teaching. They go to movies. They're movie buffs.

An Interview with Lillian Hellman

Fred Gardner/1968

This is a transcript of an audio cassette, currently available from Jeffrey Norton Publishers, 96 Broad Street, Guilford, CT 06437. Transcribed by Ruth M. Alvarez. Used with the permission of Jeffrey Norton Publishers and the Estate of Lillian Hellman.

Fred Gardner: Lillian Hellman's first Broadway play, *The Children's Hour,* was the great success of the 1934–35 season. It came after some false starts and half-hearted tries at short stories, which she later dismissed as typical lady-writer stuff, and a comedy written in collaboration with Louis Kronenberger and some odd jobs in the theater. *The Children's Hour* might never have been written had not Dashiell Hammett, a close friend of Miss Hellman's, urged her to try her hand as a serious writer. Since that time, Miss Hellman has written eleven more plays and a number of movies. She has reported on her travels to countries at war and at peace, edited an anthology of Hammett's stories, and written a book of recollections called *An Unfinished Woman.* This productivity has never kept her from an active role in American political life. I met Miss Hellman in 1961 as a student in a course she was teaching at Harvard, yet another side of her work. A year later in Boston I watched her revising *My Mother, My Father and Me,* her last play for Broadway. Does the seven-year lapse mean you're finished writing for the theater?

Lillian Hellman: I don't know. I think not, although I really am not sure anymore. *My Mother and Father and Me* was . . . well I can't say it did any clear harm. You remember we opened in the newspaper strike in New York and thus took a walloping, but I can't blame it on one play, my seeming lack of interest in the theater this minute. I think it's been coming for a long time, and I solved part of it by doing a new book. Now that the new book is finished, I'm really not very certain whether I want to go back to the theater. I want to sit down and think it over. It's a hard and difficult way to go, and I don't think I

107

like the Broadway theater very much any more. But I hope it isn't;
after all, it's what I grew up doing, what I know best how to do. I'm
just not sure.

FG: Was Broadway a more exciting place in the early Thirties?
And did it attract a livelier audience?

LH: I guess it was more exciting. I was hesitating because I think
perhaps when you're young (and I was a quite young woman when
Children's Hour was produced), everything seems more exciting
although I never thought of the word exciting. I just thought it was
what I did. I think there were better plays; certainly there were livelier
audiences. That I can be absolutely certain of. Now we get a sort of
rich expense-account audience. Then we got a totally different kind of
audience, a much younger audience, much more interested in
coming to the theater. They didn't go to movies quite so much,
nearly as much as they do now. I remember the pleasure one day, for
example, of coming down the block to the Maxine Elliott Theatre
where *Children's Hour* was playing and seeing three trucks sort of
blocking the traffic in the street in the afternoon and watching three
truck drivers get out of their trucks, go into the box office and each
buy—they were friends and evidently buying for their friends—
buying six pair of tickets. I very much doubt whether that has
happened in a great, great many years. The audience has totally
changed. And thus dictated without knowing it, of course, dictated
the nature of Broadway.

FG: To most young people right now movies and songs are the
exalted forms. Why do writers breed off one another this way, with
the best gravitating toward one medium? And why do you think
they've deserted the theater?

LH: Well, perhaps art comes in a circular form. As movies grew
better, better people came into movies; as native American music
grew better, more people came into it. The theater, the Broadway
theater, has declined in writers, has declined in the quality of writing,
I think, and thus has attracted less and fewer and fewer good people.
But I'm not sure that many very serious writers ever came into the
theater. There were endless examples of very good novelists such as
Henry James who always wanted to write for the theater and did,
never very successfully. In our time, with perhaps the exceptions of
eight or ten people (and by our time I mean say from 1910, the First

World War on . . . 1915) there've probably not been more than ten really serious writers in the American theater.

FG: Would you care to name them?

LH: O'Neill, Kelly, Clifford Odets with some reservations, I think, Miller with some reservations for me. I would have reservations, of course, about everybody including myself. By reservations I mean not on the level say with an O'Neill, although I'd even have reservations about him. Williams, certainly Tennessee Williams. I think you kind of weigh George Kaufman with the comedies, the early comedies. Albee later on. I'm only naming Americans, of course. I can't seem to get to ten. I probably left out some. A couple of the early plays of Elmer Rice. Sidney Howard. I don't seem to have reached ten, I think.

FG: A friend says you came to the theater through literature. And that even your friends were literary people. Why did you wind up writing plays?

LH: I did come to the theater through literature, and I suppose most of my friends have remained literary people rather than theatrical people. I don't really know why I did it. It now seems to me an accident, but I'm sure it couldn't have been. I was interested in the theater. I had worked in the theater as a young girl, but I wasn't conscious of wanting to write for it. I was very conscious of wanting to write novels and short stories. I really don't know how to answer it. I'm sure it was not an accident, but in time everything becomes it, and maybe in truth the form you pick can be a happy or unhappy accident.

FG: When *The Children's Hour* went into rehearsal, did you find yourself making many changes? And were these mostly at the request of the director, or the actors, or because lines didn't ring right to you in rehearsal?

LH: No, I didn't make many changes. I became known very quickly as a very difficult woman to handle for that reason. You're always difficult, I suppose, if you don't do what other people want. I decided, without really knowing that I had decided, that by the time a play went into rehearsal I had done the best I could and that any great amount of tampering was rather outside my powers. I remember the day I made up my mind to this. It was over something extremely foolish, and it caused a bad fight between the director-producer of *Children's Hour* and myself. *The Children's Hour* is about a girls' school and thus had in it eight or ten students, and one of them, a very small part, I'd written a girl in with a lisp, and somebody came to the rehearsal, some friend of Mr. Shumlin's, and objected to the lisp, and for a reason unknown to me he made a great fuss about the lisp remaining. None of the arguments was worth anything. It could have easily come out. I don't know why he made it, probably because I had been so difficult; but I think I made it because I had made up my mind that nothing was going to be done by anybody else. I came, of course, in time with enough plays to realize that lines became wrong for you yourself and didn't sound right—that when actors spoke lines that were written on a typewriter they didn't always come out the way you had thought, and your ear had gone wrong. I also began in time to see that scenes went wrong and needed occasional changes; but I really made very few changes, and I have no regrets for that even though, of course, mistakes could have been avoided I suppose by somebody more flexible. Because when it came to the musical that Leonard Bernstein and Wilbur— Richard Wilbur the poet—and I did called *Candide,* because it was my first collaboration and because what has, as you know, become a sort of great prestige success was a great financial failure in Boston. I lost my head and began to make all the changes that other people were dictating to me and at that point I knew that I had been right all along that I cannot work fast. I cannot really work on anybody else's ideas but my own and that I should never have made the changes under pressure. The *Candide* that opened on Broadway was not as good as the *Candide* that opened here. And I've never again collaborated because I've been so worried about exactly that problem.

FG: In your introduction to *The Children's Hour* when you regretted the entrance of Mrs. Tilford, the re-entrance at the very end, how come you didn't cut the last ten minutes for the 1951 revival? That seems like a change you yourself wanted.

LH: Mr. Gardner's referring to the last fifteen to twenty minutes of the play in which one of the girls, suspecting herself of lesbian desires, not lesbian acts, but lesbian desires, and thus feeling that the charge made against her had some moral truth, although no actual truth, kills herself, and the grandmother of the child who's made the charge returns to the play now having found out that the child, her grandchild, lied and that the harm she's done to these two school-teachers has in it no justice. When it was first written, many people thought the grandmother should not return. I felt that she should. As the years went on, I became convinced that I was wrong, that, of course, the grandmother should never have returned, the play should have ended on the suicide. When we did the revival, I was deter-mined to rectify my mistake and went back and worked for weeks and weeks trying to take out the last eight or ten minutes of the play which sounds very easy and as if I could have done it, but I couldn't do it. It had been built into the play so long back, so far back, that I finally decided that a mistake was as much a part of you as a non-mistake and that I had better leave it alone before I ended up with nothing. That was my reason for not changing it.

FG: After that success, Samuel Goldwyn offered you a Hollywood contract which you took, and many of your contemporaries brooded about working out there. Harold Clurman summed it up when he wrote, "For Odets at this time Hollywood was sin." Did sin cross your mind when Goldwyn made his offer?

LH: No, no, it was very common talk then. It used to be referred to as whoring. Writers would talk about themselves as whoring in Hollywood. No, it never occured to me that such a thing could be true. I was genuinely interested in movies. I genuinely did my best. I didn't come from the generation that felt any such degradation.

FG: What pictures did you work on?

LH: The first picture I did was an adaptation of *The Children's Hour,* but in those days in pictures you, of course, couldn't . . .

FG: That was *These Three?*

LH: *These Three.* You couldn't have the theme of lesbianism, so we changed it. It was important to me since it wasn't a play about lesbianism in my mind. We changed it to another situation leaving it in the same place. As you know, *The Children's Hour* was later done in what year I can't remember. You probably can.

FG: '61 or so.

LH: '61 by William Wyler and was then called *The Children's Hour* with Audrey Hepburn and Shirley MacLaine. Then I did an adaptation of a famous play by Sidney Kingsley called *Dead End.* I did the adaptation of my own play *Little Foxes.* Dashiell Hammett did the adaptation of *Watch on the Rhine,* my play, but I did the cutting on the script. I did *Another Part of the Forest,* not *Another Part of the Forest, Searching Wind;* I did my own play. And along the way I did various small jobs, rather tinkering jobs. I worked for Samuel Goldwyn for many years and cut and helped with various other pictures. The last picture I did was two or three years ago and was called *The Chase.* I think that's the list. I'm not sure; I may have done others.

FG: Would you care to comment on *The Chase* experience?

LH: Yes, it was not a happy experience. I had written what I thought was a good, small picture about twenty-four hours in the life of a Texas town, and it came out for me at least a rather botched-up job in which most certainly most of my script was there although scenes had been put in other places. Much more violent picture than I had ever intended. It was not a success in America. I'm told it's a great success in Europe. And I'm also told by a younger generation that they like it very much, but I don't.

FG: Almost all of the Depression-era plays dealing with strikes are optimistic in the sense that the militants win. Your play *Days to Come* ended with a defeat for labor and emphasized the gap between the radical leadership and the passive rank and file. It seems in retrospect the most accurate. How did you get such a good political vantage point?

LH: Well, do you mean accurate? Or do you mean something else? What I mean . . . I had the strike lose. Labor has certainly consistently, since the 1930's, won in America. I think possibly what you mean is that labor has become so conservative.

FG: The rank and file . . .

LH: The rank and file . . .

FG: . . . in your play were both conservative and near-sighted.

LH: Yes, and that's where I think I was accurate, that they were conservative and backward. And that has come out true. Certainly labor politically now is a most conservative group as somebody said recently. It's not the military-industrial complex anymore; it's the military-industrial-labor complex.

FG: What was your source of insight in the Thirties? Were you active politically in any sense?

LH: Yes, I think with the advent of Mr. Roosevelt we all were active. I was active in two of my own labor unions. One was the then recently formed Screen Writers Guild, the other was the older Dramatists Guild. But we all were politically active during the Thirties in some form or other.

FG: You went to Spain at the time of the Civil War there?

LH: Yes, I felt very deeply about the Spanish Civil War. Many of us did. My going was kind of an accident of being in Paris and bumping into a man who worked for the Spanish Republican government and being persuaded by him that my going might do some good, that people like me could write about it and have some kind of influence on other people. I don't know that that was true. I did write about it. It is included in the new book actually, but I think I really went not because I thought I might be of any . . . I don't think I had any illusions about my influence or importance because I knew America was not going to come to the aid of Spain, because I knew France wasn't going to either. I have a diary that said so at the time. I went because I felt it was rather one's duty to go, I guess.

FG: Brecht made a famous remark, "You don't paint still lives when the ship is going down." Weren't you going against the times in 1937 when you began writing a play about Southern tradesmen, really a play about your own family? Or did you know that *The Little Foxes* was going to turn out to be more political than personal?

LH: No, I still don't think of it as political except as I was. I've always been amazed that other people saw it that way. Although I should stop being amazed because, of course, the feeling that is in you comes out on the page. I was simply out to write the story of a family, a very predatory middle class family, on its climb to enormous riches. I had no political purpose. I can see now where people reading it could well think it an indictment of a predatory class, and indeed it is, but I certainly had no such intention. I'm not sure one incidentally should have such an intention.

FG: *Days to Come* had been a failure, and then the next play, *Little Foxes,* was a success; but had the legacy of a box office flop intimidated you in any way or made it harder to find backers when . . . ?

LH: Box office failures in the theater always intimidate you because they take a very high price, higher I think than say novel writers or poets or any other form of writing because the failure is so prominent, and it costs so much money. Yes, I suffered I think from the failure of *Days to Come*. And it did make for Mr. Shumlin—I don't raise the money, of course, as the author—did make it more difficult I'm sure to raise the money for *Little Foxes*. I remember his difficulties. But you get over failure in the theater too. Just as it's sharper than it is in any other form, it's also more easily forgotten for some reason.

FG: Your research notebooks for *The Little Foxes* fill two binders with a thousand typewritten pages on every subject from the economic effects of the Civil War to turn-of-the-century food fads. How much of this material works its way into a play?

LH: Very little of it ever worked its way into *Little Foxes*. It simply gave me a sense of what the rooms should look like and what the dresses should look like and what the music would have sounded like, although there is no music in *Little Foxes*. It gave me confidence in doing it. I've never done quite such a research job again, but since it was placed in a time outside my own I had to have some place to start, and it still gives me some pleasure to read that research book because it's a quite thorough one.

FG: With so much research compiled on architecture and design, did these fixed ideas you developed affect what your sets should look like, and did it influence you in working with scenic designers? What procedure did you follow?

LH: No, it didn't influence me. It would have influenced me if anything had gone wrong, but the set of *Little Foxes* was done by a man I've frequently worked with in the theater, Howard Bay. And I think we saw eye to eye on what the set in general should look like.

FG: Can you draw any conclusions about what makes a good co-worker in a director, a producer, an actor?

LH: No, I think it really so depends upon your own nature, your own disposition. I now find it easier in the theater to get along with people than I used to find it. It's just finding the right people for yourself, and that doesn't always mean the best people. It sometimes does, and it sometimes doesn't. What fits you best, what you trust most.

FG: *Little Foxes* was, of course, a vast success, but a few critics disparaged it as a melodrama. My own feeling is that the power struggle in the Hubbard family is described with a sense of purpose that has nothing to do with melodrama. Maybe you're tired of answering the whole charge.

LH: I am a little bit tired of it because it's a meaningless word unless one is using it as a put-down to mean that a play is written . . . I suppose the strict definition of it is a drama with a happy ending which, of course, is not true of *Little Foxes,* the dictionary definition. But it's usually used as a word to cheapen something, and to deny it always seems to me to defend oneself, and I don't very much like to. The play is there. It's either good or not good.

FG: What about the other . . . ?

LH: It's rather an old-fashioned charge, I think, anyway. An old-fashioned word now.

FG: There's another common criticism that your plays are too well-made. It seems that it's a feat to tell a story within the constraints of the theater, but there are always people who are asking you to break down the rules somehow.

LH: Well, I think that came about because I came at a strange period of changing theater. I was caught. By caught I mean in a time of life, not caught in any disagreeable sense, caught between a so-called realistic theater and a so-called new theater coming after the Second World War, the theater of the absurd, the theater of the imagination, whatever words one has for it. The charge of too well-made I suppose means too neat, too well put together. It's basically I think a rather foolish charge against anybody, because what is too well-made? Why should something be badly made? I think what people do mean by it is that perhaps sometimes the sewing shows, and there I think sometimes it does in my plays. I don't think too often. I hope not, but I think sometimes it does. What is amusing to me at least is so advanced a playwright, advanced in the sense of new techniques and new thought as Beckett whom I very greatly admire, writes remarkably well-made plays. And nobody uses that phrase because they're dazzled by something else. Ibsen, of course, wrote the best-made plays of all.

FG: Many of your plays revolve around transactions—libel payments, strike demands, blackmail, control of the family fortune. Have you worried at all that people might mistake money for the subject of your theater?

LH: No, no, I never worried. It seemed to me the only people who would worry about that would be people who cared a great deal about money. And I have chosen to think that I never have, which may or may not be the truth. Money's been the subject of a great deal of literature because it also . . . isn't only money of course it's power, it's sex; it's a great many other things. It certainly was the subject of Balzac and Stendhal and Dickens and Jane Austen and countless writers. It has been frequently brought up. People have asked me this question, have printed their own opinions about it; but I don't think it's ever worried me.

FG: *Watch on the Rhine* is about a man who loves his wife, and yet their love scene is brief, almost terse. In your other plays we get only intimations of love. Was this conscious? Or reaction to all the romance on Broadway?

LH: No, I don't think it was conscious. It's that I myself was first made aware of it by Dorothy Parker who pointed out once that I had never written a love scene in a play. And that there was almost no sex, except sort of off-stage sex in the plays. I think it's just my inability to write a love scene. I just don't know how to write them, except in the most indirect fashion.

FG: In 1944 during the war you accepted an invitation to the Soviet Union. There were hints at that time that the White House wanted you to go?

LH: Yes, I think they wanted me to go. They wanted to be behind the scenes in it. In my new book, I've described how my trip really began with William Wyler and I and Samuel Goldwyn deciding to make a war documentary in Russia. We had just entered the war— the United States had just entered the war—and we felt that a documentary would be very valuable. And Wyler and I were at first denied permission to go, and then when Mr. Molotov arrived in Washington the permission was suddenly given. We never went, for reasons that the book goes into but would be too long for this record, partly because Mr. Wyler was called into the Air Force and I didn't want to go with anybody else. But I did do a sort of semi-documentary script called *North Star,* and it was shot in Hollywood, and I will read to you, if I may, a little from the book because I think it was the reason why I was invited.

FG: Please.

LH: "The picture was one of the reasons" (the picture meaning *North Star*) "why the Russians invited me on a cultural mission in 1944 and why Washington—acting with faceless discretion—wanted me to go. (True, that when I got to Moscow I found they thought *North Star* a great joke, but I guess outside Moscow there were some simple peasant folk glad to find themselves so noble on the screen.)" The picture incidentally is now called *Armored Train*. "When it is shown on television, it has printed titles explaining the Russians were once our allies but haven't turned out so nice, if apologies were needed, and they were needed for the silliness of the movie"—the picture was a very bad picture—"then the picture should have been scrapped," of course. "But the convictions of Hollywood and television are made of boiled money."

"In September of 1944, I flew to Fairbanks, Alaska, where the Russians were to pick me up for the journey across Siberia."

"The trip was made on a C47, a two-engine plane capable of a maximum speed of 240 miles an hour. It carried cargo, a full crew, few instruments, and a nineteen-year-old boy called Kolya, a Russian mechanic stationed in Alaska, who had conned a ride home by convincing the top Russian brass in Fairbanks that he spoke English and was therefore a fit escort for the lady guest. His English consisted of 'and,' 'so,' 'OK,' 'hell'—I was known throughout the trip as Miss Hell—'lie up,' which he used to mean lie down or sit up, 'stockings' and 'Betty Grable.' The Russian commanding officer wished me a happy trip, said I would be in Moscow in three days, and gave me a fine sleeping bag.

"The trip took fourteen days because the crew had been instructed to take no chances with their guest. Kolya and I sat, or lay, on packing boxes in the rear of the plane, where the heating system ceased to work on the second day. (When it got so cold we couldn't stand it any longer, one of us would go into the pilot's compartment, and the radio operator would move out.) We flew only when the weather was good and that meant that for days at a time we were lodged in log cabins on Siberian airfields." And then the book goes on to describe this really quite terrible fourteen-day journey across Siberia in which I arrived in Moscow with very bad pneumonia.

FG: When you finally recovered, did you develop contacts with Soviet intellectuals for the embassy?

LH: I didn't do it for the embassy or for anybody else. I was a guest of the Soviet Union and had made clear that before I left here that I would write and say anything I wanted to, and indeed I did write a number of Russian pieces afterwards, but I saw a great deal of Soviet intellectuals. Of course, the war was on, a great many people were away, but I certainly saw a great many of them. And I think that the trip was in that sense valuable. They were friendly toward me.

FG: You spent time with Eisenstein?

LH: I spent a great deal of time with Eisenstein. We became close friends. He was a remarkable man, and I was most impressed with him.

FG: Did you see any of your wartime friends on your return trip twenty-one years later?

LH: Yes, I did. I hadn't been back as you know in those twenty-one years, but I did see a good number, including several women I had known, one now a quite famous critic and one now a quite famous translator, and I saw a good many other people; some, of course, were dead in those years. But I saw a great many people I knew and was very moved, as one frequently is, by seeing people in one atmosphere where the last time I'd left them, of course, they'd been miserable and hungry and cold and war weary. Now, of course, they're much better off economically; some of them are not very well off intellectually.

FG: What has your assessment been of recent Russian theater and Russian writing?

LH: I don't think I have any. Last two visits I, with the exception of three times, didn't go to the theater. I don't very much like to go to the theater even here, and I certainly don't like to in a language where I can only pick out one word in twenty-five. There is a remarkable company in Moscow now and a very remarkable company in Leningrad called the Gorky Theater. But I didn't go very much. Writing seems to be booming. I did meet Mr. Solzhenitsyn who's a most impressive man. I had met Yevtushenko here. I'm told Voznesensky is a good poet I think. I can of course only read in translation. And then I'm told by Russian friends that the most remarkable of them is a young man in Leningrad called Brodsky, who is in, I think, some political trouble . . . off and on in political trouble.

FG: Your first play after the war, *Another Part of the Forest,* isn't the sequel but a prelude to *Little Foxes.* You chose to examine the Hubbards when they were younger. This is the direction in which a psychoanalyst explores. Had you been under the influence?

LH: Well, I suppose my whole generation as well as yours has been under the influence. But I don't think that was my reason. I had started *Little Foxes* intending to do a trilogy and, of course, intending to go forward. When I came down to thinking about the trilogy, I realized that I had to go back in order to go forward. So I went back but, having done it, never wanted to do the third play of the trilogy, which would have been later, of course.

FG: You directed *Another Part of the Forest* yourself. What was behind that decision, and how do you feel it worked out?

LH: What was behind that decision was that I had left my old director, felt that there was nobody else that I trusted. Playwrights very often make good directors. I did a good job with *Forest,* but I later found out that I didn't make a good director when I directed *Montserrat.* And I didn't even like it very much. So I stopped it.

FG: Howard Bay recalls that you used to, as a director, treat actors as though they were normal logical people, as if you just had to explain something and that was that. Did you stick with that approach?

LH: Yes and I'm afraid that's one of the things that went wrong. He's quite right that that's exactly what I did do, forgetting, of course, that most of us aren't normal and logical people and certainly people in the theater . . . that's not the way one should speak, but I have no other way of speaking, so I decided that was one of the reasons it wasn't right for me.

FG: In the heyday of Senator Joseph McCarthy you learned that you were among those blacklisted writers who couldn't get film jobs because of their politics. How did you get this word?

LH: I don't any longer remember the exact circumstances. I remember that William Wyler wished me to do an adaptation of *Sister Carrie.* And I returned from Europe where he and I had been talking about doing the picture together, only to find that the studio wouldn't have me. This bewildered both of us, and then Wyler was told that I was now on a blacklist and probably couldn't be employed again. I think it was the first knowledge of a blacklist . . . my first knowledge that one really existed. We'd all heard rumors of it, but we didn't know that it was in actual existence. It was indeed to be in existence for many, many years, for a great many people.

FG: How did the House Un-American Activities Committee respond when you told them that you were willing to testify but only about yourself?

LH: Mr. Gardner's referring (just for those of you who aren't old enough to remember) to the House Un-American Activities Committee habit, by this time a long habit, of calling various witnesses before them to ask them about their beliefs and about their associates in whatever beliefs they had. It was interesting that they never called anybody but so-called liberals or so-called radicals. I think they called one man in their history on the charge of a Fascist connection, but nobody ever after that. I came quite late in this disgraceful series of badgering that the House Un-American Committee was doing. I came in 1952 . . . was called in 1952, and I offered to testify about myself, to tell them anything they wanted to know, but I refused to testify about anybody else, not that I knew too much about anybody else, but I felt that whatever I knew, whether it was personal or political or any other way, I could not do. They refused this offer. They wouldn't allow me to testify only about myself; but happily for me they never recalled me even though I had broken the rules of the committee.

FG: It could happen that the people who as you say aren't old enough to remember that habit of the House Committee might live to get a first-hand look at it. Do you think if another repression came that the liberals would run as fast and as far as they did in that period?

LH: I'm sorry to say I do think so. I think there's one hopeful sign which is that, whatever one's opinions are of young people (and I've now had several weeks of many dinners where I hear middle-aged people talk sometimes sympathetically but very rarely), whatever else they think and however they justify, they are . . . since I think a great many of the present insurgent group of young people may be stupid or fools or even fakes, I think of a great many that is not true. There is a solid idealism behind the present cutting up and more courage than perhaps the people of my generation would have. I believe that; I hope it will turn out to be true.

FG: Do you think staying in the United States during this McCarthy heyday affected your own writing?

LH: The fact that I stayed?

FG: Yeah.

LH: No, I don't think so. It affected my finances very greatly. I couldn't do movies which I had not only liked but had made a living, a steady living. But I don't think it affected very much what I did. I suppose I felt depressed and saddened by it all. In that sense one could say I was affected. We all were who went through it.

FG: In the post-war decade you did three adaptations: *Montserrat,* by Emmanuel Roblès; *The Lark,* which made Jean Anouilh's name on Broadway; and the book for *Candide,* of course, which was drastically cut to accomodate the songs. Was there the same investment in and gratification from adaptations?

LH: No, I don't think that there ever is, but in all three cases . . . I suppose because it would be an impossibility for me I wouldn't like it if anybody did it to me, and I don't think I would allow it . . . but I changed the plays a fair amount so they became in a sense in part mine at least.

FG: At the time it was written you called *Autumn Garden* your favorite play. Does that still hold?

LH: Yes, I think so. I think it's the fullest play. It's the most rounded play. I see things wrong with it now that I didn't see then; but, of course, that's always true. No, I like *Autumn Garden.*

FG: So do I. In 1953, you edited a collection of Chekhov's letters confirming what many critics had guessed, that he was one of your favorites. But how precisely did he influence your work? Did you read Chekhov and say to yourself, this is the way to write plays or this is a style I can adapt somehow?

LH: No, oddly enough, I never read Chekhov at the time I first started to write. One has forgotten that Chekhov was very late in being translated. Earlier in England than here but very late here. I really think I only began to hear of Chekhov . . . well, I began to read the short stories . . . I'm sure that when I was in college I never read a Chekhov play. I think they'd been translated by then, but they hadn't reached my level; and since I started to write not so many years afterward, they couldn't have influenced me. I'm his great admirer, of course, have become an even greater admirer; but I don't think they influenced me to any large extent.

FG: At Harvard you taught a writing course in which you said that good writers know how to steal. What kind of stealing have you done in your own work?

LH: Well, you remember that the course I taught you (as is true of the course I'm now teaching) was based on taking a short story or a play and using the plot or the characters and making them your own. I did this really not because it has much to do with me but because I think it's best for young people to have some solid ground on which to stand. The only time I can think that I did it was *The Children's Hour* which was based on an actual case in Scotland in the nineteenth century. I'm sure I have borrowed a great deal from a great many people, but I'm not conscious of it. I don't know who they would be.

FG: Did you ever try your hand at the fiction that Dashiell Hammett always urged you to write?

LH: No, no. I wrote fiction before I ever met Dashiell Hammett. I wrote short stories and didn't think they were very good, and then tried once or twice later at short stories again. I don't think it is a good form for me. I've often thought of it and told myself, now, it was too late but . . . but maybe not. I'm not sure.

FG: Is it true that you wanted Mike Nichols, who till then had never directed, to do *My Mother, My Father and Me?*

LH: Yes, I wanted him very much as the director for *My Mother and Father and Me.* Mr. Bloomgarden, my producer, perfectly understandably felt that somebody who had never directed a play was a dangerous chance to take on so expensive a production, but I did want him very much. I had a very strong sense that Nichols was going to make a first-class director, and I wanted him very much to do it.

FG: When you finally did work with him on the 1967 revival of *The Little Foxes,* did you have any generation gap problems?

LH: No, no. I don't believe in the generation gap problem. I think it's only made by an older generation. So I don't have a great deal of it with people younger than I. It seems to me only a problem in the sense that I might not understand the way people wear their hair or what dress they wear or possibly some slang which I don't understand. In nature I don't think I have any problems. We had one minor, and I think rather interesting, problem. He now says that he thinks he was wrong. I've come to think he was rather right. We had one very sharp disagreement about . . . there are two negro servants in *Little Foxes,* and they were as written in the play. One is a very fine lady who is one of the few so-called good people in the play, the other one's a rather foolish sort of semibutler, the younger man, and Mike Nichols wanted them played, and they were played, as rather conscious present-day negroes, conscious of mocking white people, conscious that white people were their enemies. I did not want this. This seemed to me an historical untruth. He says now that he's sorry he did it. I, in turn, have come to think perhaps it was wise to do it, that it might have added something to the play.

FG: That's a happy ending for a dispute.

LH: Mr. Nichols and I got along splendidly as you know and are old friends. He would be a hard man not to get along with. He knows what he's doing; any other quinks and quirks can be put up with.

FG: Your forthcoming book I'm told is called *An Unfinished Woman.* It's a book of recollections. Do you tell the story of your life chronologically? Is it a conventional autobiography in any sense?

LH: No, no, it's not an autobiography at all. I've chosen the word memoir which is an old word and a not very good word because I couldn't find any other word that seemed to me right for it. It starts at the beginning so called and does all kinds of jumps. I did a jump of eight years in one place and a jump of nineteen in another. It has no chronology because in that sense it isn't . . . while I'm certainly all through it, it isn't about me in the usual sense, in the auto-biographical sense. So it moves from say Spain with some various small connecting chapters so that there won't be too much confusion, say into 1944, a seven, eight-year gap.

FG: Well, I look forward to reading it, and thanks very much.

Lillian Hellman Reflects upon the Changing Theater

Dramatists Guild Quarterly/1970

From *Dramatists Guild Quarterly,* 7 (Winter 1970), 17–22. Reprinted in *Playwrights, Lyricists, Composers on Theater,* ed. Otis L. Guernsey, Jr. (New York: Dodd, Mead, 1974), 250–57.

Here is an edited transcript of a discussion with Lillian Hellman and Dramatists Guild members at Guild Headquarters. At Miss Hellman's request, following Jerome Weidman's introduction, the discussion took the form of a question-and-answer session (questioners are quoted but not individually identified so that we may hold the transcript's focus upon Miss Hellman).

Jerome Weidman: Lillian Hellman and I both had a friend named Margaret Case Harriman who was a brilliant writer for the *New Yorker.* One day I had a date to have a drink with her. She was writing a Profile at the time, and she looked rather glum when we met at the Algonquin. "What happened?" I asked.

"Well, I have made a very bad mistake," she said. "Miss Hellman and I had a lovely lunch and a great afternoon, and then I referred to her as a *woman* playwright. Miss Hellman told me, 'I'm a playwright. I also happen to be a woman, but I am *not* a woman playwright.'"

So, honoring this marvelous distinction and without further ado, let me present to you one of the great writers of English of our time and one of the great ladies of all time—Miss Lillian Hellman.

Q: I was intensely interested in a recent piece you wrote for the New York *Times* in which you indicated that the Broadway theater has had it. Would you like to go into that for a bit?

Miss Hellman: I didn't say the Broadway theater has had it, I said *I've* had it. *I've* been tired of it for a great many years—deeply tired for the last eight or ten years. It's a dangerous, losing game, not

124

worth the candle. The last play I did, *My Mother, Father and Me,* opened during a newspaper strike. I wanted to do it as an off-Broadway production, but, understandably, Kermit Bloomgarden didn't and I'm not even sure that off Broadway is the answer.

Q: What's the alternative?

H: I don't know. Maybe if there was an economic change in this country—and there might well be—there could also be an economic change in the theater. And if there was an economic change in the theater, there might be an artistic change. But my interest in the theater was always in being *alone* with the play. I certainly had great pleasure and rewards from the theater, but I don't think my nature ever fit too well with it.

Q: Do you enjoy theater in places other than New York?

H: I enjoyed it a little in London last year. I saw a few things I liked. Once in a while one does here, too, but so seldom . . . .

Q: How about university theater?

H: It's often too slick. It's neither one thing nor the other any more. None of you should be depressed by my feelings about the theater. It's an old story for me, a new story for many of you.

Q: Does writing a book satisfy you, as opposed to writing a play?

H: I've always had great satisfaction out of *writing* the plays. I've not always had great satisfaction out of seeing them produced—although often I've had satisfaction there. When things go well in producton, on opening there's no nicer feeling in the world—what could be nicer than watching an audience respond? You can't get *that* from a book. It's a fine feeling to walk into the theater and see living people respond to something you've done.

With a book, there's every chance that it may fail, but you've failed alone, and that's easier, somehow. I don't think that I'm a collaborator by nature—nobody else thinks I am either.

Q: Dashiell Hammett once said that you never really enjoyed the theater except when you were alone in your room with a pad and pencil. Isn't that what *all* writers feel?

H: Perhaps, but I'm not so sure it's what *theater* writers should feel. It may have been what was always the matter with me as a playwright.

Q: Let's go back to beginnings. What is the initial passion of playwriting?

H: I've learned something about that from teaching, something that is a denial of what I believed most of my life. I was always convinced that any *good* writer could write a play, given time. I once raised money from a producer to commission five plays by five well-known writers. I was absolutely convinced that each of them could write a good play, particularly if I would read the first draft and offer a few suggestions. Well, I was *totally wrong*. Not one of the plays turned out well.

One finds in students almost the very same thing. I've never taught playwriting, but I've taught many writing seminars. I pick out a novel or short story and ask the students to re-work the plot as a short story or piece of criticism or even a one-act play. Many of them choose to do plays. Some are interesting, except that they are not really *plays*.

So I have finally come to the conclusion that instinct for the theater is not to be defined or taught. I don't know what makes it. Why does one child learn to play the piano at six and another, given the best lessons in the world, never learn? It must be something instinctive, something that can't be taught. The knowledge of poetry, the formation of a poem, for example, is to be learned, but I am not sure the formation of a play can be learned. I can't remember what made me write my first play (*The Children's Hour*). What made me write my second play and the others, was that I was a playwright.

Q: Didn't you once say that no serious writer would work in the theater today because it is such a foolish medium?

H: No, you're misquoting me. What I said was, the plays of Henry James are bad plays, the one play Hemingway wrote was a bad play, but once upon a time it was normal for good writers to try the theater at least *once*. It's appalling to me that today this is no longer true—that's what I said.

Q: Why has this happened?

H: Maybe the writers of today understand that playwriting is something you have to come by instinctively, to be born to. Maybe they feel it's too hard, or not worth it, or a combination of both.

Q: You wrote marvelous plays, you were part of a strong, thrusting theater, you left quite a legacy of literature, and now you want to abandon it?

H: Abandon it? No. Do realize that I speak only for myself. I've tired of listening to the theater's money troubles—when I started, I didn't even know about them. And I don't like the idea of success or failure depending on one newspaper.

Q: Why don't more young people turn to the theater?

H: Perhaps they can't afford to, and maybe they don't like it very much. Movies are their thing. They know all about movies, even how they get produced. I ended a writing seminar last January by asking how many students had read any of my plays (I picked myself because I was their teacher). Only four out of eleven had read me, but they knew every movie I had done.

Q: Doesn't the theater actually require dramatists rather than writers?

H: Yes, and they have always been in short supply. They're probably in shorter supply now than ever before.

Q: The greatest writer in the English language, I suppose, was Shakespeare, and he chose the theater as his medium.

H: That's right, and it's perfectly possible to make a case that the theater was, or might be, the greatest medium of all—even though in our time it has gone steadily downhill. Even musical theater isn't as good as it used to be. Maybe it's just me, but I don't have much fun in the theater any more.

Q: A long time ago I heard a lecture in which you said you intended to turn the Hubbards into a trilogy. You hadn't yet done *Another Part of the Forest*. I'm still waiting for the third play.

H: I am, too. I always intended the Hubbards as a trilogy, but I got tired of them. I realized after the revival of *The Little Foxes* at Lincoln Center that certain work belongs with a certain time of your life, and when that is past you are finished with it.

Q: Do you think maybe the theater's audiences have outgrown the theater's producers?

H: I think audiences have grown very special. I went to a musical the other night, and there was the most specialized audience I ever saw. It really belonged en masse in a restaurant eating caviar. It had nothing to do with the theater.

Q: Do you think film writing is more exciting?

H: Yes, films now are more exciting than plays. I'm sad to say this, because I have certainly changed my point of view. I was one of the few people who liked writing for pictures years ago, but most of my generation made fun of pictures.

Q: The atmosphere, the ambience of going to the theater used to be thrilling.

H: Yes, I remember when *The Children's Hour* opened at the Maxine Elliott Theater at the height of the Depression, I was fascinated with the audience and its reactions. I used to stand in front of the theater to see what kind of an audience I was getting. I remember a happy day when four trucks drew up, taking up most of Thirty-ninth Street. Each truck driver got out and conferred with the others. Then one of them came to the box office and bought forty-four tickets. I asked him what he was buying them for, and he said, "We're buying forty-four tickets for our families and friends in Queens." It was a happy minute. I very much doubt that many truck drivers have attended the theater since.

Q: We used to go to the theater with high hearts, all excited.

H: I don't see many young people in the theater any more. True, I don't sit in balconies, but you can't sell tickets there any more, nobody sits in balconies. I couldn't guess at the number of students I've taught by now, but it has to be five or six hundred over the years, and while some of them are interested in *writing* for the theater you'd be shocked at how many famous theater names they don't recognize. They will know the name of Arthur Miller or Williams or Albee, but they will not have read their plays, let alone *seen* them.

Q: Young peole don't think anything of spending $25 a ticket to hear Joan Sutherland sing or Horowitz play.

H: That's not the same thing. They go to *one* concert of Sutherland or *one* concert of Horowitz. A play has to go on *every* night.

Q: Don't you think there's something to be said in favor of appealing to adults?

H: Don't misunderstand me. I'm not using young audiences as a standard. This generation is rather ignorant about literature. They may be respected on social or political grounds, but not on literary grounds.

Q: Then you are in favor of a playwright writing for adults?

H: I am for a playwright writing for whomever he wants, adults, children, anybody.

Q: Isn't it the writer's function to concern himself with what works?

H: I can never answer a question about what a writer's function is.

I don't know what it is, and I hope never to know. As far as I can tell, his function is to do the best he can. That's all, nothing more mysterious, the best that he can do in this world. Whether you are good or not is something else again.

Q: So when you write you aren't thinking of the audience—in other words, of how your play will work?

H: Worrying about audiences is a dangerous and losing game. A game that American movies played and lost. Who knows about audiences? They like one thing this year and another thing next year. Good writers will write what pleased them.

Q: Miss Hellman, how many plays have you written?

H: Fourteen, including three or four adaptations.

Q: Do you feel a sense of responsibility toward the theater now that it's fallen apart?

H: A sense of responsibility? No, I don't think I feel any responsibility. I want to do the best I can do. The writer's only moral obligation is to be as good as he can be. You don't have any *moral* responsibility toward any medium—theater, novel or poetry. The best one can is, perhaps, the greatest moral responsibility.

Q: Miss Hellman, are you writing plays that we are not seeing?

H: No, for the last ten or fifteen years I haven't liked the Broadway theater.

Q: If *The Little Foxes* were written today by a playwright who is not well established, what do you think his chances would be for production? Harder now than when it was written?

H: I don't think so. The money for *The Little Foxes* was very difficult to raise. I was established in the sense that *The Children's Hour* had been a big hit, but the next play had been a big failure, and at the time of *The Little Foxes* the Depression was only just coming to an end.

Q: Was the play's title your own idea?

H: No, it was Dorothy Parker's four days after we went into rehearsal. I've always had trouble with titles.

Q: Miss Hellman, you say you're not a good collaborator which means, I think, the problems of compromising with a director in production. Do you think that today's playwright has to do more compromising than when you were writing *The Little Foxes*?

H: I don't know. I only know my own experience when I found I was not a good collaborator on *Candide,* the first real collaboration I'd ever done. I went to pieces when something had to be done quickly, because somebody didn't like something, and there was no proper time to think it out, I couldn't go away for a month to decide whether it was right or wrong. Twenty people would be saying, "It has to open Thursday" and I was saying, "It doesn't have to open Thursday," I realized then that I was not fit for collaboration. I had never been through that kind of experience before, and everything I had learned about the theater, all my instinct went out the window. In looking back on *Candide,* I realized that I panicked under conditions I wasn't accustomed to. I wasn't accustomed to five or six people saying such-and-such a scene wouldn't do and had to be fixed, and I was trying terribly hard to both be myself and be accommodating, which is not the way collaboration should work. It took me a year or two after the failure of *Candide* (if it *was* a failure because, you know, it has now become a cult show) to understand that it was truly not my nature, that I must never go through it again. During my early days in the theater, good or bad, failures or not, I had sense enough to say to myself, "That's all I can do. That's as good as I can make it now." But during *Candide* I was saying "Yes" when I meant "No" and "No" when I meant "Yes," and all kinds of personal things were coming into it. I would act too disagreeable, and then I would be agreeable because I had been disagreeable . . . I don't think it was a unique experience. It's probably very typical of theater. Anyhow, it never happened to me in the theater before, maybe because I was a very stubborn young woman.

Q: Do you like actors?

H: I like some of them, some of them I don't like. They don't like *me* very much. Not because I've been disagreeable to them, but there's a common language in the theater, and I've never learned it.

Q: Do you ever feel that a collaborator makes a contribution . . .

H: Oh, certainly, many times, I don't mean that I was right all the time. Many, many times suggestions were made that were better than my own. It isn't a question of whether or not other people come up with excellent ideas, it's whether you can act on them or not, whether you can write them. When *The Children's Hour,* my first play, went into rehearsal I had made up my mind that the play was as good as I could do at that minute of time. It wasn't that I thought other people were wrong. It was that I couldn't do any better than what was already on the page, although by the time *The Children's Hour* had been in rehearsal a few days I knew that the last ten minutes should not be in the play. But I didn't know how to alter it, so we had to ride with what was wrong as well as what was right. For my kind of nature, that was a sensible decision.

Q: Were you able to approach the material with any freshness when they revived the play?

H: No, but I tried very hard to change the ending. I went over the play for a year before the revival, but I still couldn't do it. I finally came to the conclusion that you might as well accept what's bad about your work along with what's good. Maybe they are one and the same. To try to make it perfect is often to muck it up.

Q: In other words, it's better to stick to your guns?

H: Unless you're sticking to your guns only because you don't like the blue eyes of the actress or the wife of the director.

Q: But can we hope there will be another play from Lillian Hellman?

H: I hope there will be. I don't mean to make a declaration of retirement. I think there will come a time when it might be fun to write another play.

Lillian Hellman Walking, Cooking, Writing, Talking

Nora Ephron/1973

From *The New York Times Book Review,* 23 September 1973, 2, 51. Copyright © 1973 by Nora Ephron. Reprinted by permission of International Creative Management.

Lillian Hellman is 67 years old now, and as I arrive at her house on Martha's Vineyard, the new house she built on the beach just below the one she shared with Dashiell Hammett, she is standing at the door saying she hasn't been feeling well—she has a bronchial infection that worried the doctors because of her emphysema, and the emphysema has weakened her heart, and she has been on antibiotics for the last two weeks and they make her sleepy.

"I'm not used to having anything wrong with me," she said later on. "I'm totally unequipped for getting older. Nobody ever told me I was getting older. The doctors say I shouldn't smoke, which I go smack on doing. They also say I shouldn't be in a bad climate in winter, but the trouble is, I don't know any warm places I like. I had a great deal of energy when I was younger. Dash used to say very peevishly, 'For Christ's sake, sit down for two minutes and give my eyes a rest.' Now much of that is gone."

There is a cough every so often as she speaks, and she can tick off the things she can no longer do because of her age—she speaks nostalgically about the fishing boat she sold because she could no longer manage it alone; she logs only one work period a day now, instead of two—but it is difficult for anyone who spends time with Lillian Hellman to do anything but take her word for the ill health and loss of energy.

At the end of two days of following her around with a notebook as she tramped down the beach, cooked dinner and talked nonstop, I was exhausted; she, on the other hand, was preparing for a houseful of guests and a weekend full of parties and was about to sit down with her secretary to work on a mass of correspondence—there are letters from former students, producers about to stage her plays in revival, publishers with requests for reprints. There are business matters dealing with the Hammett estate, which she owns, and with the Dorothy Parker estate, which she worries about.

The new book had just arrived, all black and sleek, and was sitting in a carton on the upstairs landing. *Pentimento,* a collection of portraits, is her second memoir; the first, *An Unfinished Woman,* was published in 1969 and won the National Book Award. The new book took her just over a year to write, a length of time she seems to feel was too long. "It wasn't difficult," she says by way of explanation. "I'm just slow."

Q: Was *Pentimento* your first title?

A: Yes. I always knew I wanted it. But there was a problem. Most art experts say pentimenti, which would have been a mess. I started calling around. The Metropolitan people said pentimenti. Other people said pentimento. I had to make up my mind as to which one I believed.

Q: You refer frequently in the book to notes and diaries you kept as a child. Did you save all of them?

A: No. Not all. I had a terrible time digging them up. Anyway, I don't have them all. I have a few years and then nothing for many years. I kept very young girl diaries. It was my way of learning to write. Exercise books. Some are unreadable now—they were in pencil. And I tore up a lot of them. I decided nobody should see them.

Q: In the new book, everyone you write about is dead. Was that a conscious decision?

A: I didn't know it until I was in the middle of writing the book, and then I thought, Oh, my, everybody's dead. But you feel freer that way. Except for interviews, I'm not sure live people should be written about. It's too hard to write about the living. I'm not talking about pulling your punches, that's not it. It's hard to tell the truth about the living. It's hard even to know it. And you don't want to hurt people out of a blue sky. Although everybody's hurt by everything. One word of reservation and that's all people remember. I'd've never been able to do the Parker portrait [in the first book] if she'd been living.

She'd have been pained. We had an elaborately polite relationship—I don't think we ever said an unpleasant thing in all the years.

Q: How did you come to write *An Unfinished Woman*?

A: It was *faute de mieux*, that book. I decided I didn't want to write for the theater, so what was I to do? I didn't want to do an autobiography—that would have been too pretentious for me. I had a lot of magazine pieces I'd done that hadn't been reprinted, and I started to rewrite them. But I didn't like them. I thought, maybe now I can do better with the same memories.

Q: I wondered why you've never written about the McCarthy period and the blacklist.

A: I tried it this time, and a number of times. I never can say what I mean. I tried in this book to say it in the theater piece. I wasn't shocked in the way so many people were. I was more shocked by the people on my side, the intellectuals and liberals and pretend-radicals—and that's very hard to explain. I'm not really saying it right even now. I mean, I wasn't as shocked by McCarthy as by all the people who took no stand at all. Many of them now think of themselves as anti-McCarthy when they weren't. If they say they were anti-McCarthy, what they mean is that they were anti-Joe McCarthy himself, not what he represented. I don't remember one large figure coming to anybody's aid. It's funny. Bitter funny. Black funny. And so often something else—in the case of Clifford Odets, for example, heart-breaking funny. I supposed I've come out frightened, thoroughly frightened of liberals. Most radicals of the time were comic but the liberals were frightening.

Q: In the new book, the chapter on your cousin Bethe is extremely romantic about you and Hammett. I wondered why you had never married.

A: In writing about it I suppose I've forgotten many of the bad times we had. I think it was my stubbornness that kept us together. We did have two periods of planning to be married. The first time he disappeared with another lady. That's not really fair—I was disappearing too. We were not faithful to each other at that time—we were different generations, but we were both of that nutty time that believed that alliances could stand up against other people. I should have known better because I had a jealous nature.

Q: Yes. There's an episode in *Pentimento* where you destroy an entire soda fountain in his house because he was with someone else.

A: Well, he deserved that. One of the reasons we didn't get married the second time was that he was drinking so heavily those years. I was frightened. After a time we never spoke about marriage. It was just as well. I don't think either one of us had natures that were certain of the future. Dash to the end of his life never had any certainty about anybody and never had any ill feeling about it. He'd made up his mind that there was no certainty in any form anywhere and he totally accepted that. I've never seen anyone else who did that.

Two months before he died, the doctor said he had to go to the hospital. We sent for an ambulance. They came to the house and put him on a stretcher. I put on my hat and coat and was holding the door, when he looked up and saw me. "Oh, are you coming with me?" he asked. I really think if he had not been sick I would have put a knife through him. He was surprised that I would come in an ambulance with him, surprised that life had turned out as pleasant as it had. It was shocking to me. "What's the matter?" he said. "I'm very angry with you for thinking I wouldn't come," I said. He said, "Don't be angry. I only meant it's nice of you." *Nice* of me—after all those years. He had a remarkable nature. Maybe it was what made it possible for him to go to jail without too much pain.

Q: What is the status of the Hammett estate?

A: I own it. Arthur Cowan [a lawyer who is the subject of one of the portraits in *Pentimento*] arranged it. The estate went up for auction because of the Internal Revenue Department—they wouldn't allow him a nickel after he went to jail, and they garnisheed everything he earned. They didn't come to enough so the estate had to be auctioned. I didn't think I could afford it, so Cowan said, very kindly, never mind, I'll buy it. He bought half and I bought half, and after Cowan's death his share came to me. Hammett's books do well. I like that. Bertolucci is doing *Red Harvest*—that worries me. I guard what he wrote as carefully as I can, but I'm really violating what Hammett wanted. He didn't want to see the short stories published again. That was just the sickness, I think. And I think that he thought 'til his dying day that he was going to publish new, different, better stuff.

Q: And the Parker estate?

A: It's a bad story. She left everything to Martin Luther King, and on his death it was to go to the N.A.A.C.P. It's one thing to have real feeling for black people, but to have the kind of blind sentimentality about the N.A.A.C.P., a group so conservative that even many blacks now don't have any respect for, is something else. She must have been drunk when she did it. I was executor, as you know. When King died, it turned out I was no longer executor—everything passed to the N.A.A.C.P., of course. I was so stupid that I assumed I would be executor of the estate until I died. Now the N.A.A.C.P. has sold the rights to all her work for a Broadway musical. Poor Dottie.

Q: What do you read now?

A: I read a fair amount of poetry. I've come to like biography and poetry and letters almost best. I don't read any novels any more, I'm sorry to say. A writer should read novels. When I do I go back to the ones I've read before. Stendhal. Dickens. Balzac. Melville. I teach Melville, but there's not much response among this generation. I find now when I go to get a book off the shelf I pick something I've read before, as if I didn't dare to try anything new.

Q: Ever since *The Children's Hour* opened, you've been called a woman playwright and a woman writer. How do you feel about that?

A: Irritated.

Q: What do you think of the women's movement?

A: Of course I believe in women's liberation, but it seems to make very little sense in the way it's going. Until women can earn their own living, there's no point in talking about brassieres and lesbianism. While I agree with women's liberation and ecology and all the other good liberal causes, I think at this minute they're diversionary—they keep your eye off the problems implicit in our capitalist society. As a matter of fact, they're implicit in socialist society, too, I guess. It's very hard for women, hard to get along, to support themselves, to live with some self-respect. And in fairness, women have often made it hard for other women. I think some men give more than women give. The world seems so sharply divided into people who get so much for giving nothing and those who get nothing and give so much. Dashiell Hammett used to say I had the meanest jealousy of all. I had no jealousy of work, no jealousy of money. I was just jealous of women who took advantage of men, because I didn't know how to do it.

Q: Do you ever worry about what will happen to your work or your papers after you die, or worry that someone will write a bad book about you?

A: I've worried a great deal because I've stopped biographies of Hammett. I was not able to stop that awful biography of Dottie. But in the end, you can't stop biographies, and maybe the best thing is to leave as little as possible. I hope I can bring myself to destroy all of it. But in any case, I hope I've protected myself by choosing a few friends who will fight for me. It's a silly point, because what do you give a damn when you're dead. Any life can be made to look a mess of. Mine certainly can.

Lillian Hellman: The Great Playwright Candidly Reflects on a Long, Rich Life

Bill Moyers/1974

This is a transcript of an interview telecast on National Educational Television in April 1974 and available on audio cassette from the Center for Cassette Studies. Transcribed by Ruth M. Alvarez. Used with the permission of Bill Moyers.

Hellman: "Old paint on canvas as it ages sometimes becomes transparent. When that happens it is possible, in some pictures, to see the original lines: a tree will show through a woman's dress, a child makes way for a dog, a large boat is no longer on an open sea. That is called pentimento because the painter 'repented,' changed his mind. Perhaps it would be as well to say that the old conception, replaced by a later choice, is a way of seeing and then seeing again.

"That is all I mean about the people in this book. The paint is aged now and I wanted to see what was there for me once, what is there for me now."

Moyers: In the next hour, Lillian Hellman looks at the canvas of her own life and talks about what was there once and what is there now. This is the definitive edition of Lillian Hellman's plays. The first, *The Children's Hour*, was written forty years ago to be followed by a succession of major works that twice won her the New York Drama Critics' Circle Prize for the best play of the year. *Watch on the Rhine, Toys in the Attic, Another Part of the Forest, The Autumn Garden,* and, of course, *The Little Foxes.* This is her first memoir, *An Unfinished Woman*, winner of the National Book Award in 1969. And this is her most recent triumph, *Pentimento*, portraits of people who have touched her life with indelible results. Her life has been filled with people—anonymous people, celebrities, some fools, and not a few of the great people like Ernest Hemingway and Dorothy Parker and the man she loved and lived with so many years, Dashiell Hammett, who created Sam Spade and wrote among others, *The Maltese Falcon* and *The Thin Man.* In recent years, Lillian Hellman has been Regents Professor at the University of California in Berkeley and Distinguished Professor at Hunter College in New York. I found her in Florida where she had rented a house for the winter months in one of those occasional retreats into privacy that have always marked her life.

M: There's one question that I have wanted to ask you for a long time. And it has to do with why, when you had a chance, in 1945, on the front with the Russian army, to go at the invitation of the Russian general with his army into Warsaw, then onto Berlin, you said no.

H: I'm afraid the answer is too simple; I was too frightened. I had been on the Russian front by that time about two and a half, three weeks, and I was already frightened enough but the idea of moving into Warsaw . . . that the Russian army, as you know from reading the book, was at that point on the other bank about to go into Warsaw, and then they were absolutely certain they were going through to Germany which they indeed were right about. And I used every excuse I could find such as I didn't have enough clothes and I couldn't go, and he would say never mind we'll liberate some clothes for you, and it just was plain fear. There was nothing, nothing else.

M: Fear of death, fear of conflict?

H: Fear of death . . . I don't know whether I thought so much about death. It's my belief you don't think that much about death, but fear of the hardships of the trip, I think, or that I wouldn't be able to do it.

M: It would have been an historic passage.

H: It certainly would have been, and it's been the regret of my life that I didn't.

M: You do regret it? I've wondered about that.

H: Oh deeply, deeply deeply regret it. Two years later if it had happened I'd have been able to make the trip, but I was so frightened of my own reactions. And my inability to stand deprivation. The deprivations were very great even at the front.

M: You always wanted a certain degree of comfort, didn't you?

H: I evidently thought I did anyway. I found at the front that I was not as uncomfortable as I thought I would be. It was much easier for me to take it. But I somewhere had in my head that a day's long journey in a truck or on a horse was going to be too much for me and that I'd start complaining, and I'm sure I was also frightened of death, but I think most people particularly in a war can't afford to think about death. I couldn't afford it on the Russian front. I stopped thinking about it after the first day.

M: They didn't want you at the front at first and yet they then turned around and invited you?

H: I don't know whether they wanted me or not. They had never allowed a foreigner at the front. And when I first got to Moscow . . . I went . . . it was a great secret for years because I don't think either Mr. Hopkins or Mr. Roosevelt wanted it known. I really went because they wanted me to go. The Russians had said they would accept somebody, and Harry Hopkins and Roosevelt I think both wanted me to go, and I went with very great reluctance.

M: What was the purpose of the trip?

H: Well, they wanted somebody from the so-called cultural world. You remember Eric Johnston had gone on . . . I've forgotten why Eric Johnston went . . . even forgotten Eric Johnston. They were accepting people from various worlds. And since they'd done a number of my plays, I was the obvious cultural choice, I suppose. And I didn't really very much want to go at all. But I did go, and when I first got there, the foreign office called me in and asked me what I would like to see and do. And I said I didn't care, it didn't matter if I didn't do anything. And that sort of shocked them—I was meant to ask for things. And one of the things they asked me whether I wanted to do was go to the Russian front, and I said, oh no, I didn't want to go to the front at all, it wasn't necessary. I wouldn't know what I was seeing. I didn't want to go. That was paid no attention to so when I'd been there about two months, the news came that they would very kindly allow me to go to the front. This caused a sensation among the journalists in Moscow because nobody had been allowed to go. Such a sensation that they finally arranged a trip for the rest of the journalists to go in another direction to the Polish army. My old and dear friend John Hersey to this day makes bad jokes about why he wasn't allowed to go to the Russian army and I was allowed to go to the Russian army.

M: Certain things have always seemed to happen to you against your will, and yet you were drawn to them ineluctably.

H: I suppose so. I suppose one makes one's own dramas and doesn't know it.

M: Did those experiences on the front affect you as much as say your experience in the Civil War in Spain when you visited there?

H: I don't think they affected me as much emotionally as the Civil War in Spain did, because it was such a sad and moving war. It affected me far more, in terms of watching an army and watching a fighting army, the details of a fighting army. They were very important weeks in my life.

M: What do you mean the details of a fighting army?

H: Well in Spain, while we were all under bombardment a great deal, I was only for one half of a day anywhere near the Spanish front and then I wasn't that close. Here I was really very close; the Germans were shooting, oh perhaps, five hundred yards away. We were really in dugouts, and I was put up in a small village I think called Anja—although they had taken down all of the signs so that I wouldn't recognize where I was. But we were very, very close to the front. And every day we moved forward a little bit, and I would move forward with the army.

M: So many people have moved through and in and out of your life, obviously having left a part of themselves with you. In memory, are there any heroes left?

H: I don't know. I'm not sure I think of people in terms of being heroes or not. There are people who are sort of better in my mind than other people but whether they're heroes or not. . . . It's such a large word, isn't it?

M: It is a large word and yet so many of the figures who moved through your life were large people . . . Hemingway.

H: I'm not sure I'm capable of judging heroism or heroes. I wish I was because I think they're very badly needed; they're particularly badly needed in this country now when I don't know how you feel, but one is almost dying to see a hero rise up in America now. It's a terrible lack too that there are certainly many decent men but that's about where it is; there's no large figure to say anything for any of us anymore.

M: Other than Norman Mailer, who is as much actor as writer I think, there aren't any writers today who are as dominant in a personality sense as there were in that gang you knew so well. How do you account for that?

H: I don't know and maybe it's a good thing. Maybe the personality of the writer doesn't matter quite as much as all those people thought. Maybe it's just what you write. Maybe it doesn't. It was a wilder time one mustn't forget. A wilder period. They were all cutting up about society, or about themselves, or about women, or about men, much more than people are now.

M: Were they conscious of being personalities? Celebrities?

H: I think so; I think so. I'm not sure that I don't think it's better now. I'm not sure why writers should have remarkable personalities, or, they're not actors, they're not society people; they're not automobiles, there's nothing, no reason for them to be seen so much or be so interesting. Most very good writers I think are rather uninteresting in a room.

M: Did you ever make up your mind about Hemingway? I remember your writing that you weren't sure he liked you, and you weren't sure what you thought of him either.

H: Uh, no, I wasn't ever sure what I thought of him. I suppose if I had to be truthful, he was an extraordinarily attractive and interesting man. I was very impressed with him. I don't really think I liked him entirely. He was a difficult man to like, I think. But he was an extraordinarily impressive man, and I don't mean the talent, he just was an impressive figure.

M: A sense of presence?

H: Not only in what he looked like, which was very remarkable, but there was a power in the personality which was enormous. And I don't think it was the power that came from fame, because many famous people are not very impressive. He was a man of extraordinary instincts. I saw him one night do a very interesting thing in Paris. We were sitting at a table in a cafe, and gradually through the evening two or three people joined us. Two of the people I knew, and two of the people I'd never seen before. And within about three or four minutes he leaned across the table—he had never seen any of them before—to tell me what he thought of them. And he was not only right about the people I knew, he turned out to be absolutely right about the people that I didn't know. It was the most extraordinary sort of instinct I'd ever seen operate.

M: But the two of you seemed to have a kind of tension between you.

H: I think there was a sort of tension. I told a story in *Unfinished*

Woman about reading a manuscript of his. And Dorothy Parker said a very wise thing. I read the manuscript and said there's a part missing here. I was reading the galleys of the manuscript. I put the manuscript down and said there's some pages missing, aren't there. And he said no there are no pages missing at all, just go on. And the next day when I told Dorothy Parker about this she said you've made an enemy for life, that was the place that the editor cut, and you never should have guessed it. But it wasn't an enemy for life. I don't think he ever really liked me, but he was kind to me in Spain; he was thoughtful to me in Spain.

M: What about Thurber? There's a mention in the book about his throwing a glass at you in a speakeasy.

H: Yes, he threw glasses at everybody. I don't think he cared very much about me one way or the other. He just threw a glass at me.

M: Were you the target? Did you know him well?

H: Yes, I knew him better than I knew Hemingway. We all used to hang out at a famous speakeasy called Tony's. I was much younger than anybody else, but everybody else was very famous. I wasn't. I used to go with Hammett. And everybody when they got drunk enough was very often bad-tempered, and Thurber was certainly bad-tempered when he got drunk. We later on . . . when we saw each other once years afterward got along perfectly well.

M: But was he like . . . was he as witty as say . . . Dorothy Parker was in conversation?

H: No. But almost nobody was. She was an extraordinary wit.

M: And the two of you had an extraordinary relationship?

H: Yes, we did have an extraordinary relationship.

M: How did that happen because the two of you seem to me from a distance quite different people?

H: We were; maybe that's why we managed it. I really don't know how it happened. We had met in New York and just at a party, and we weren't to see each other again until four or five years later, and then we met in Hollywood. And I really don't know any longer how we got to know each other. And I certainly don't know how we got to like each other. But it was a long-lasting and very good relationship. I think she was as devoted to me as I was to her. And it was strange that two not very easy ladies got along so well.

M: Did your occasionally infamous temper explode at her as well as it did at . . . ?

H: No, never. Never. We never had an unpleasant word.

M: That was unusual for you, wasn't it?

H: In my memory.

M: Are the stories about the temper exaggerated?

H: No, I don't think they're exaggerated. They're exaggerated. I only had tempers at work, really. Once in a while they would be tempers outside of work. They were usually tempers in the theater. Tempers that had to do with my own work, when I couldn't bear anybody interfering with it. Once in a while they would explode in social situations but not very often. I'd like to have some of it back again.

M: You once wrote, "I used to have silent angers." What were they, and do you still have them?

H: Well, I shouldn't have really said that I suppose because they weren't always so very silent. They're much more silent now than they used to be. Yes, I still have them. I don't have them with the force they used to come, but I don't have anything with the force the way I used to have, I suppose. I was very ashamed of temper because I had been taught to be ashamed of it. In looking back I think it had great troubles and caused great troubles, but I think it had certain virtues.

M: What were they?

H: Well, it kept you from doing certain things. It carried you in bad situations very often that you might have collapsed under. I didn't know any of this when I had them but now in looking back I think that, for example, before the House Un-American Committee I was so silently angry that it carried me through the whole day. I might have collapsed otherwise.

M: You don't think it would have been better in retrospect to have expressed that anger?

H: There?

M: Uh huh.

H: No, I think it would have been very dangerous to have expressed it there. It didn't really matter about expressing it. I was so angry anyway. It was for me, that anger. What I mean is that I think I might have taken a totally different position if the anger about the whole thing hadn't carried me like a lifesaver.

M: You don't like confrontations. I assume that because you used to rush from rooms. You would even fly out of cities to get away from. . . .

H: I don't like confrontations I can lose; I think that's it.

M: Well, welcome to the human race.

H: Yes. If I can win them, I don't mind them at all.

M: But what was behind this, this often indescribable lure of just moving on, of getting away from some place in a hurry?

H: I think, perhaps, in a sense the fear of anger, that if I stayed, I'd be out of control. And that I better move as fast as I could, and as far as I could and forever as I could.

M: Did you ever lose a good friend because you fought with him or with her?

H: I think so. It wasn't one fight, if you know what I mean; it wasn't dramatic. But I think a couple. I have regrets for one; I don't have regrets for the other. It seems to me when you reach my age that kind of regret is nonsense. There's nothing to be done about it.

M: Is it too personal to ask which one you regret?

H: I can't name him because I think it would pain him. But it was an old friend, a rather distinguished literary man whom I grew up with. And I'm sorry that we don't see each other any more. But I don't think that it was all my fault, by any matter of means. We had just been very young together and very fond of each other. Times changed. It's very hard now perhaps having spent most of my younger life blaming myself too much. It's very probable I don't blame myself enough now.

M: You wanted success. You've admitted that. But you snarled at it when you got it. Why?

H: I don't know. I think I've asked myself this many, many times. I can't answer that question. I wish I could. I spent my life wondering about it. I don't know that I snarled at it. I had a sense of disappointment, I suppose, or maybe just a sense of fear that it would never happen again and what was I celebrating so much.

M: But you didn't feel at home in the world of the theater, did you?

H: No. I don't feel even at home in the world of success, I think. I'm not sure I was made for what people thought. I'm spoiled enough; I don't mean that. But I don't think I was made for the world of very successful people or the houses or the cars or the boats . . . . Not that I don't like them, I do. It's just that I'm not entirely comfortable.

M: You write most movingly about simple anonymous people, although you know so many of the great figures. Did you feel more comfortable with the . . . ?

H: I think I must have; I think in some way I possibly still do. I know a great many famous people and really like most of them. But I think . . . I'm making this too simple . . . I'm sounding as if I don't like success when of course I like it very, very much. And like all the benefits and the money and the rest from it.

M: What about the requirements of getting there? The discipline, the limits?

H: Well, I never thought of it that way. I've thought of it as just work. And since I've worked all my life, I go on working.

M: Well, the puzzle is that you did question glamor at least.

H: Yes, that I certainly have questioned, that I certainly have questioned. It's kind of comic to me, glamor.

M: And yet you were in a world of glamor, Hollywood and then Broadway.

H: Yes, I was. I was. I guess I still am to some extent. But it's always been faintly amusing to me, glamor. It's just such a funny word, isn't it? And it passes so rapidly. And I don't mean I wasn't impressed by it . . . an enormous number of people . . . and still aren't. But it's such a childish word really. It's a childish state.

M: What moved you to write the first play?

H: It's a long dull story. I don't think you want to hear it. I had started out as a . . . to be as brief as possible, I had started out . . . I had gone from college to work for a publishing house. And then I wanted to be a writer all my life, and I had written short stories. And one or two of them were published in unknown magazines, and they weren't very good. I'm not being modest; even I knew they weren't very good. And then I stopped writing and thought well this isn't any good, and I'm not meant to be a writer. And I was married then and went to Hollywood with my husband and got a job reading in the Metro-Goldwyn-Mayer reading department for the magnificent sum of fifty dollars a week where you had to read in two languages or you didn't get the job, and you worked from 9 until 6 at night, and then I got a divorce, and I went to live, as you know, with Dashiell Hammett. And I suppose . . . I don't know . . . I think he encouraged me to start again. Although I don't remember any words of it. And why I chose plays I haven't any idea since I really didn't know very much about the theater except I had gone to it during my lifetime. And had worked in very cheap jobs in the theater. I had worked in a Rochester stock company and taken tickets at a box office and done press agent. They were all very shabby jobs. I think I just started to write plays because I didn't know what else to write. I knew I wasn't a short story writer.

M: The beguiling paradox is that your plays, the early plays, were preoccupied with the terrors in the human heart, with evil. And yet *An Unfinished Woman* and *Pentimento* both deal with people, with the recognition of civility and decency, even among those people you didn't always like. How do you explain the preoccupation with evil in the early plays and the reflections that seem more encouraging about the race?

H: Well, I'm not sure I agree with you. I do know what you mean, of course. I would say—it doesn't mean I'm right because I don't think one ever looks at one's work very accurately, or even perhaps has any right to—that I'm still looking at evil but perhaps through another set of glasses. I don't think all the plays did look at so-called evil but some of them certainly did . . . you're quite right. And I think both books in a sense look at it but through perhaps a different age, perhaps not glasses, perhaps a different time of life.

M: You seem to be looking in *Pentimento* in particular at the people who pass before us . . . at the hopeful qualities, at the encouraging attributes, whereas in *Little Foxes*, for example, you seem to be looking for whatever it is that lurks inside of us that is dangerous and awful.

H: But, but, of course, from my viewpoint which as I said before doesn't at all mean anything because I think I said once I think I'm a moral writer and looking at evil is a form of morality, isn't it? *Little Foxes* of course were people I knew to some extent very, very altered. And I was in an angry period of my life. In any case I was very angry about such people. I still am angry about such people, but I suppose it would have a different form now. If there's any hope for a writer in the end, there can only be hope for some sort of change. Otherwise you do exactly what you always did.

M: Your last play was when, 1960?

H: 1962.

M: *Toys in the Attic?*

H: No, it was an adaptation called *My Mother, My Father and Me.* It was a failure.

M: Why haven't you written a play since then? Why did you turn to memoirs?

H: Well, not with that play, but long before that play, the Broadway theater began to be sort of sickening to me. I got tired of the talk about money and tired of the fact that the *New York Times* without any evil intention at all, it can't help it, it's not its fault by any matter of means, simply controls the success or failure of a play and if you get a bad review you might as well close the show. And it began to seem like nonsense to me, such pressures and so much money spent. And I think it really began—my leaving the theater—long before I left. It began with *Candide* which Leonard Bernstein, Richard Wilbur and I did as a musical. Somewhere in the middle of those rehearsals and that time in Boston I thought there's something crazy about a show that can't stay on the road because it hasn't got any money and is coming into New York before it should. And everybody's staying up till 6 o'clock in the morning and then going to work at 10 and making wild decisions, and I don't want my life to be this anymore, I don't know where I am anymore. I don't know whether I'm saying something is good because I think it is or just to please other people or. . . .

M: Have you seen a good play lately, one that moved you?

H: No, I've seen, you know, plays I liked to some extent, but no I haven't. I don't go to the theater very much anymore.

M: Why is that?

H: I don't think it's very good anymore. I much prefer going to movies. I've seen things that I liked and were interested in.

M: Why do you suppose there aren't more women writing plays or writing for the theater today?

H: Well, of course, there always should have been. God knows why there weren't early. I think there are a lot more women writing now, not only for the theater; there are a lot more women writing now than when I began or certainly fifty years before me when there were very few women writing anything. There're more women poets, there're more women novelists, aren't there?

M: You once said I think that women's liberation is a matter of economics. Would you elaborate on that?

H: Yes. I was misunderstood when I said it in a forum. I don't have to tell you how deeply I believe in women's liberation. I think some of its cries are rather empty cries because I think it all comes down to whether or not you can support yourself as well as a man can support himself and whether there's enough money to make certain decisions for yourself rather than dependence. In that particular discussion that was quoted one of the ladies brought up the point of she was not willing to do the cooking and lift the garbage cans. It seems to me it's not a question of who lifts the garbage cans but whether you have enough money to get somebody to lift them for you or enough money to say to your husband look I've worked as hard as you've worked today, please lift the garbage cans for me; or please do the cooking, I've worked perhaps even harder than you've worked today. I doubt if there'll be any true women's liberation until women are capable of even being paid for bringing up children which I think should carry a salary with it.

M: God knows you were liberated before, in the current sense of that word, it was ever in currency. Rebellious girl, rebellious woman. Where was the rebel born?

H: I don't know. Where are rebels ever born? I was rebellious when I was four years old, I think, and a nuisance too. All rebels are nuisances too.

M: Most rebels are nuisances.

H: They are.

M: Useful, but a nuisance.

H: I must have been the prize nuisance child I would guess. I often wondered how anybody put up with me. One asks oneself that always, where are rebels born? Where are non-rebels born equally?

M: But were you aware at an early age of wanting to be on your own, of wanting to be dependent upon no one?

H: No, because I think I was very dependent. I think I'm very dependent now. I was conscious of not liking it. I preferred to be left alone. I also think I knew early that I wasn't going to be. But I don't think that's the only kind of rebellious I was. I was very rebellious and that I think in part I inherited. You know that I grew up in part in the South, and I was very rebellious.

M: New Orleans?

H: Yes, the way negroes are treated . . . it seemed to me very unjust and ugly. I wasn't only rebellious about myself. I suppose I got that to some extent from my father, but not entirely. Maybe because I early fell in love with a negro nurse and stayed in love almost all my life I guess.

M: You said you were dependent and yet you strike me as always being a fugitive from commitment. I know you lived with Dashiell Hammett for thirty years off and on.

H: Yes.

M: And I guess one could say that's a commitment, and yet in your writings and in your life there seems to be a hanging back from commitment.

H: I don't think from commitment; I think you mean from marriage.

M: I didn't mean it, but I'll accept that amendment . . . from both. Why from marriage? Then I'll move on.

H: I've been, as a matter of fact, I think a little too committed. I don't know. I don't know. It isn't even that I had a very bad first marriage. I had a very pleasant first marriage to a very pleasant man called Arthur Kober. It wasn't at all a mean marriage, and we still see each other and are very fond of each other. I suppose I decided that it wasn't right for me. I don't mean that so many people urged me into it, but I thought I was better with no formalities. I was better if . . . I would stay longer if I felt free to go any day. I suppose that was it.

M: What did your father mean when he said you lived with a question mark?

H: Oh, I think he didn't mean anything more than I was just a damned nuisance with the questions I talked when I was young . . . in nothing but questions. Absolutely nothing. I never said a declarative sentence. I formed everything in the form of a question. And I would pull at everybody's coats or dresses to tell me what I wanted to know along a street. I don't know whether my father got it right or not but there was a play long before I was born called *Jimmy Valentine,* and he evidently was a question-asker. My father used to refer to me as Jimmy Valentine. Let's leave Jimmy Valentine alone for a while. Till she stops asking questions.

M: Well you can begin a few.

H: I still ask a great many questions.

M: What was there about Dashiell Hammett that enabled you the question-asker to really give yourself to him?

H: That's a very complicated question. What enables anybody to love somebody else? God knows, he was a very remarkable man, no question of that. He was also a very difficult man. Maybe . . . probably he was willing to answer the questions; I don't know. But it's a very hard question, isn't it, to ask anybody why they loved one person and didn't love another and. . . .

M: Respect often cancels out romance as I think you said of Dorothy Parker's marriage.

H: Yes.

M: But in your case?

H: No, in my case it didn't.

M: There was respect and romance.

H: Yes, there was. I had a great respect for him. I hope I didn't ever write that we had an easy life together. We didn't.

M: Oh no.

H: We had a very difficult life together nor did we ever live it twelve months a year together, very, very seldom except the last four or five years of his life when he was very ill. We usually skipped places, and I went away a great deal. I went to Europe a great deal. Hammett would never move. He never went out of America.

M: Why was that?

H: I don't know. I have a feeling he was an extraordinarily American kind of man in an almost provincial sense. He not only had for a radical a rather great dislike of foreigners; and people who accused him of having sympathies for the Soviet Union didn't quite know what they were talking about because, while he was interested in what they were doing, he had a sort of feeling that no foreigner equalled us really in the end.

M: Did he help you with your writing?

H: Oh yes, enormously, enormously. I can't ever pay him enough gratitude for what he did beyond the obvious things that writers can help with. He was so enormously patient. And more than patient, he was honest, sometimes rather sharply and brutally honest. Without that I don't think I would have done very much.

M: Did he tell you this is no damn good?

H: Oh yes, indeed. In stronger words than that. In very strong words.

M: Did you take it from him?

H: Oh yes, I took it. Once in a while I would get terribly pained and miserable about it. Yes certainly I took it because I recognized that it had . . . I think you can always take what people say if you know there's no malice in it or no self-seeking in it. Then whether they're right or wrong, they've shown that amount of love to take the chance on your hating them which has always impressed me in people.

M: Why did he ask you to stop reading *Li'l Abner*?

H: He hated *Li'l Abner*. He thought it was a fascist comic strip. He hated it. I used to be very amused at his violence about *Li'l Abner*.

M: I wonder what he would think today about Al Capp?

H: Well he sure guessed it long before. Because this was years ago. I was a great comic strip reader. And he used to be violent about my reading *Li'l Abner*. How could I stand it? How could I stand what a picture this was of people? It was a low-down mess. He was violent. And he wasn't a violent man, he was a rather good-tempered man.

M: Did you keep your promise to him to stop reading *Li'l Abner*?

H: Yes, I never read *Li'l Abner* again.

M: I guess that's the ultimate tribute.

H: Once in a while I'd try to sneak back, and I was so inhibited and so superstitious that I don't read it. I took to reading *Orphan Annie* instead.

M: I guess that's the ultimate tribute to commitment. I was wrong all along about you. You will give up *Li'l Abner* for the man you love.

H: Oh I loved *Li'l Abner*, I was crazy about it. I didn't even know what he was talking about. I think I know what he's talking about now.

M: But Hammett saw politics in it.

H: Yes he did, he did. I was amazed that he did. It turns out to be right.

M: He was right. You've never written extensively about your own political beliefs or activities. And yet you say that the McCarthy era changed your life.

H: Yes, I've tried to, Mr. Moyers, a number of times, and I tried for *Unfinished Woman*. I tried long before *Unfinished Woman*. I tried for *Pentimento*. It seems to be something that at least at this period of my life I can't do. I write ten or fifteen pages, and I then tear them up, and they seem to be the wrong tone. I can't seem to say what I want to say.

M: Why is that? You've expressed yourself on the stage, you've expressed yourself precisely in two memoirs, and yet when it comes to political views this hesitation.

H: Well of course it's such a complicated period, because it simply wasn't just McCarthy; everybody now uses this word to sort of blame one man or ten men or fifteen men. It was much more pervasive than that. It even includes many, many liberals, still living. And I suppose perhaps I feel more sharply about them than I do about McCarthy.

M: Why?

H: Well I had foolishly told myself that they would stand up in such a period, and most of them did not. And that evidently is still so difficult for me to understand. Many of them were my close friends. I suppose that's so difficult for me to understand that I don't. And I'm so frightened of it happening again in some form that I can't. . . . It's all so difficult because many of them now deny it. Maybe they believe what they're saying. I don't think they do, and perhaps that isn't my only reason. I was very ruined in that period, financially very ruined I mean.

M: When you were blacklisted?

H: Yes. And what money we both had went. And I don't think I like to think of . . . I don't enjoy periods of pain. I find it a little embarassing to talk about it. Particularly since I did all right afterwards. Maybe if I never had it would have been.

M: The country's recovery from that period, your own recovery from that period, is a sign of hope isn't it?

H: Yes, indeed, indeed. Indeed, indeed it is. I hope we're not entering another one but it could never be the same. It could be much worse. But it could never be the same. Of course, it is; and I think I sort of always knew that if one lived long enough and had any kind of break, and I did have a break, many people didn't of course. It depended on what age you were, what talents you had, I suppose, and what health you were in, many things. Many people didn't survive. I suppose I always thought that if one just could hang on long enough one would survive. I wish I knew why I couldn't write about it. If I knew it I could do it.

M: You've said it in snippets here and there. You said for example that Hitler had shaken so many of you in the Thirties into radicalism, and I remember your describing staying in a London hotel after you came out of Spain and saying that those were the root days of your radicalism. Yet did you really become a radical?

H: No, it's a loose term. No, I never belonged to any political party. No, I didn't become a radical, I'm afraid. Since I admire many radicals, I'm rather sorry to say I don't think I did have either the interest or the commitment. But no, I didn't. And I don't ever want to fake that I did.

M: That's another difference between you and Dashiell Hammett.

H: Yes.

M: He was very committed.

H: Yes, indeed. He was certainly the last fifteen to twenty years of his life totally committed. We had frequently bad times about that.

M: Arguments?

H: Yes, sometimes arguments, but more often my . . . I think my fears; once he went to jail, I was terrified he was going back again.

M: He was sent to jail because of his radical activities.

H: He was sent to jail because he refused, quite honorably, to supply a court with the names of people who had contributed to something called the Civil Rights Bail Fund. As I've written before, he never in his life had seen the names; he never had even been in the office of the organization, he didn't know where the office was. But he'd agreed to be a trustee and decided that he was not going to turn over the names, and he went to jail. Once he got out of jail I was always terrified he was going back. He was by this time quite a sick man.

M: So that was a source of tension?

H: And we used to have arguments about it. He finally said quite clearly that he intended to do what he wanted to do and that if I didn't like it that was too bad but he'd understand. We'd move away from each other then. He understood it was some danger to me too and that he wouldn't have any feeling about it if I chose to leave, and I didn't choose to leave so. . . .

M: You said once I think we were younger in our twenties than people are today. Why?

H: Well I think education is better today for one thing. I think the average parent is better informed, less stuffy about what children can or cannot know. But chiefly I think education is better today than it was. I still don't . . . as somebody who teaches very often . . . I still don't think it's the dream . . . it's better than it was with me. And customs and manners in America are less stuffy and inhibited than they were.

M: I take it than they were when you were in New Orleans growing up?

H: Yes, exactly. Or even in New York by the time we moved to New York. I came, of course, it's perhaps not very fair to say from a very middle class family. Maybe they were, my mother and father weren't but everybody else was, and maybe they were stuffier than most. But I think people don't hide from children and know more about children. Freud's had a good deal to do with this too. Don't you think so?

M: Yes. Do you fear age, old age?

H: Oh yes, yes, indeed. I'm furious about it. I'm not furious so much as I'm so angry about it.

M: Angry?

H: Yes, I hate not being . . . and I've seldom been really sick . . . I hate not being able to do everything I could do or getting tired or having to think about my body or myself. It's childish of me; I just can't possibly get through my head it's happened to me.

M: That's a common ailment. How do you deal with it? How do you come to terms with it?

H: Go to bed. About all one can do, lie down, just tell myself there's nothing to be done about it.

M: Where do you go from here?

H: From here in age?

M: Uh huh.

H: Getting older.

M: From where you are intellectually?

H: Oh God knows, God knows. I hope okay but who knows. I go around telling myself how my memory is going, you know. I give myself a little talk everyday about it but so far I suppose it's better than I could have expected.

M: You accused yourself once of making larger symbols out of things than should be made out of them, and I'm guilty of the same thing. Which prompts me to ask you, do you remember the fig tree?

H: Yes, indeed, indeed.

M: Tell me about the fig tree.

H: Well, I think you mean the fig tree I wrote about in *Unfinished Woman* where I spent a great deal of my New Orleans childhood, when the weather would allow it. My aunt had a boarding house, and the boarding house had a fair amount of grounds, and there was a quite large, exceptionally large fig tree. It was sufficiently removed from the house and heavy in limb and leaf that you couldn't be seen. So I rigged up a seat for myself and baskets I used to put on pulleys and books that I kept up there and food that I took up there. I lived many a day and sometimes part of a night in that fig tree. I would skip school. Since I partly went to school in New York and partly went to school in New Orleans, I was behind my class in New York and way ahead of my class in New Orleans. So in New Orleans they wouldn't even care if I showed up or not. Nobody'd mind if I showed up two or three times a week. Nobody said anything. So I would frequently take all my school books and go round the block and get on the streetcar and get off, come right back to the fig tree.

M: I'll show you what I mean when I say I make perhaps too much of something, but this is the way you describe the fig tree in *An Unfinished Woman*: "The fig tree was heavy, solid, comfortable, and I had, through time, convinced myself that it wanted me, missed me when I was absent, and approved all the rigging I had done for the happy days I had spent in its arms." And the question becomes has Lillian Hellman spent the rest of her life looking for another fig tree?

H: Yes, of course. All of us . . . whatever that fig tree has been in everybody's life. I'm not sure one finds it after childhood; one is very lucky to find it in childhood, isn't one? Most children don't find it. I was at one with that tree.

M: Have you ever felt that way again about anything or any place?

H: I don't think, to that degree. I felt it in a large measure about the farm that I owned before the McCarthy period and had to sell because of it. I felt very comfortable and at home because I had worked very hard on it. I did work physically very hard on it. But I don't think in the sort of mystical way that child felt about that tree.

M: Do you miss those fat, loose, wild years that you once described and lived?

H: Sometimes I do, sometimes I do. Yes, but now of course it would be almost impossible. Every once in a while I have a great dream of it. I don't drink very much anymore and once in a while I get great feelings about the days when I did, and then I think how silly when I don't really want to drink anymore. What nostalgic foolishness that is. I couldn't in the first place and don't want to in the second. About four or five years ago, I guess I was in the Vineyard by myself in the autumn, and I thought I haven't been drunk in twenty, twenty-five years, I guess. I'd really like to be very, very drunk again. And I was by myself and I got very, very drunk, and I started up the stairs. My house has a rather large landing in the middle of the stairs. And I thought wouldn't it be nice not to go to bed in this sort of formal way I go to bed every night now. To go back to just going to sleep where I was, which is what I used to do. So I went to sleep on the landing, had a very bad cold in the morning, was terribly uncomfortable . . . and a back ache and thought well that's enough of that nonsense forever. Now I'll go to bed for the rest of my life. It was a very good night for me. Good teaching. I felt awful for a couple of days.

M: Worse than giving up *Li'l Abner?*

H: Much worse. It's more painful.

M: You wrote once, "We were suspicious in those days of the words of love."

H: Yeah.

M: Did you get over that suspicion?

H: No, I still have it. I think I'm still doubtful about all statements of emotions. I have some feelings that they better be proved before the words are used. I like the words. I would like, of course, like to be told the words. And I think one can make too much fuss about not saying them, but it seems to me we all talk too loosely very often about what we feel. I'm a little frightened of that, I must say, rather than acting it out or proving it in some way.

M: Was Hammett reluctant to use the words of love?

H: Oh, terribly reluctant. Hammett was a very taciturn man. Very reluctant. He had far greater suspicions than I had of emotion.

M: But the two of you never really seemed as far as I can discern from reading to have a great deal of doubt about the vitality of the relationship.

H: No, I don't think we did. I don't think we did. I think we both knew. Well, it took a long time to find out, but we both knew in the end . . . long before the end . . . what we felt. We didn't talk about it a great deal. We both were very . . . . I think we were good to each other. I think. I'm sure. I think I would have liked far more words. All women like far more words. I'd have liked poems written to me, but I wasn't getting them, so I did without them; I'd still like a poem written to me if you know anyone who'd like to write it.

M: A poem. Lillian Hellman's life has been its own poem, with its special cadence of love and loss. Poetry acted out rather than merely written. And like the woman herself, still unfinished.

Lillian Hellman on Lillian Hellman

Janet Chusmir/1974

From the *Miami Herald,* 17 March 1974, sec. F, 1, 10. Reprinted by permission of the *Miami Herald* and Janet Chusmir.

Sarasota—Still, I will always remember that when she opened the door of the tree-hidden house she'd rented near the Gulf of Mexico she was worried the "damn cat" would get in. She didn't like it. And it didn't like her.

And I will remember she was much shorter than I expected, maybe five feet two inches, with such a large head and broad shoulders and bust that the slender legs were a surprise as if God had changed his mind partway about the size Lillian Hellman would be.

She was born in New Orleans on June 20, 1905. And then again in the literary sense in 1934, the night they stood and shouted "Author! Author!" when the Broadway curtain fell on her first play *The Children's Hour.*

It was written, she says, on Key Largo. She and "my closest, my most beloved friend," writer Dashiell Hammett, spent two winters and two springs on Key Largo when only a fishing camp and two houses were there.

Now there are trailer camps and gas stations and restaurants and bars. And lots of other plays, most of them great successes: *The Little Foxes, Watch on the Rhine, The Searching Wind, Another Part of the Forest, The Autumn Garden, Toys in the Attic.* With them came honor and awards.

In 1969, a memoir, *An Unfinished Woman,* won the National Book Award. And now there's *Pentimento,* a book of portraits. Because of them a new generation is getting to know her father's family, the German-Jewish Hellmans, and her mother's, the wealthy, bickering Newhouses—often thinly-disguised characters in her plays.

Her childhood was divided between New Orleans and New York, a city she dislikes to this day because it's so big. Her first job was in a publishing house. While she was working there she had an abortion

159

and then married the father, writer Arthur Kober. Then easily divorced him and not so easily spent a good part of 30 years with Hammett, author of *The Maltese Falcon* and *The Thin Man*. In fact, he modeled the bright and witty Nora Charles after her. She found out later, the villainesses and the silly girls in his plots, too.

He died in 1961.

She doesn't know why they never married. In the past she's said she supposes she's forgotten many of the bad times and she's talked about the two times they planned to marry and how the first time he disappeared with another lady. And then she's said. "That's not really fair—I was disappearing, too," and she's explained how they believed that alliances could stand up against other people although she had a jealous nature and should have known better.

She's also talked about his heavy drinking. She stopped hers "because I was going to pieces, because I grew frightened of what would happen to me."

Not getting married "never was a problem one way or the other. I got a divorce first; he got a divorce shortly afterwards and I suppose that was the intention. I think it's really quite wise we didn't get married. It's fine, you know, to say that because it lasted in any case. So all one can say when something lasts is it's just as well not to have married. If it hadn't lasted, I suppose my answer would have been the opposite, that if we'd gotten married it would have been better."

Though once she flew across the country to smash the bar in his Hollywood house because a woman answered her phone call in the middle of the night, now she says his "great many ladies" are not the reason. "Those are the reasons that young women tell themselves.

"It's very hard, years afterwards to say with any truth why you did something or why you didn't. I wouldn't like to hear most people telling why they got married."

Nor is she sure that she really regrets never having children. "I'm sorry never to have had children, but whenever I say that to myself I say that's the biggest nonsense ever talked because it's too late now to bother regretting it and if I'd wanted them enough I would have had them, I suppose."

Regret, anyway, is a waste of time. But, she does regret that she still doesn't own and run the farm in Pleasantville, N.Y. "But it's too late for that because I don't think I'd be capable of doing that and the world has changed so much that I don't think I could do it. I don't think you can find the Farm Labor anymore.

"Yes, that I would have liked to have gone on doing. I was good at farming and I would have liked to have gone on trying it anyway . . ."

There was no choice. It went with everything in the McCarthy era when she was blacklisted for suspected leftist leanings and Hammett went to jail because he wouldn't give the House Un-American Activities Committee a list of names. He wouldn't tell the committee either, that he didn't know the names.

Bitterness, like regret, is a waste of time. "What good does it do?" she asks. But she still feels an overwhelming bitterness about the aimlessness and sort of comedy of it all and how much it affected her and other people. It's one of the reasons she's never been able to write about the McCarthy period.

She doesn't single out Joe McCarthy. He couldn't possibly have gotten away with what he did without the time being proper for it "and people aiding him including Mr. Nixon, and Pat McCarran and all the rest. None of it came out of the blue. They came along at a proper time."

She speaks in a low, cigaret-hoarse voice, sometimes interrupted by rasping coughs. A cigaret addict, she wakes up with a "cigaret hangover" each morning and vows to give up the much more than two packs of Marlboros, but then an hour later is lighting up again. She once quit for four days until she decided she didn't want to live her life that way. "It's so disgusting. I'm not undisciplined about other things. To find something that's totally outside of my hands is a shocker to me."

As you get older, you get frightened of what you can't do physically anymore. She can't handle a boat alone anymore. Her work periods have gone from two a day to one.

She did have an enormous amount of energy and she supposes there's a fair amount left. But to her it's diminished. "I've gotten to sort of come to grips with that, too. Nothing so terrible. It just means watching one's self.

"The one thing I shouldn't be doing I go right on doing. So it gets kind of silly to say I have to go to a climate when I go right on smoking . . ."

She has emphysema. It has already affected her heart as well as her lungs. It is the escape to warm weather, made with the doctor's warnings to stop smoking ringing in her ears, that takes her South— away from the house in Martha's Vineyard, where she spends most of her time, and the apartment in New York.

She also goes right on being hard on herself. She never came to peace with herself. There's no chance of that. "I'm much too critical of myself to ever be at Peace with myself. I could do with a little less of that I must say. That gets to be a bore particularly since it doesn't go very far anymore and I don't correct myself much anymore. But in my kind of nature, I think peace with one's self would be age. I daresay I'll get there. I have no desire to get there."

It's not just her writing. "Nothing on God's earth am I totally pleased with, certainly not myself.

"That would be awful. Imagine being pleased with yourself! My God, that would seem to me death and I don't want to die."

A power boat pulling a surfer roars by on the bay. Two startled seagulls flee their dock-piling-perch. And Lillian Hellman, admired for her lack of hypocrisy and for her integrity, deftly fields the question: How did you come out with the integrity you have?

"I don't know that one has the right to think of one's self as having integrity," she says.

"When I was a child my father once said something that I've always remembered and liked. Evidently I used the word honest a great deal and he looked up from a newspaper one morning at breakfast and said, 'I have something to tell you. Honest people don't talk about honesty.'

"I've remembered that. That seemed to me a very profound statement. He said, 'People who don't lie don't say they don't lie. Honest people don't say they're honest.' "

You do something by instinct, she supposes. She never thought of it as integrity or not integrity. It was just what she had to do and she's delighted if other people think it is. She has a theory that whatever is that quality, one doesn't know about it, but probably gets it very, very young. Or the lack of it.

"My father had a kind of integrity, I suppose. My mother did, too. What does the word mean? A difficult quality to put one's hand on, isn't it?"

Then, let's say that she never sold herself.

"I don't know if I did what was right. That I couldn't say. I don't think I ever sold myself. But then I never had any temptation to do it. I suppose it's a matter of temptation. I never wanted money enough to do it, I suppose. It must be awful for people who want something very badly. I don't think I ever wanted anything enough, maybe never needed anything enough. Maybe that's all it is."

Asked to relate that to Watergate, she says, "They wanted everything and nothing else mattered. Nobody else but their own desires mattered. But that's a shabby, shabby crew, isn't it? And they are so pious about it all. I'd much rather have open villains than those pious villains. Every single day there's a pious statement from one of them. One of them's found God or . . . Too bad they didn't find Him earlier."

She spent her life hard at work in a world, the theater, that was not her world, although it has been her life.

Her world, she says, was a strange mixture through the years in the theater of rather simple people—more literary people than theater people.

She lost interest in the theater 11 years ago. "I lost it for a number of good reasons not all of which can be explained," she says. "But the Broadway theater seemed to get to be increasingly a question of money and it occurred to me that I didn't want to live in a world where one was a wild success one minute and a wild failure the next and it seldom depended upon the worth of what one was doing."

But she's rather pleased she did one thing—plays—and turned to another—books. "There's no reason why you should go on doing the same thing all your life. It never occurred to me that would happen. I might go back to the theater. I don't have any rules about it."

She finds it very hard to write about the living. "You step on toes and you're less free. When I first started *Pentimento* I had no idea I would do mostly dead people—80 percent dead people—and I suppose I did it because it's easier to do it."

It's more than not stepping on toes, it's not causing too much trouble and fights. And it's also "since you see people through your own eyes, how do you know if you're telling the truth? Dead people can't deny it."

But the dead do not always stay buried. Even now, she worries would the dear friend, the heiress of great wealth who was killed by the Nazis because she fought Fascism and helped get people out of Germany have wanted her story told in *Pentimento*?

She strikes a match and lights another cigaret. There is silence as she inhales for awhile.

Has it been a happy life?

She hates words like that. She's scared to death of them. She doesn't know what they mean. "It certainly hasn't been a bad one, though. It's been mostly fun.

"It depends on your nature. Mine has not been a very unhappy nature. It's very often a gloomy one, but not an unhappy one so it would be hard for me to say what was happy and what wasn't happy."

Would it be hard to say what she means by gloomy?

"Well, I get into depressions, but I get out of them very fast."

She takes a few more puffs of the cigaret and goes on to say that she gets great pleasure out of small things and doesn't need large things to cheer her up.

"But I don't know that anybody has a right to look at their life and say it's been happy or unhappy. As you can see, I have a great disbelief in large conceptions about yourself. I always wonder if I'm telling the truth.

"You can stand not knowing the truth about yourself. You'd kill yourself if you did, probably. But it's not knowing the truth about anything else that's so worrisome and as you get older it's more worrisome and you think, 'I must be a fool.' I go around with that so much that . . ."

She never finishes the sentence because it reminds her that Hammett used to have a theory that she made up her mind too fast, that she would come far nearer the truth if she didn't have to make up her mind so fast. "But that was his nature to go slow. My nature is to go fast.

"He understood most people and I don't. He used to say about people, whenever I'd say how wrong I'd been, he'd say, "It's not a question of wrong. You just have to make up your mind for some reason in the first 10 minutes. If you'd go slow and not make up your mind at all and wait to see what happened . . ."

"And then it would occur to me years later that it took too long. It wasn't worth all that trouble."

"Sweetest Smelling Baby in New Orleans"
Jan Albert/1975

This is a transcript of an audio casette which is available from Pacifica Tape Library, 5316 Venice Boulevard, Los Angeles, CA 90019. Transcribed by Ruth M. Alvarez. The transcript has been edited to include only the interview portion and not the excerpts from Miss Hellman's works. The interview was conducted by Jan Albert, WBAI, New York, 1975, and is used with permission from the Pacifica Radio Archive, Los Angeles, CA.

Jan Albert: You grew up half in New Orleans, half in New York, and it must have caused a lot of strange influences, different influences from both sides. I wonder if we could start by your telling me a little bit about that and about the people you were surrounded with as a kid.

Lillian Hellman: Well, it's always hard in a few sentences to sum up one's childhood. New Orleans and New York were of course very different. New Orleans particularly when I grew up, because it was a rather poor city. It's now a boom city, of course, and a quite rich city. When I grew up it was not, in general, a rich city. The school systems were quite different. I think New Orleans systems in those days were way behind New York systems. This naturally made a little girl uncomfortable going from one kind of school system into another kind of school system. I rode ahead of my class in New Orleans and way behind it in New York. And I was moved from one school to many other schools, I mean many others in a single place like New York. As far as the children went, I don't know that one as a child makes much difference. I think I liked my friends here better, because, of course, in the end we came to live here. But I was at least fifteen, sixteen years old before we stopped this commuting that we did.

JA: What caused the commuting back and forth?

LH: Well, my father took long business trips of four and five months a year, and then they thought it best to go back to New Orleans for that time. My mother did. I guess he did too, and we'd stay with my aunts. As I've written, my aunt has a very pleasant boarding house, and I guess my mother liked it there (probably it was lonely in New York without him). I suppose that was the reason; I never asked, of course.

JA: It must have been quite incredible living in a boarding house, certainly a child's fantasy, imagining all the lives of the different boarders.

LH: Yes it was. It was fun, but now that I look back on it. I was so interested in everybody of course. It wasn't always fun. You didn't have very much privacy of course. Boarding houses in New Orleans . . . in much of the South were not boarding houses as one possibly knows them now but more like French pensions. You took two meals a day and sometimes three meals a day. So that there weren't people just in rooms. You ate with them most of the time; sometimes we ate privately *en famille*. My one aunt did a great deal of the cooking. My other aunt worked at an outside job.

•   •

LH: It had been my plan to be a writer, as well as my plan to be an architect. I soon realized I wouldn't ever be an architect. But I had written all my life till I was about twenty-two . . . twenty-three, and then I decided I wasn't any good, so I stopped. I didn't think I was any good so I stopped writing and never really resumed it until after I met Hammett. Dashiell Hammett.

JA: You got back to writing after you met Hammett?

LH: Yes.

JA: You represent him as being the person who started you writing again. How did that come about?

LH: I don't think there was any plan or plot to it. I think he just encouraged me to. I don't remember any hour or minute. I think it was just an encouragement to start again.

JA: Your first play, *The Children's Hour,* was a huge success, and I wondered how you came to write it. How you came up with the topic of the play, the subject of the play. It's such a powerful subject, and it would be even if the implied lesbianism wasn't there because of the evil children spreading stories and ruining adults' lives. The sort of "bad seed" concept.

LH: *The Children's Hour* was actually based on a real case written by . . . it happened in Scotland in the nineteenth century and written by a man called William Roughead who was a lawyer and who wrote a number of quite good books about Scotch law cases. And the actual case was two middle-aged ladies who ran a boarding school in Scotland and who took into their school an Indian girl, an Indian Indian girl, half Indian, half Scotch. And she seems to have made accusations about them. And they brought suit and sued to the end of their lives . . . evidently broke themselves and died without ever winning. I don't remember really what they won or lost. And I obviously did a great deal of changing there; but certainly that was the basic idea.

JA: I was looking back through articles about your plays, and I found one that spoke of a woman having great difficulty in dealing with the changing sexual mores of the time. And I wondered did the subject hit? What was the reaction to the subject of lesbianism? Was it as hard as *The Night Porter* is to a lot of us now? Was it that strong? Or was it an accepted topic?

LH: No, I don't think it was an accepted topic. The play has nothing to do with lesbianism, of course; it's just one of the side issues. It's just the charge of the girl, that's all. But Mr. Shumlin, the producer, was very worried; everybody was very worried, because a play called *The Captive,* a French play, had played in New York a few years before and had been closed up by the police department. So we took every precaution. The children, the so-called children, were all over eighteen years old in the play. And we observed every possible fire law, which no theater does—people smoke backstage. We were very careful to be . . . it was banned in many cities. It was banned in Boston for many years. It was banned in Chicago for many years. Here we had no trouble at all. Because I really don't think people who saw it ever thought of it as a lesbian play. But it was banned in many places. We finally won both the Chicago and Boston suits, but after many, many years. Yes, it was a forbidden topic.

•   •

LH: *The Children's Hour,* which was my first play, was backed by the Shuberts, and I so little knew it because Mr. Shumlin produced it that I didn't pay any attention to the fact that we were rehearsing in a Shubert theater, and I was quite young. I was twenty-six, I guess, which doesn't explain why I had the habit of putting my feet up on the seat in front of me. But I did have a habit of sitting that way all day. And suddenly a little man came down an aisle one day and tapped me on the shoulder and said, "Take your feet off that seat." And I turned around in absolute shock that anybody would speak to me this way. And I said, "Who are you," and he said, "Just take your feet off the seat of my theater." And I strode to the stage and said to Herman Shumlin, who was the producer-director, "Somebody has come down the aisle and told me to take my feet off the seat." And Mr. Shumlin said, "Mr. Shubert, get out of here. This is the author. Get out of here." And Mr. Shubert left. And then I said, "What right beyond owning the theater did he have." And Mr. Shumlin said, "Well, I must tell you he put up the money for the play," which I had never known before, and I never saw Mr. Shubert except the opening night of the same play, which turned out to be a great opening night but was a kind of mess because the Shuberts had decided that we weren't worth very much. We were put in the Maxine Elliott Theatre on 39th Street, shortly to be demolished. Downstairs got proper programs. Upstairs where I sat to look at the play they handed out a program I still have called *Sunset Grove,* which was the play that had opened and closed about eight days before, and people were just going around handing. . . .

JA: Your second play, *Days to Come,* which I liked when reading it in the *Collected Plays . . .* the line I liked best was that "things start out as hopes, but end up as habits." I guess it hit something in me, but it sort of got me thinking to very early big huge successes that can't be followed up, and people are just sort of sunk into terrible depression about not being able to follow up their first super hit of some kind. And I further thought that you and Dashiell Hammett were sort of late starters in the field of writing. You didn't have your first success until you were twenty-eight; that was when you first wrote a play.

LH: It's a late start to start writing, but I don't think even now it would be considered a late start for success. There are very few writers that I know who have been successful very much earlier, maybe twenty-five, -six, somewhere in there. I don't think it's very late in age now. I don't know how old Dash was when he first . . . he certainly wasn't very young when he was first successful. He must have been in his early middle . . . near to middle thirties, but he had been writing for many years.

JA: All the time he was a Pinkerton man he was writing?

LH: No, not all the time; after he quit Pinkerton.

JA: People you knew as writers, Fitzgerald, had very big successes at first, and I guess couldn't follow them up afterward.

LH: Yes, he was quite young. Hemingway, I think, the first book was published I think in 1925. And he must have been a man twenty-five or -six then. That's young. I don't know of many writers now who are very great successes before that age. It's nicer to have it young, of course, but. . . .

JA: Not if you're forced to have to top yourself every time, I guess.

LH: Well, there are other penalties for the other way around. I suppose if you don't have any kind of recognition I don't . . . I'm not talking about money success because that's something else, but if you don't have any recognition and get to be in your forties things must be very . . . rather tough going. It must take a great deal more courage than it does if you get some recognition before then.

JA: Your family is incredible. You could have a few books on just your family.

LH: Everybody's family is incredible.

JA: Oh, I don't know. But you speak of your grandmother as the type of person who would break people's spirit for the exercise of it, as a very strong lady. And you spoke of your feelings about your family's wealth, sort of a self-hatred . . . your respect of the wealth. And I wondered if *The Little Foxes* purged you of this at all? After you'd written it?

LH: I think to a certain extent, yes. Yes, I think I wrote it out. I think so. I've always thought I had.

JA: I wondered if writing worked like that? Like dreams sort of. Once you'd gotten it down. . . .

LH: I think it very often does. I don't think you're ever finished really with anything that's the matter with you or even right about you. But you often can work out things that have been painful to you in writing, I think.

JA: *The Little Foxes* is when you met Tallulah. I wonder if you could tell us a little bit about your association with Tallulah. How she got involved with playing Regina in *The Little Foxes.*

LH: Well, Herman Shumlin thought of that casting.

JA: He was the director?

LH: Yes, the director-producer. And I had never seen her so I had no opinions at all. She turned out at first as I've written many times very very very good. And later on in the run of the play, not very good. But she certainly the first six months was perfectly splendid.

JA: You adapted *The Little Foxes* to the screen. Was it difficult to do this, adapting a play for the screen? Was it hard to get into writing movies? Especially adapting your own work?

LH: No, I liked writing movies. I was one of the few people who sort of in those days genuinely enjoyed it. No, I liked it, liked doing it.

JA: Did you adapt *The Children's Hour* also?

LH: The first *Children's Hour* was not *The Children's Hour*. We took the basic idea of the school and took the lesbianism out. It wasn't allowed. And it made a very nice little picture called *These Three* with Merle Oberon and Miriam Hopkins and Joel McCrae. The second *Children's Hour,* which was done only about eight or nine years ago, I didn't have anything to do with. It was done by somebody else.

JA: Did you like the way it showed up on screen?

LH: Not entirely, no. I think perhaps Mr. Wyler was over-respectful of me—William Wyler who had directed both pictures—was over-respectful of the play. And it would have been better to have altered it more on movie terms.

JA: Can you give me some of the movies you wrote? Besides the things you adapted of yourself. *The Searching Wind* I know you adapted for the screen. What else have you written? I know you wrote *The Chase.*

LH: *The Chase.* I did *The Little Foxes.* I did a first picture called *Dark Angel.* Uh, what else did I do? I did a picture called *Dead End,* Sidney Kingsley's play, which is shown on television still a great deal, I think. And then, of course, I also wrote what turned out to be a bad picture called *North Star.* On *North Star,* Goldwyn and I had a fight and then not long after that, of course, I was banned in Hollywood during the McCarthy days. And then when I wasn't banned anymore I found I didn't very much want to work there.

JA: You didn't want to go back?

LH: No, not much.

JA: Dashiell Hammett helped you the most you say with *The Little Foxes.*

LH: Yes.

JA: How did he help you, just with his sharp criticism?

LH: Yes, sometimes real suggestions about what should happen and what shouldn't happen. Yes.

JA: Did you work well together? I notice he wrote the screenplay for *Watch on the Rhine,* and I was thinking it must be really hard to have somebody so close to you adapt one of your own works. Was it? Or did you just work fantastically together?

LH: Well, we didn't work together in the sense that you mean. He did *Watch on the Rhine* screenplay because I was . . . I've forgotten now . . . I was doing something else. I've forgotten what I was doing and couldn't do it. And he did it as a favor to me. He wasn't crazy about doing it. But we didn't work together in that sense. I mean we read each other's stuff, but we didn't work in any kind of collaboration.

JA: Did it work the other way also? Did you help him with suggestions and stuff of his?

LH: No, no, very seldom, very seldom. He didn't want it, and I didn't offer it. I knew he didn't want it, no.

LH: You must have had a huge amount of trust in him to allow him to adapt your work.

LH: I had a great trust in him. And it certainly was very difficult; at times I was very angry often. And he, I guess, must have been quite angry as well. But we worked it out. It was a kind of anger I got over and quickly saw that it was for my benefit. Sometimes I didn't agree with him, of course, and had to go my own way, but the criticism was always given without any malice which is what one is frightened of in criticism of any kind, I think. Either malice or too much desire to please which is almost the same thing. And there was none of that, and I was grateful for the very professional help.

JA: Yeah, I guess you had that.

LH: Yes, he was a real pro beyond everything else.

JA: How did you feel when he told you that Nora was based on you, Nora Charles?

LH: Oh, I was very pleased. She's a charming character, I think.

JA: She's swell, yes. It seems like the nicest character to be based on, yes.

LH: Yes, it is.

JA: And they have a jolly life together.

LH: Yes, they liked each other.

LH: I went on what was called a cultural mission. I was invited during the war. There'd been a business representative. Eric Johnston, I think, had gone on a business mission, and I was invited as the cultural representative. And I don't know that the State Department was too anxious for that. But I think the While House was, and so I went.

JA: It sounds incredibly exciting. That's one of the most exciting parts of the *Unfinished Woman* book. Your trip to Russia flying in this little plane over Siberia.

LH: It wasn't a little plane; it was what we know as a DC3 C47. It's a little plane now, but it was a quite big plane then, and it still is you know is known as the workhorse of the planes . . . a great plane. It was very little compared to the plane you get into now, of course. It was more than exciting; it was a very dangerous trip. If I'd ever known how dangerous it was I wouldn't have gone on it. But I'm so ignorant that I didn't have any knowledge. I never would have gone in a thousand years if I'd have known.

JA: Well, it got even more dangerous because you contracted pneumonia.

LH: Yes, it got terribly dangerous, terribly dangerous. Kind of a miracle I lived through that trip and the pneumonia as well.

JA: You went back to Russia several times, but this first time you went the Russian State Department for some reason chose you to go to the front line. They called you into their office and said you were allowed to meet anybody in Moscow that you wanted.

LH: Yes.

JA: And you couldn't quite understand why they had chosen you?

LH: Well, no, that isn't quite the way it was. I was a guest, and I had refused to go as a journalist because I realized that as their guest in a sense I would be far better off. I'd be allowed to see more. I did do pieces, but I did them when I came home. But journalists were very restricted, and I knew that before I went . . . realized that I'd be less restricted. I was right because I was the only person ever allowed to go to the Russian front.

JA: That sounds incredible. It really does. I guess that is the closest you've been to war. I guess you were closer there than you were during the Spanish Civil War. Although you were in Spain.

LH: Yes, I think so. I think so.

JA: At times you could actually see the German army across the way, right?

LH: I couldn't see German soldiers; I could see German trenches and German gun emplacements. I don't think I ever saw a German solider except ones they were taking prisoners. They were very close to each other; they were within two hundred yards of each other, where I was.

JA: The Russian army invited you to accompany them on their invasion of Warsaw.

LH: Well, not the Russian army. One of the generals invited me to come along. He said they were going into Warsaw and then straight on to Berlin which they did do. And I was too frightened to accept. I only found out in '67 that he had been killed about eight days after the invitation. So I suppose I would have turned back in any case.

JA: Do you regret not having gone?

LH: Oh yes. I regretted it all my life, of course, very much regretted it. But in looking back I'm not sure it would have worked or that anybody would have allowed me to go very much further. It was done as one of those jolly offers after a good deal of vodka, and I'm sure I'd have been a nuisance and been turned back.

JA: Well, I can't imagine what you would have done there, but it would have been an experience.

LH: It would have been very exciting to go through, of course. It was an exciting fight all the way to Berlin.

JA: When you got back to Moscow they invited you to meet with Stalin. And you decided no you were going to go home at that point.

Was it just because you had experienced so much, and you didn't want an overdose at that point or . . .?

LH: No, I've never understood why one just wants to meet the great or the famous because they're great and famous. If I'd wanted to do an interview then I could have understood it, but I didn't want to, and it seemed to me we would have nothing to say to each other.

JA: Right.

LH: And I don't think they really wanted me very much. My own belief is that they already knew I was going home. I wasn't going home I was going to England. And that that's why they asked me. But I couldn't see what I could possibly be doing except taking up his time. I would have had nothing to say, and I've never had any very great desire just to meet the famous.

JA: That seems pretty straightforward, yeah. I guess a lot of people do.

LH: Yes, most people do, I think.

JA: But. . . .

LH: They're chatterers. I'm not a chatterer I'd hope.

JA: I don't know what I would say to Stalin either, now that I think of it, but it just seems like. . . .

LH: How do you do, how are you?

JA: Amazing.

LH: How's your health?

JA: If somebody said how would you like to meet Stalin. Well, here's this big offer.

LH: I said that's very kind of you, I'm leaving.

JA: What did you do during the McCarthy years that hit you both very hard? Mr. Hammett went to jail for a year because he refused to name names.

LH: No, six months.

JA: Six months. You appeared before the House also?

LH: I appeared before the House Un-American Committee, yes.

JA: And you were blacklisted in Hollywood.

LH: And I was blacklisted for a long, long time, many years.

JA: What did you do during those years? How did you survive?

LH: Well, we survived in various ways. I owned a farm which we sold, lived on that money for a while. And then when Mr. Hammett came out of jail, he owed the Internal Revenue Department some money; and they never let him have any income after the day he came out of jail. They took it all. And, well, we sold a great many things we owned, pictures, furniture; all the things people do to survive, I guess.

JA: You've never been able to write about that in both of your autobiographies.

LH: I wrote a little, but not very much. No, it's a very difficult period for me to write about. I haven't any idea why but. . . .

JA: Still too strong, I guess.

LH: Perhaps, perhaps; I don't know, perhaps.

JA: What is your favorite play?

LH: *The Autumn Garden* is my favorite play of my own. I don't know why except I think I said more of what I felt in *Autumn Garden* than I ever said before or afterwards. I think it's the most mature play I ever wrote. It was not the most successful play I ever wrote. But I like it better than any other. It was me being all I knew at the minute rather than me only being a certain part of what I knew at the minute.

lst Questioner: May I ask a question about what you think of the possibility of the future for the perfect play, the well-made play?

2nd Questioner: He wants to know whether you think it has a future?

LH: Oh, sure, it has a future.

lst Questioner: In spite of the trouble you have with the connection, with the younger generation and so on?

LH: Oh sure, everything's got a future. It doesn't matter about the form of something. Really form doesn't matter. You say something in the best form you can say it in. It doesn't matter whether it's the theater of the absurd, or the well-made play or whatever it is. It's newspaper idiots who make these distinctions between well-made plays, or magazine idiots. It seems to be a very dull idea to worry about. You write in the form you write in. It doesn't matter what form it is. It's good, it's not good.

JA: You have a big gap. You haven't written a play in fourteen years. What made you decide to go ahead and write . . . I guess you weren't very excited about the idea of writing your autobiography, but you came up with *An Unfinished Woman* and followed it with *Pentimento?*

LH: I hope it wasn't an autobiography. I don't like to hear it referred to as such.

JA: No, yes; I know that.

LH: Because it wasn't an autobiography. It doesn't follow any plan or place. It was in my mind a memoir, which I think is quite different. It seems to me the word autobiography should be about yourself and have some space control—when this happened and how it happened and what followed next. I made no such attempt as you know. It skips all over the place.

JA: Right.

LH: So I hope it isn't an autobiography. I have no interest in writing one.

JA: *Pentimento* is like a whole different form it seems to me that you've come up with. It could be really incredibly well-written exciting short fiction. And you've never written a novel, and at one point you say that you wrote bad short stories when you were younger. Well these are just incredible. They're portraits of people. Jane Fonda's involved with making a movie of "Julia," one of the portraits in the book.

LH: Yes.

JA: Are you pleased with this idea?

LH: Yes, very pleased, very pleased with it.

JA: When do you think it's going to go through?

LH: I think they're working on it now. Matter of fact, the gentleman who just called me is the producer.

JA: Oh, really?

LH: Yes.

JA: Oh, how exciting.

LH: It's a true story. Of an old friend. It's never easy for me to have to do this story because I hesitated for many, many years of my life before writing it. I suppose out of fear that a woman who was dead wouldn't like it. It's called "Julia."

JA: Bethe is my favorite portrait in the book. Julia is the most touted, but Bethe it seems to me is sort of otherworldly. It's a child's sort of first like to-the-heart look at a relationship between a man and a woman, a strong feeling between them. Bethe was a distant cousin of yours.

LH: Yes.

JA: And she became a Mafia moll; I guess that's what she was.

LH: Yes.

JA: And it was sort of that versus your high idealistic theory of love as a kid and your aunts on the other side, and it's just an incredible, incredible story. And I wondered what was it you wanted to tell Hammett that Bethe had to do with you? Did you ever sort it out?

LH: No, I think I just would have stumbled around explaining what I explained in the story. I don't think it ever could have been drawn up in one sentence. I probably would have had to tell that whole story to him. I think that's why I came to write it. I was wondering how I would have told it to him.

3rd Questioner: Miss Hellman, I welcome this opportunity to say a few words to you. I was so impressed by your book *Unfinished Woman*. It seems so timely—your description of the different characters and particularly your relationship with Dashiell Hammett. And I wonder if you'd be kind enough to say a few words on that—to describe how a woman keeps a man interested in her for thirty years or how you really maintain a relationship like that without the conventional marriage as we know it.

LH: Well, I wish I could tell you. I wish I knew. I'd try it all over again if I knew. How does one know who is going to be interested and stay interested? One of those guesses. It certainly was no wisdom of mine. Maybe it has something to do with my having always been interested. That's as close as I can come to it. And one meets a . . . at least I did . . . a remarkable human being and responds to it and stays interested might have something to do with it, but I wish I knew that answer. I sure would try all over again. I don't know it. I deeply wish I could answer that question. He would be terribly pleased by your question so I thank you for it.

JA: Most plays have one really good character that stands out if you're lucky. But *The Autumn Garden* has seven or eight people involved that are just all incredibly remarkable and diverse, spurting great lines at every second. And one of the characters, Mrs. Ellis, is talking about how she likes to be alone and has liked to be alone more as she got older. And she says when one wants to be alone a room of one's own is not nearly enough. A whole house, or better still an island. Are you a person who guards your solitude a lot?

LH: Yes, to a certain extent. Yes, yes, one has to. There wouldn't be any time to write.

JA: Well, a lot of people don't like to be alone at all ever.

LH: Oh no; I've liked to be alone all my life

JA: Do you still have definite work periods every day? Are you working on something now?

LH: Usually in the morning, uh-huh.

JA: The morning. What are you working on now?

LH: I don't know.

JA: But you're working on. . . .

LH: I'm just gambling around, yes.

JA: Well I'm glad. I hope we see something soon.

LH: Thank you.

JA: *Pentimento* . . . I got it a year ago; I read two of the portraits, and I lent the book immediately to a friend because I wanted to save it and not use it up all at once. And, of course, I read the rest before I came to see you but I guess that's the best compliment I can pay you.

LH: Thank you.

JA: That I saved it for so long.

LH: Thank you.

Lillian Hellman

Rex Reed/1975

From *The Sun* [Baltimore], 9 November 1975, D 3. Reprinted in *Valentines & Vitriol* (New York: Delacorte Press, 1977), 103–08. Copyright © 1977 by Stet, Inc. Reprinted by permission of The Dorese Agency.

Mark Twain used to say honor was something you get after you're dead. But tonight on Broadway, the lights will go on at the Circle in the Square, honoring Lillian Hellman at the height of her life and craft "for her contribution to the theater, to literature and to the protection of civil liberties." No tribute has ever been or will be more deserved. Lillian Hellman is an oak among saplings.

Warren Beatty, Jane Fonda, Ellen Burstyn, Jason Robards, Maureen Stapleton, Irene Worth and Mike Nichols are some of the people who will be reading and performing excerpts and songs from her plays (*The Children's Hour, The Little Foxes, The Lark, Another Part of the Forest, The Autumn Garden, Watch on the Rhine, The Searching Wind, Toys in the Attic, Regina* and *Candide*) and books (*An Unfinished Woman* and *Pentimento*). The applause will all be for a great American writer, but the money will go to the Committee for Public Justice, an organization she founded five years ago to support the Bill of Rights and protect private citizens against threats to their constitutional rights and liberties.

"Times are getting dangerously close to McCarthyism again," she was saying a few days ago over coffee in her book-lined eagle's aerie above Park Avenue, "and some group had to be formed to wake people up. We've existed on peanuts, but we've done good work. We held a conference on the FBI that so disturbed J. Edgar Hoover he wrote a seven-page letter to us. We did others on the grand jury, Watergate, the CIA, invasions of privacy and the Justice Department, and we hope to expand to cover everything that menaces the public of this nation. We're even investigating fish toxins. We've had a few grants, but foundation money is scarce now, and we're not always the most attractive group to ask for aid. But it is my belief that we need every protection we can get, and this group carries more than its own weight. McCarthyism was resurfacing under Nixon, but thank God some of us saw the handwriting on the wall."

When trouble surfaces, so does Lillian. From the Spanish Civil War to the McCarthy witch hunts, she has always been on the front lines. She herself was blacklisted from 1948 to 1956. She worked in the theater but was wiped out in Hollywood. "I was very broke by that time, and the scars of that period still show today. Some people have a forgive-and-forget attitude, but I feel very sharply about it. I've never seen any of the people who testified against me. I even try not to speak to them, but that gets embarrassing at parties. Too many lives got mangled for the wrong reasons. It was a very cruel time, and if it ever happens again, it will make McCarthy look like a runt. Everyone you know who ever signed any bill on civil rights will be in big trouble. We have to fight to make sure that never happens. The tribute is really to the work the committee has done. I was worried and embarrassed at first, but I've worked very hard for this cause and if we can raise some money, it's worth it."

These are dog days for Hellman. She's just returned to the city from her pastoral home in Martha's Vineyard to put the finishing touches on a new book about the McCarthy period, and her life is at sixes and sevens. "It's very short, about thirty thousand words. I call it *Scoundrel Time*. It's mostly about me. I've tried to write about that ghastly period before, but this time I've forgotten about historical backgrounds and stuck to personal feelings, and I think it's worked out better."

She rises at dawn, markets at eight, works from nine to one and knocks it off for the rest of the day. "The older I get, the more tired at night I am. I don't go out much anymore. I don't enjoy small talk, and people bore me. I go to parties and find myself walking out of the room in the middle of a conversation."

Those hard-drinking years with Dashiell Hammett are long ago. She has a scotch before dinner or maybe a martini, but "I haven't been good and drunk in eight years. It's very funny. One night in Martha's Vineyard, I said to myself, 'Who says you have to go bed?' So I got good and drunk and woke up the next morning on the staircase. I thought my neck was broken, and I couldn't move my arms and I had a cold and the hangover of the universe, and that's when I knew I wasn't young anymore."

But despite her formidable reputation for being tough and tyrannical, there's another side to Lillian Hellman that is not often publicized. She is very emotional and feminine and easily moved by the plight of others. In many ways, she's younger than the first thrush of spring. "I am sixty-nine years old, and *Who's Who* is always getting it wrong. I hate being sixty-nine. I'd like to be young again, and I pay heavy penalties for that. I am my own toughest critic. I look back on the body of my work and see so many, many things I'd redo. I've grown rather frightened of rereading myself. It makes me inhibited. Sometimes I can remember what emotion was going through my mind at the time I wrote certain scenes and passages. Other lines and chapters seem to have been written by someone I've never met.

"Two years ago I did a TV interview with Bill Moyers, based on an agreement that I would read parts of *Pentimento* aloud. He had selected passages from the 'Julia' chapter. Now, I had written 'Julia' with enormous difficulty for too many reasons to go into here or anywhere else. But when I started to read, I started to cry, and we had to stop the program. I had to take an hour off and rest. It was the most shocking thing that ever happened to me in public. Verbalizing your own words—something triggers emotions you can hide when you're at the typewriter. A psychiatrist once told me something very revealing about myself. I was too young to understand what he meant at the time, but now I see the insight. He said I look at myself as though I'm a total stranger."

She always had her own mind, her own wits and instincts, and has never been easily influenced by the fads and fashions of the day. She can be very temperamental and stubborn, as many former colleagues in the theater can testify, but she doesn't suffer fools easily. "It's really hard to see yourself as others see you. If you're not a fool, you don't see yourself as famous or great or a genius or any of those tags. I've been told I accept praise ungraciously, but the truth is I simply don't know how to say thank you in an interesting way. I want to be praised and flattered desperately, but when it happens, I feel embarrassed. I've been loathed and dismissed by so many people through the years that I tend to be suspicious. It might not last, I tell myself, and it usually doesn't. I've had too many failures to get a big head this late in life. My problem is I always took the successes for granted and worried too much about the failures."

She's a woman of great wisdom, a strength that shines through in her work. But she's suffered for what she's learned. "I pick up a newspaper and read about the two or three greatest American playwrights, and I'm not listed as one of them. That's painful. But the theater is a place of fashion and whim. I think I knew that from the beginning, but it's hard to recognize the weaknesses in something when you love it so much."

Lately, she's getting the kind of praise usually reserved for funeral orations, though a friend recently visited her mother's home town, Demopolis, Alabama, and looked up an elderly aunt at Lillian's request.

"I'm a friend of your niece's," he said when the old woman came to the door.

"Which niece?" she asked suspiciously.

"Lillian Hellman," he said.

"We don't like her," said the aunt, slamming the door in his face.

Neither did Tallulah Bankhead, who feuded with Lillian from the opening night of *The Little Foxes* until the day she died. "That hatred was mutual," admits Hellman, "but we did have a brief reconciliation at Truman Capote's famous party. I was sorry about the reunion later because it had been so boring." She has always spoken her mind.

She tries to hide it, but a bitterness creeps through when she talks about the theater. "I was an instant success with *The Children's Hour,* and it was hard to duplicate success after that. There was a long period of my life when I was totally ignored and then forgotten. I kept picking myself up and trying again. The sad truth is that now I've had enough and I never want to go near the theater again. The disillusionment set in with *Candide.* I was forced to work fast, which is against my nature, and told how to work in a form I didn't care for. The show was a spectacular failure, even with Dorothy Parker, John Latouche and Leonard Bernstein all working together with me. It certainly did not feel like we were creating a cult show at the time. It was a very upsetting experience. I have seen the Harold Prince revival, and it is not the way I ever saw *Candide*. It's too gimmicky and cute for my taste. But very pleasant."

The final nail in the coffin came with her last play, *My Mother, My*

Father and Me, which flopped in 1963. "It was a black comedy that was ahead of its time. Gower Champion was replaced by Arthur Penn, so we had two different styles of direction; the casting was wrong; we opened during a newspaper strike. I began to see that timing is everything in theater, and I have to work at my own pace. I'm not one of those people who can sit in a hotel room in Boston and bang out a new scene in one night. I began to see myself in relation to the theater as a stranger in a hard, alien world. I didn't see life the way other people did; I didn't laugh at the same jokes others found amusing. When you're young, you tend to blame other people for these things, but now I blame only myself. With books, I stand as the lone creator of my work, and the result is much more rewarding."

She prefers movies to plays now and rarely goes to the theater. "The past eight or nine years have produced very few things on the stage I've wanted to see. I get bored and irritable and walk out impatiently after the first act. It breaks my heart. The theater has got to improve in some country, somewhere. It can't go on being dull and irrelevant, in this sad decline forever. But I don't think the change will occur on Broadway. I used to think I was the only one who felt this way, but last spring I had a pair of tickets to something, and I couldn't find anyone to take me. Everyone I called said, 'Thank you, but I can't bear the thought of being trapped in a theater all evening.' The theater requires a formal commitment I am no longer prepared to make."

Born in New Orleans, she's one of that special breed of southern Jews with dignity "and none of that junk about proving yourself. Dashiell Hammett always said I was the only Jew he knew who was also a Puritan." Last year, she was sitting in the Pontchartrain Hotel staring from her window, when suddenly she exclaimed: "I'm looking right down on the house I was born in. I had diphtheria when I was three years old and spent an entire year on that porch!"

It's the constant rediscovery in herself that charges her work with distinction. She has pruned away the clutter. Tallulah Bankhead used to nastily say Lillian Hellman looked like George Washington. Tallulah was wrong. She only lives like him—with humility, courage, truthfulness and, after tonight, the honor that is justly hers whether she wants it or not.

Lillian Hellman: She Never Turns down an Adventure

Stephanie de Pue/1975

From the *Cleveland Plain Dealer*, 28 December 1975, sec. 5, 2, 8. Reprinted by permission of the *Cleveland Plain Dealer.*

Q. Many reviewers, in discussing your books, have commented that, partially, they're so interesting because you've led such an extraordinary life. One said, "in biography, experience matters, and it is not altogether an accident of history and geography that determines who is where: inevitably, spirit creates experience." When you were young, perhaps, did you dream of such a life?

Miss Hellman. I think it wasn't that, I didn't think of it in those days, that I was adventurous. I didn't think of it in those terms. I just thought—I did what came to mind to do. It wasn't I will now go away and have an adventure.

I think, it seems to me, that I didn't turn down adventure, if you know what I mean. I didn't. I suppose that means I accepted it.

I don't know whether I always accepted it with any great knowledge of what I was doing but, I suppose that's still true. I suppose I still don't hesitate very long about what might be a certain kind of danger.

But I don't think you think that out, I think that's just sort of your nature, and you've had it since you were four years old, or something like that. I certainly never planned any adventures, if you know what I mean. I didn't even plan to go to Spain, the summer I went to Europe.

I had no intention of going to Spain. I was talked into going to Spain. And the Russian thing came along because, as has been printed 20,000 times, they wanted me to go, and the White House wanted me to go. The White House didn't want to be associated with it very much—they wanted somebody to go on a cultural mission, and the Russians were willing to take me.

I was told later that I had been in enormous danger on the trip going over. It's a good thing I know so little. Robert Lovett, who was the Secretary of the Navy, I guess,—was it Navy or Air, I've forgotten what he was Secretary of—said that if he'd ever known I was going to cross Siberia on one of those planes (an unheated 2-engine C-47 cargo plane capable of 240 mph, maximum), I wouldn't have gone.

But I didn't know. Mine was partly, I think, wanting to do things, and partly ignorance. I didn't know what I was doing. Once I was there, I did the best I could.

Q. There's a line in your play *Montserrat* where a character says, "Faced with danger, we are ourselves, to our surprise." Could you amplify that?

A. Well, of course, that wasn't my play, you know, it was an adaptation.

Q. I know.

A. And I can't remember any longer whether that's my line or his line. If it was my line, and I'm not sure it was, I would agree with it anyway. It's really no more than saying, and not saying anything very brilliant, that faced with danger, most people act by instinct, and the instinct has long ago been built up.

And some people act more easily, some people act quietly, that's really all I meant, that you become some part of yourself, and the part that's probably deepest down. I don't, I suppose it also depends on what form of danger it is, I find, when I've been in danger, that I grow very, very quiet, exceptionally quiet.

But I wouldn't like to be faced with a kind of danger, because I think I would grow very noisy. I wouldn't like to be faced with watching somebody hitting somebody and wounding them, because I think I would be in a panic. I think it very much depends on, you know, the kind of danger and your own nature.

Mine just happens to go far quieter than it really is any other time. It's my way of saving myself, or trying to save myself, I suppose.

Q. And yet I found a line in a piece you did some time ago, about a journey to Budapest. You were having trouble getting your visa at the airport, and you said that your voice went into "the high-scale notes the South teaches all women to use when they are angry."

A. Oh, yes. I think that most Southern ladies have very high voices, and when they get excited, their voices rise. I find that I, who have a low voice, whenever I get very upset my voice begins to rise, in exactly the Southern fashion.

Q. So you consider yourself still Southern, rather than a New Yorker?

A. Well, I have no right to, because the New York years now far outweigh the Southern years, but I suppose most Southerners, people who grew up in the South, still consider themselves Southern.

Q. Yet, as a child, you spent, you say, half of each year in New York.

A. Well, I came from a family of Southerners. It wasn't simply a question that I was brought up and down from the South. I came from a family, on both sides, who had been Southerners for a great many generations.

Q. I had the impression your father's family had come from Germany fairly recently.

A. No, no, my mother's family came about 1825, my father's family came about 1848. My grandfather was in the Civil War as a young man, so . . .

Q. Well, another critic has described your work as quintessentially Southern in the amount of inefficient housework that goes on. She commented that there couldn't be any plays in the world with more mops and brooms on the stage, and anyone of Lilllian Hellman's households would have horrified a proper New England house-wife . . .

A. Laughs. I wasn't conscious of that. It's usually a way of getting somebody to do something in a play, you know. Give them, of course, a reason for doing it in another room. One wouldn't necessarily like to see a whole room cleaned in front of you on a stage. Laughs again.

Q. It's such a nice quote, "disorder and dirt, unscheduled meals, slovenly and shrieking women, rude servants, blatant but pointless housekeeping."

A. I don't think I had been aware of that review. An interesting review. I don't know, I'm not conscious of that, it would be very hard for me to comment on it. I think she missed the—I don't know about the slovenliness, where would the slovenliness have been?

Q. Well, in *Toys in the Attic,* one of the sisters is walking around with her blouse undone, carrying a plant . . .

A. Well, I meant them to be two old maids living alone. Very seldom women living alone get very dressed up. Coming home from work, weary.

Q. In that New Orleans heat . . .

A. At least I wouldn't, I know.

Q. You were recently named Ladies Home Journal Woman of the Year, in the Creative Arts, and cited for "embodying woman's potential as an artist since the production of your first play."

So many women seem to have the conflict, "Shall I be like mommy, and be safe, or be like daddy and do something?" I recently read an article which notes that women of noticeably great achievement have often been raised by, or particularly close to, their fathers . . .

A. Well, I suppose so, but then most girls are closer to their fathers.

Q. It's an awful, sociological phrase to use, but do you feel you've made a valuable contribution to younger women by being a role model, a woman of accomplishment?

A. Oh, I wouldn't answer that question for anything in the world.

Q. You wouldn't?

A. No. Certainly I don't think I've been—how can you look at yourself that way, looking in the mirror to say "I've been something." I don't do that, I don't look at myself that way. If it's happened, I'm delighted, and if it hasn't happened, it doesn't worry me. I don't see myself in such terms, they're too high for me.

Q. Well, you have now lived through two women's emancipation movements. Do you think the second will stick better than the first?

A. My youth couldn't have been called a women's emancipation movement.

Q. There were a great number of women who became doctors, lawyers, etc., and in the 40s—early 60s they got lost . . .

A. Yes, but I don't think it was a movement, in the sense of women's liberation. There were a great many women for the first time, not even for the first time, it began in the 20s, beginning to work, beginning to sleep around, beginning to live with people they weren't married to.

But I don't think there was any real movement, just a pocket of people in certain cities. Most of the people I went to college with, for example, I don't think went to work.

Q. Well, it's a common aphorism, that one of the greatest temptations for women is to think they can simply be rather than do. Have you found that so yourself?

A. I think women almost have to be more sort of interested in a personal life than men have to be. I don't mean because men don't want one, any more than women do, because I think they do.

But I think women, no matter how liberated they are, feel more pressed to look for a personal life, whether it's a husband or a lover or a house or children or whatever it is, than men feel pressed to.

Q. Well, you've written 12 plays and 2 books, which is quite a bit by any one's standard, yet you say at the end of *An Unfinished Woman* that you think you could have accomplished more if you'd been less interested in looking for truths, in going around and doing things, in wasting time. Do you still feel that way?

A. Yes, I think I wasted time. But I didn't quite mean looking for truths. I meant, I think, I was slow in coming to certain conclusions. Slow in knowing myself, and sometimes lazy, just plain lazy.

Q. You've said many times that perhaps your most famous Southern plays, *The Little Foxes* and *Another Part of the Forest,* were to be parts of a trilogy. Are you still planning that?

A. No, I've decided not to do it. I intended to do it always as a trilogy, but I've decided not to do it. I don't think I want to go back to them any more.

Q. The Hubbards, you mean? I don't know, I've just reread them before coming to see you, and I remember, as a child, hating Bette Davis as Regina when *The Little Foxes* was on TV.

A. Everybody does that. I never meant her as bad as everybody. I never meant—I just meant her as a cold lady, I didn't mean her as bad, particularly. I was very shocked when everybody said she was. But there's a great deal of hypocrisy in this world, with everything bad that's going on.

Q. But then, when I was rereading, I kind of liked her and Ben, they had a certain insidious charm.

A. Oh, I like them. I didn't mean that I don't think it's right for me now. We're going to do a revival of the play next year.

Q. I've read a lot of criticism that money, the getting, the spending and the willing of it, seem to be very central to your plays.

A. A lot of people have said it, I'm not really sure it's true. Going back to the plays, *The Children's Hour* isn't—everything in the world has to do with money, but politically, *The Children's Hour* certainly doesn't. The second play was about a strike. I suppose that has to do with money but in a very indirect way. *Little Foxes* certainly did. *Watch on the Rhine* did not. *Searching Wind* did not. *Another Part of the Forest* did. *Autumn Garden* didn't. People have been saying that for a long time.

They certainly are good things to be concerned about, I don't at all deny it. I'm not ashamed of it, because they're very good things to be concerned about.

Q. In *Toys in the Attic*, Albertine says, "the pure and innocent sometimes bring harm to themselves, and those they love, and when they do, the injury is often very great." It has sometimes occurred to me that there's nobody more dangerous than a truly naive person—

A. I don't think I meant naive so much as I meant somebody rather convinced of the purity of their motives, which is a form of naivete, I suppose, but naivete means stupid and I think I meant somebody more than stupid. I meant somebody—I didn't mean to make fun of the purity, I meant to make fun of the dangers of the purity.

People convinced they were right. She was talking about her daughter, wasn't she? I meant the daughter to be quite a pure girl, rather high-minded, pure, romantic girl, who didn't stop often to examine her reasons for things because she was convinced that they were rather pure. Naive comes in there, but I don't think it's the exact word for purity.

Q. Everybody in that play treats the girl, Lilly, as if she's half-mad—

A. Well, I meant her to be sort of half-bats. Not bats, but sort of on the edge of some sort of mysticism, some kind of—well, I said it actually, she's just been off to a sort of fortune teller.

That wasn't a bad guess, so long ago, that that generation that later became convinced of Guru Ma Jolie, I don't know, or somebody else . . .

Q. Maharaj Ji? He seems to me, sometimes, to be symptomatic of a period of insanity our society went through in the late 60s, with all the hippie, and greening of America stuff. In some ways, I think we're getting more realistic again, but there's still great interest in the occult, isn't there?

A. Yes, there certainly is. It particularly seems to be attractive to what were once the young radicals of the 60s. They seem to be all going for the occult . . . It probably did start out as a very good business of getting away from Mama and Papa's values. That it had to take the form of some dopey religion led by some fat boy doesn't . . . There's always a singular amount of nuttiness going around, you know.

We've forgotten all the nuttiness of other days, and rather than concentrate on anything that's really wrong with the country, it's very nice to concentrate on your plants, you know. Or your dogs, or saving animals, or—don't bother with human beings, you can save animals.

Q. They don't talk back.

A. They don't talk back. They're easier to handle. This country's in trouble, and I suppose, when people feel powerless about it, and, in an effort to get away from their recognition of the powerlessness, they find things they have got some possible control over, or they think they have, like a plant, or an animal, or . . .

Q. Someone said that in your writing you often emphasized the importance of honesty of motive. Would you say you did?

A. I suppose to some extent I have. I've long been fascinated by villains who very well knew they were villains, who didn't give a damn, if that's what you mean. Yes.

Q. We seem to be in a period now where a relativistic morality is riding high—I sometimes get this nightmare of an updated Adolf Hitler, shaving before his mirror in the morning, telling himself he was just doing his best to make Europe safe for civilization. . . I can see him crooning a couple of choruses of Frank Sinatra's song, "I did it my way . . ."

A. I think that's just what he did do.

Q. I find it kind of frightening.

A. Yes, that's exactly what I mean. I think it's much less dangerous if the so-called villain, or liar, or deceiver, knows it. That's what I meant really in *The Little Foxes* that they were all rather amused by it,

the fact that they knew they were, and were thus, in a sense, less
dangerous.

I'm sure Adolf Hitler did think he was 100% right. The brilliance of
his, must have been certainly based on an intense belief that this was
best for Germany and best for the world. I don't think you can fake
that kind of thing.

Q. Another of your reviewers said, "unlike many Americans today
who dread a hassle, Hellman faced up to battle, and went in. I
believe you said, in talking about Dorothy Parker, that one of the
things that made you uneasy about her was that she was so pleasant
to people, while being nasty about them behind their backs.

You then said that a certain sort of "pleasantness" was thought
very highly of then, and that you thought the wheel had turned
again, so that the same sort of "pleasantness" is currently very highly
valued.

A. Forgive me, I think that's jumped a step I didn't mean. They're
unconnected, my saying the one thing about, in my mind, at least,
they are. She did the—what I didn't like—to be funny, and to amuse
herself. To amuse other people as well. The second thing you're
asking, I think, is quite different. That we have mostly in the last—
well, most of my lifetime—put a great price on charm.

Too great a price, for me. I mean, I like charming people but, and
everybody else likes charming people, and they should like charming
people, but having said it, I don't think there's much more to say
about it, if you know what I mean. There's been an enormous—
incidentally, Dotty, by herself, was an enormously charming person—
but I think we've been so anxious to like that we automatically dislike
anybody with a rather sharp personality.

Because it's not fashionable, it's not pleasant . . . I think (the) upper
and middle classes in America have made up some dimestore version
of human relations.

A Still Unfinished Woman:
A Conversation with Lillian Hellman

Christine Doudna/1976

From *Rolling Stone*, no. 233 (24 February 1977), 52–57. By Straight Arrow Publishers, Inc. © 1977. All Rights Reserved. Reprinted by permission.

Lillian Hellman has been a literary institution for nearly 50 years— long enough, as she put it, to undergo a revival within her own lifetime. She was 27 when her play *The Children's Hour* was proclaimed a smash success in 1934, and she almost immediately acquired the label "America's foremost woman playwright." (Her reaction to that honor was typical: she was quick to point out the discrimination of the phrase.) She survived the failure of her second play, *Days to Come,* and went on to write such major dramas as *The Little Foxes, Another Part of the Forest, Watch on the Rhine, Toys in the Attic* and *The Autumn Garden.* She has relished her many successes (after *The Little Foxes* opened, she carried some mink skins for a coat she had just ordered to a cocktail party in her honor to prove she had made it; last year she modeled a fur for a Blackglama ad which has appeared in several magazines and which is reproduced on page 54.)

A woman of fierce temper and fiercer loyalties (the most remarkable thing about her stormy 30-year relationship with writer Dashiell Hammett seems to be that it endured), she dared to lecture Joe McCarthy and his cronies about the immorality of their actions when the most likely consequence was her own imprisonment. As Hemingway once told her, she had "cojones." Perhaps most impressive, she started a new career at the age of 62 and wrote a string of memoirs— *An Unfinished Woman, Pentimento* and *Scoundrel Time*—that became instant classics.

Lillian Hellman has become, in short, an icon in an age of iconoclasm. But she resists becoming a standard-bearer for any movement. When I asked her how it felt to be adopted as a matron saint by the women's movement, she laughed and said she wasn't sure she was, but if she was she guessed it was fine. At times she has been more caustic: in a recent article she referred to "the new army of lady journalists who have chosen to interpret women's liberation as the freedom to attack other women." She's a self-proclaimed rebel ("I cannot and will not cut my conscience to fit this year's fashions," were her now famous words to the House Committee on Un-American Activities). It's a role that she obviously enjoys, but one that's given her the reputation of being a "difficult woman."

So it was with a mixture of fear and admiration that I first approached her. We had a series of rather ill-fated phone conversations over a period of a couple months trying to arrange a time for the interview. Some of these calls left me feeling I had been through an intense sparring match and would never reach the main event. It seemed I was never able to satisfy her—I either called at the wrong hour, or at the right hour on the wrong day, and once made the mistake of addressing her in a letter as "Ms." rather than "Miss."

But we finally met over last July 4th weekend at her summer home on Martha's Vineyard. The house faces the harbor of Vineyard Haven, and next door is the Revolutionary War-era house where she and Hammett spent several summers before his death in 1961.

Hellman was watering her rose garden when I walked up. We shook hands and she greeted me warmly in her inimitable wire-rake-on-gravel voice. She's smaller than I expected—about 5'2", energetic, tough. Her face is deeply lined with age; her eyes are intelligent and engaging. We talked for several hours that afternoon on the patio overlooking the harbor, then later over dinner. The furniture in the house—mostly antiques, including the early-Victorian sofa from the original set of *The Little Foxes*—came from her beloved farm in Pleasantville, New York, which she was forced to sell when she was blacklisted. She loves the island ("I'm crazy for salt water and boats") but her doctor won't let her spend more than summers there because the dampness is bad for her emphysema. Nonetheless she chain-smoked during the entire interview, interrupted only by coughing spasms.

Throughout our conversation she projected the sense of control that comes across in her writing. There were certain topics she adamantly refused to discuss, and gossipy anecdotes were not forthcoming (doubtless a matter of instinct to a writer whose own life is her best material). At a certain moment she announced that our conversation was over for that day ("I get bored talking about myself"). The next day, as we finished up our conversation, she was impatiently waiting to go for a boat ride with her old friend and neighbor John Hersey, and once his boat came into view I knew the interview would be terminated. Typically, the grande dame had arranged a proper exit.

When I spoke to her in Los Angeles last week, Hellman said she had no current plans or projects—but that's what she said last summer. Since then she's traveled around the country with Rosalynn Carter for a magazine piece, taken a trip down the Nile and negotiated for various film projects based on her memoirs. And the day we spoke, CBS was about to film and interview with her for their program *Who's Who*. At 69, Lillian Hellman stubbornly refuses to act her age. Clearly, she is still an unfinished woman.

Q. Why did you turn to memoir writing after a long and very successful career as a playwright and screenwriter?

A. I don't know. I decided I didn't want to do another play for a while. I'd been thinking about this kind of writing for a long time, wondering whether I could do it. I had started off as a short-story writer but never liked the stories very much. I had to find some other form to write in.

Q. Did you find it very difficult to shift gears at a late point in your professional career?

A. No, I didn't find it too difficult. I had no plans. I knew that I didn't want to write a play, but I knew that I wanted to go on being a writer. I had no intention of publishing. I didn't make a contract for *An Unfinished Woman* until the book was a third finished. And then I made the contract with a clause that I could give back the advance if I chose to, and have no further ties. I was worried that I wouldn't like it when I finished it.

Q. You seem to use a lot of the principles of fiction in your memoirs.

A. Yes, I wouldn't have chosen the people I chose without a feeling for fiction, some belief that what I was writing about was interesting or dramatic. The structure was difficult because I didn't want to alter facts, and since in none of the portraits did I go steadily through a life, then it became a way of finding out *how* to tell it. In no portrait except Hammett's and Dorothy Parker's did I know any of these people over many years. So there were long gaps: I had to make use somewhere of the gaps and had to find some method of doing it. Julia was particularly hard. But nothing on God's earth could have shaken my memory about her. I did finally look at whatever notes I had left, but I didn't need to.

Q. Is there any particular pattern to what you find you remember easily and things you have a bad memory for?

A. I remember what people say fairly accurately, but I don't remember where they said it or when they said it.

Q. How much of the dialogue in your memoirs is reconstructed?

A. Well, much was reconstructed but I have a good memory for the way people talk. That was my job for many years, that's what the theater is. If you sit through enough rehearsals, you get trained.

I remember most rooms I've seen. But I very often can't place what city the room is in. Everybody's memory is tricky and mine's a little trickier than most, I guess.

Q. What kind of research do you do when you're writing? Do you call up friends and acquaintances to help you remember?

A. Sometimes. Very seldom. When I was doing the piece about Hammett which I used in *An Unfinished Woman,* I wrote to 11 people about his stay in the Aleutians and I got back eight answers. Seven had him in places he could never have been, and the years were all wrong. I'm sure something remained in their head of the truth, but it was checkably inaccurate. I heard last night someone repeat the Henry Wallace story in *Scoundrel Time* and do it completely wrong, completely wrong. And he said he'd read the book only last week.

Q. The critics of *Scoundrel Time* have argued that the issue of who cooperated with the House Committee on Un-American Activities was a lot more complicated than you allow in your book, particularly for disillusioned former members or sympathizers of the Communist party.

A. If you were a member of the party, you could have had good reason for leaving the party. That certainly must have been a complicated situation. But that doesn't have anything to do with supplying people like HUAC with information. No sane person can doubt what HUAC was out to do. It's comedy even to discuss it. It's there on the record.

Q. Nathan Glazer suggests that if people like you had spoken out at the time about the evils of Communism there might have been no McCarthy.

A. Oh, nonsense. McCarthyism came from powerful places; the famous China lobby and the anti-Red scares had nothing to do with people like me—nothing whatever. McCarthy is a very inaccurate name for a shameless period. McCarthy only summed up the angers and fears of a great many people.

Q. Several reviewers, including *Rolling Stone*'s, have taken exception to the tone of the passage in which you talk about American intellectuals finding in the "sins of Stalin Communism" an "excuse to join those who should have been their hereditary enemies." The passage continues: "Perhaps that, in part, was the penalty of 19th-century immigration. The children of timid immigrants are often remarkable people: energetic, intelligent, hardworking; and often they make it so good that they are determined to keep it at any cost."

A. I meant nothing snobbish. My family were immigrants once upon a time, too; everybody's were.

I didn't mean that the oldest Wasp wouldn't have acted just as badly, but not so many of them were involved. And because Jews have always been persecuted, it is my belief they should fight it anytime, anywhere.

Q. So you were referring primarily to Jewish immigrants?

A. No. I'm a Jew and I don't know how they could have thought a Jew could be snobbish about other Jews. Perhaps I worded it badly. I don't know.

Q. You've never dealt specifically in your writing with what it was like to be Jewish in the South.

A. I'm sorry I had no religious upbringing. Maybe it would not have mattered but it might have been interesting to have it. Southern Jews, particularly New Orleans Jews, had different histories than Northern Jews. New Orleans Jews, just as New Orleans people, were a breed apart. They had a pleasant community of their own and in turn the community allowed them to have it, although they never accepted them into their own circles. No Jew has ever been allowed in the best Carnival balls, as far as I know, to this day. But it never seemed to worry them. I heard about one Jewish family—they used to be a joke—who left town during Carnival balls. But everybody laughed at that.

Q. Are you very conscious of being Jewish now; is that a part of your identity?

A. Oh yes, sure. I don't clearly know what it means to me, I just know that I would rather be a Jew than not be. I think Nazism had a great deal to do with that. It suddenly became very important to me.

New Orleans had a live-and-let-live quality about it. That was rare in the South.

Q. Were you conscious when you were writing *The Little Foxes* of incorporating parts of your family into it?

A. Oh yes. Part of my family threatened to sue after they saw the play. They never did. I think *The Children's Hour* worried my mother a little bit. She was puzzled by me anyway—I turned out to be a writer. And then my father scared the daylights out of the poor lady. She was a very naive woman. He told her that he'd never read the play and didn't know anything about it, but he was shocked to hear that I'd put a toilet onstage and somebody actually used it in front of the audience. My mother was a wreck the opening night and for a long time after.

Q. How did your plays fare in film adaptation?

A. I think *Little Foxes* turned out very well, and *Watch on the Rhine;* I think the first *Children's Hour* was better than the second.

Q. What about *The Chase*?

A. It wasn't the picture I wrote and I was upset by it. Its accents were totally different than what I wrote. I didn't mean that kind of violence: I meant a Texas town gone wild on a Saturday night. Evidently the film is quite well thought of in Europe.

Q. What do you think of having Jane Fonda cast as yourself in the film version of "Julia"?

A. I was very pleased to have her, but I wan't involved in the casting.

Q. Do you feel any apprehension about seeing yourself portrayed on screen?

A. I know it's hard for anybody to believe me, but when I sold the rights to "Julia," it never occurred to me that my name would be used. I don't know why it didn't occur to me; it was very stupid of me. But there it is. The first I knew of it was when I read the script of the picture, when of course it was too late to say, I don't want my name used. They were—and are—perfectly within their rights to use it. But I would like to have seen my name changed. I don't want to be represented on the screen as me.

Q. Do you think Hollywood scripts were more interesting in the Thirties and Forties than they are today?

A. The age of comedy certainly was better. Except for the great Woody Allen, pictures today don't seem to have much sense of comedy. You think of the great comedians of that time—they were remarkable.

Q. In *Scoundrel Time* you said of move executives like Louis Mayer, Samuel Goldwyn and Harry Cohn that they didn't have interesting natures. Didn't they nonetheless have a kind of appealing vitality?

A. Once somebody is powerful or rich you see vigor where it might not exist, or where it might have existed once long ago.

Q. You didn't find them creative?

A. Not creative . . . daring, maybe. And also very timid and often cowardly. Gamblers is a better word. They were good gamblers. But then I'm no great judge. The longest I ever stayed in Hollywood was six months, I think. I knew it well in the sense of work but not in a sense of who was who, or why.

Q. Why do you think F. Scott Fitzgerald was so taken with a guy like Irving Thalberg in *The Last Tycoon*?

A. I think Fitzgerald was a romantic man. I only met Thalberg once and he didn't appeal to me. Fitzgerald was a very good writer but I think he was overromantic about many people and places.

Q. What films do you like today?

A. Besides Woody Allen, I like Altman very much. I like some foreign pictures.

Q. Lina Wertmüller?

A. With reservations. I like certain parts of her pictures. I like some Bergman.

Q. What about writers?

A. I won't talk about other writers. I've always believed writers have a tough enough time without my making it tougher.

Q. Anaïs Nin said she always consulted people before including them in her published diaries. What are your rules about what you exclude in your memoirs?

A. A great many of the people quoted or included are dead. I change names if I think the story is going to be painful to the person. I don't think you can injure the dead very much, unless they have wives or children who might be harmed. I haven't changed the dialogue as I remember it but I've sometimes changed the circumstances or the place. Sometimes lawyers wanted changes. I had to change names and places in "Julia." Because her family is still living, I could have had a lawsuit. I was really saying they had never wanted to find her baby.

Q. Do you find things you once didn't consider important become important as you're writing about them, or vice versa?

A. Yes, I think so. You see or hear something you know will be useful to you, and you will use it. Some of the time it sails by you or you put it in a third compartment, which is the one you don't know anything about. It's very probable that "X" is the compartment you most use. As you get older, you more easily recognize the people or the events that will interest you, that you think you can handle. I often find myself bewildering people. They talk about one thing and I make an immediate connection to something entirely different. I would have to write it to make clear what had happened. If the word creative means anything, that's perhaps what it means.

Q. Do you ever surprise yourself with what comes out on paper?

A. Sometimes you can make discoveries. Things you didn't think you knew anything about. When I did *An Unfinished Woman,* which was the first time that I'd ever fooled around with the memoir form, I had no idea where I was going. I just thought, I'm doing the book for myself. In the opening story of *Pentimento,* for instance, called "Bethe," I don't think I'd thought about Bethe in 25 years. And why I did at that minute—I was lying on a bed half asleep—I have no idea. That certainly is the "X" part of the mind. Then every time I finished one section I'd say, what's next, I don't know what's next.

I certainly don't say that the people in the books are the most interesting people I've ever known. I don't even remember many of them clearly. Very tricky business, the business of oneself, plus memory, plus what you think you can do plus what has moved you,

sometimes without your knowing it. Very often the things that you
think have most moved you, you find have not moved you very
deeply at all. They may have been sharply painful when they
happened. And very often they are the first to pass.

Memory, of course, is not the same thing as what really happened
in the real minute of pleasure or pain. Pain can almost totally fade.
And another much lesser pain is much more easily remembered and
more important to you. What is intensely important can, when the
years have passed, fade, disappear.

Q. Can you give an example?

A. Examples are too dramatic. "The failure of work," or the
"success of work" or the "loss, the disruption of a great love affair,"
too arbitrary, such things. They are not really the necessary stuff of
life. We all lead more pedestrian lives than we think we do. The
boiling of an egg is sometimes more important than the boiling of a
love affair in the end.

I had a very comic example of that recently. A very old friend of
mine was divorced about eight or ten years ago. He was telling me
he wished he'd gotten divorced ten years before he did. I said, "You
almost did." He said, "No, never." I said, "Yes, you did. You told me
that you were leaving your wife, that you'd fallen in love with a
woman and what did I think because you were worried about your
two little boys." My friend said, "What are you talking about? That
never happened." I said, "You're a nut! Of course it happened, the
girl's name was Dorothy." He said, "What was her last name?" I said,
"I don't know. I'm not sure I ever heard her last name, but her name
was Dorothy." He said, "I know you're not making it up but you're
mixing me up with somebody else." A few months later I found an
old diary. Her name was Dorothy, and her last name was also there,
incidentally. I called my friend and said, "Her name was Dorothy
Smith." He said, "My God, I wonder whatever happened to her." He
had totally forgotten the importance of this woman to him. It's a
comic example; most people aren't that nutty. I suppose the woman
wasn't of any major importance. What was important to him was
leaving his wife.

Q. You seem in some ways a reluctant memoirist. The reader
senses your control over your presentation of your life.

A. Well, I don't always like writing about myself or talking about

myself. You've probably sensed that in this interview. I don't ordinarily talk about myself very much. That's why I try to write
memoirs without being a central part of them. I get bored with talking
about myself and with people who talk about themselves a great
deal.

Q. Boredom is one thing. Do you think you find personal revelation difficult?

A. Yes, I find some kinds of personal revelation difficult. I've never
been through the experience of spending nights talking about myself
with anybody, or listening, because nobody's ever done it with me. It
seems to me that summation of what you feel, not of what's
happened but of what you *feel,* is a dangerous game to play. The
words become too simple.

Q. Did you find therapy very difficult for that reason?

A. Yes, I had a very hard time. The man who analyzed me once
said I was the only patient he'd ever had in his life who talked about
herself as if I were another person. He meant no compliment. He
meant that I had too cold a view of myself.

Q. Could you talk about what analysis meant to you?

A. It's a very private business even if one wanted to talk about it. I
suspect people who talk about it when they're having it and I suspect
the people who talk after it because it's a stew, the details of which
should be forgotten. Things are changed without your knowing
exactly how. It's an evolutionary process, not an operation on the
appendix. I wouldn't know how to talk about it. It cured me of heavy
drinking, that's enough. I used to talk a little bit about it with
Hammett, not very much but a little bit. Hammett used to say he
learned more about himself through my analysis than I learned about
myself.

Q. Do you think it affected your ways of analyzing relationships?

A. Oh, yes, all the rest of your life you apply it, but I don't know
whether you apply it to other people. If it's been a good analysis, you
apply it a second before something happens, rather than the second
after. That's a big step forward. It took a very long time in my
particular case. I started it in the days when I was working in
Hollywood so I used to leave it often for four or five months at a
time. And for a long trip to Russia during the war. So it was

constantly being interrupted, which is not the best way to be analyzed.

Q. Drinking was the main reason you entered therapy?

A. It was the main reason. It wasn't the only reason. It never is the only reason because you have to say, what am I doing the drinking for? Somewhere, by instinct, I had sense enough to know that I was going to have a crackup. I don't know *why* that was, because *Little Foxes* had just opened and was a great success. The doctor I went to said I didn't have the stamina of my drinking friends, even though they were much older than I.

Q. It seems like a lot of that generation grew old rather gracelessly. You say they had stamina but in fact a lot of them died quite young.

A. Well, Fitzgerald, of course, died very young, and Lardner . . . Faulkner died too young but not that young. Hammett died too young but he wasn't that young, either . . . neither was Dottie Parker . . . and all three of them had given themselves bad beatings for a great many years. Yes, many of them did die young.

Q. Why did they live so self-destructively? Were they fighting off fears of aging and death or of success?

A. No. I think it's Woolworth Freud to make such guesses. I'm not sure you ever know more than a few people well enough to know why they do what they do. Maybe experts do; I ain't no expert. I knew Dorothy Parker very well. I wouldn't possibly know why she drank.

I always thought that the reason Hammett drank so much was that he was basically a shy man and the drinking made him less shy. But I don't know whether it's true or not.

Q. Do you think the generation of the Twenties and Thirties romanticized drinking in a way that the generation of the Sixties and Seventies romanticizes drugs?

A. Oh, I don't know. There were drugs in the Twenties and Thirties too. I tried smoking grass several times. It never did anything to me. I found myself always getting sleepy. I still do when I try it.

Q. You talk in *Scoundrel Time* of your disappointment with what "the good children of the Sixties have come to." What has survived of that decade?

A. Most of those kids have retired to communes or taken on one of those dopey California . . . whatever you have out there . . . some of your semireligious crap.

I don't understand personal salvation. It seems to me a vain idea. Conscience includes the fate of other people. In the great movements—the early Christian movements or the early Jewish movements—there was more than personal salvation involved. But there were mysteries then, inexplicable mysteries in the world which are no longer so mysterious. You can understand man turning to mysticism for what he couldn't understand. Very hard to understand it in an age of reason. And this would certainly seem, scientifically, to be an age of reason.

Q. You've said that you have enjoyed men more than women. Did you have difficulty forming friendships with women?

A. Oh, no. I've had a number of women who were close friends. I like women. I think men are frequently more interesting than women, that's all. That's quite different—liking and finding interesting. I've never felt very competitive. I've felt jealous of certain women but that is quite different. I was always jealous of great beauties. With jealousy you can feel upset, angry, but you give up when you know you're not in the same class. But competitiveness means you're in the same class.

Q. You never felt any sense of competition with Dorothy Parker, say?

A. Never. And I don't think she did with me. I've never felt competitive with anybody. Men or women. Maybe I am too arrogant. The only times I've ever felt it was when somebody very second-rate got praised and I had just taken a beating.

Q. What kinds of battles—professional and othewise—have you had as a woman?

A. I don't think I had any battles as a woman. I know I didn't get paid the same sums for jobs as men. That was an economic fight, not a battle as a woman. I didn't run into men who put women down. It was not the kind of man who attracted me.

Q. You wouldn't classify Hemingway as that kind of man?

A. Oh, I don't mean people I bumped into. Yes, of course I would classify Hemingway that way. He didn't worry me, who worries about people you bump into? I meant men with whom I had real relationships. I was lucky. I was successful early, I was 27 years old. Women *have* been put down, there's no question of that. For centuries and centuries.

Q. In a speech you said of the women's movement: "Some of its cries are empty cries." You talked about someone who was complaining about carrying out the garbage.

A. I don't think it's of any great moment who carries out the garbage. I think it is important that people be economically equal. So that if somebody feels like walking out, there's a way for her to earn a living rather than suffering through a whole lifetime because she can't. Most people of decent manners, living together, automatically divide the jobs anyway, whatever they are. My own nature would have forbidden anybody depriving *me* of what I thought were my rights. I would have walked out.

Q. Isn't that an extreme way of resolving a problem? Suppose you don't want to walk out over who carries out the garbage?

A. I would think in a decent relationship you don't have to keep a daily score of who does what. It doesn't matter who washes the dishes. It seems to me a thoroughly middle-class argument and I have no interest in it.

Are you going to legislate this? Is every mother in the world going to bring up a son who says, I won't put my wife down? And is every mother going to bring up a daughter who says, I don't dislike men and won't make them pay? A great many women put men down very badly. Particularly upper-class ladies.

Q. Do you think some women use the women's movement as an excuse for letting out hostilities which are really a lot more complicated?

A. I guess many do. But I don't know any. Most women want everything. They want "leadership," they want to be darlings, they want to be Marilyn Monroe and they want to be Madame de Maintenon. At the same time they want to be president. There is no oneness about any movement.

Q. Does the fact that young women have an easier time of it today than 50 years ago make you unsympathetic to their concerns?

A. I'm not sure young women do have it easier. Yes, there are more jobs available, but for whom? I'm not sure Negro women have it any easier than they did when I was growing up. I'm not sure poor women have it any easier.

Q. As a writer and a woman, how do you feel about the alterations in language that many feminists advocate?

A. I hate "Ms." There really isn't anything like making small battles in order to lose big ones. That's what the whole women's movement has been about to me. The big battle is equal rights, whether one likes to face it or not. Even that may never solve it, but the small battles just won't do. These are diversionary movements.

Nobody can argue any longer about the rights of women. It's like arguing about earthquakes.

Q. Do you think there's such a thing as feminine sensibility in literature?

A. Sure. I think sometimes it's extraordinarily good and sometimes it's awful. The present crop of feminine porno writers is below contempt. Masculine stuff is very seldom porno in quite as nasty a fashion.

Q. Erica Jong, for example, is somebody who . . .

A. I'm not going to discuss people by name. Whoever thought sexual liberation had anything to do with liberation?

Q. Anaïs Nin talked about how a lot of her creativity had been taken up by personal relationships. Have you ever experienced that as a conflict?

A. Oh Christ, what a silly thing to say. That's like saying a lot of creativity has been taken up by drinking or going swimming. It's your choice. Silly, self-pitying remark. You chose it, you wanted it.

Q. What was it like for you and Dashiell Hammett, as two writers, to live together? Was there any sense of competition?

A. There was no competition whatsoever. He was proud of me and I was proud of him. There were other kinds of trouble, but never that. That's why I'm always bewildered by competitiveness between people who live together. I don't think I could stand it.

Q. There were no ego problems from the fact that your career was on the rise while his was on the wane?

A. If there were, I never recognized them, and I don't believe he did. He was very sharp with me about what he didn't like and terribly pleased when he liked something.

Nobody ever gave more aid to anybody than he gave to me, and you can't do that if you feel competitive. You can start that game but it breaks down very quickly if you feel any anger or competitiveness.

Q. During that long period when he wasn't writing did you ever try to get him to write?

A. No. We didn't have that kind of relationship. He was a quite forbidding man, Hammett. Writing was one of the things you didn't talk to him about. I wish I had. I don't think it would have done any good, but it seems now to have been cowardly of me not to.

Q. Did you in some ways find Hammett's harshness appealing?

A. No, I found it sometimes awful and I found it sometimes admirable and brave. If you mean was I a masochist, I'm not. The harshness wasn't ever about anything but my work. And there, if you ask for help or opinions, you have to take what's coming.

Q. You said that he was very important to the writing of your plays but you also said that there was a chance that you made the dependency greater than it was. Do you ever have moments of doubt that you haven't got the nuances of that relationship exactly right on paper?

A. Of course. When you come to feel dependent upon people it may be that you exaggerate the dependency—it blinds you to what you could have been without it.

Q. Was that a question which haunted you in your relationship with Hammett?

A. No, it didn't worry me at all. I was perfectly willing to have the dependence. He said he never agreed with my formulation of it. I've been told by other people that maybe I'd have been okay without it, I don't know—I liked it.

I think between men and women there should be dependency, even between friends. Dependency has very little to do with independence. Independent natures aren't worried about dependency. It's a ridiculous thing to worry about anyway, because you're dependent on some things all your life.

Q. Do you ever feel that you romanticized that relationship with Hammett?

A. Yes. Then sometimes I feel that I haven't romanticized it enough.

It's very hard to tell, when a relationship is over, what you saw and what was fact. If by romantic one means invention, then I didn't invent it. If by romantic one means maybe time has dulled the bad parts, then I don't know.

Q. How much of yourself do you see in his character Nora in *The Thin Man?*

A. Some of the dialogue is almost direct quotation from me, but she is Hammett's picture of me. I don't see myself. Some of the dialogue is exact because it amused him.

Q. Do you like her as a character?

A. Yes. It's an affectionate portrait of a woman; but what pleased me more than anything else was that it was an affectionate pair of people. A man and woman who amused each other and got along.

Q. Nora often tries to get Nick involved in various detective cases and I think he once said she was always trying to get him in trouble.

A. He used to accuse me of doing that. I was interested in his past detective career and I was anxious for him to go back to it occasionally. He never went back to it.

Q. Why do you think Hammett has become so voguish these days? Do you think you had anything to do with it?

A. I had nothing to do with it at all. The Hammett renaissance was long before I wrote a word about him.

Q. You talk about how much Hammett influenced your life. Do you think that you influenced his life to the same degree?

A. No, I don't think so. He thought so, but I don't think so. There can be all kinds of reasons for that—he was a different age than I was, different kind of nature. He was a man, I was a woman, the old business. He wasn't a very easily influenced man. I was a rather easily influenced young girl.

Q. Did Hammett have many close friends other than you?

A. No, he had none that I know of.

Q. You talk about your fear of marriage . . . do you think that was an outgrowth of the kind of relationship you had with Hammett as much as a fear of marriage itself?

A. No, I don't know why we didn't marry. We thought of it but then after a while it became silly even to discuss it. Well, my guess is that neither one of us could have deeply wanted it or we'd have done it.

Q. Is the fact that you've never had children been an experience that you miss?

A. Oh, sure, of course, very much. And I don't know why I didn't but . . . it doesn't matter anymore. It's too late to cry about it now. Of course, I should have; I like children very much.

Q. You said that you only realized that you loved your mother five years after she was dead.

A. I began to see that I had liked her very much and had more respect than I had thought. I was far more touched by her than I ever thought I was. Too bad I didn't know that when she was alive.

Q. Do you know what helped you to see that?

A. I suppose the classic business of when the rival is gone you really don't want your father. Classic Freudian sense. After she died, I was able to see what a really interesting and moving character she'd been. But if she came back tonight I would probably find her a difficult lady to take.

She was an odd woman, and her oddities were difficult to accept. I think she loved me too much but I don't think she had any real understanding of what a child was. But there comes a time when you must put aside your parents. You can't, of course, ever, but you must make an effort to. If you stay with them and your grievances too long, then—well, it's destructive.

Q. Do you ever find your celebrity a mixed blessing?

A. I don't think about it. You see that I live quite simply and I don't very often see people I don't want to see anymore. People who want to meet famous people have asked me places and then quickly found themselves rather bored and disappointed by me. I don't fit in with what they expected. I suppose you're meant to be interesting or funny or something. That's amused me for years.

Once in a while I get a feeling that my life is too limited and I go clumping off for a week and then that feeling is over with. But there's just so much energy by the time you get to be my age. I had enormous energy once. . . .

Q. How do you come to terms with aging?

A. Best I can. The only thing good about it is you're not dead.

Q. Do you think about death very much?

A. Sure, everybody does and everybody forgets it. I haven't had any tendency to stay with it very long. I deeply resent the idea that I physically can't do certain things I used to do. I told this to a doctor recently, who said, "I have news for you, Lillian. The only difference between you and other people is it happened to you 15 years later."

Q. You're still very active physically? You used to garden an enormous amount. . . .

A. I don't think I am anymore. I used to do everything an enormous amount. Hammett's most often used sentence was "Please sit down, will you?"

A Profile of Lillian Hellman

Dan Rather/1977

Barbara Howar: You may recognize this face from an ad that's
appeared in national magazines—not exactly your standard cover
girl, but the ad shows her as "a legend" in a mink coat. Well, Lillian
Hellman started writing her own legend 40 years ago when she
turned out hit plays and movies like *The Little Foxes* and *The
Children's Hour.* Well now she's the subject of a movie herself, with
the part of Lillian Hellman played by Jane Fonda. But Hellman has
not always been Hollywood's idea of a heroine. In the 1950's—the
McCarthy era—she was blacklisted, an experience she wrote about
recently in the latest volume of her memoirs, a best-seller that stirred
up the kind of controversy her life always has. Dan Rather recently
paid a visit to this controversial legend.

Dan Rather [looking at Hellman self-portrait, Hellman laugh-
ing]: Deep blue eyes—natural deep blue eyes, blond curly natural
hair—this sketch that you drew of yourself. And it says, "What I
wanted to look like and don't," Lillian Hellman. [Laughter] Is that
how you wanted to look?

Lillian Hellman: I guess I did when I was a child, yes, I guess so.
I wanted blond curls and great big blue eyes, tiny nose, rosebud
mouth. That comes from that book, doesn't it?

Rather: The rosebud mouth. Now, I hadn't noticed that.

Hellman: Well, that is because I don't draw very well. That's—
That's what I—that was my version of a rosebud mouth. [Laughs]
You can see that I didn't get any of what I wanted.

Rather: What Lillian Hellman did get was a quick string of hits early in her career. This film, *Watch On the Rhine,* starring Bette Davis, was voted one of the best in 1943. Like much of her work, it carried a strong moral message.

[Excerpt of *Watch On the Rhine*]

After *Watch On the Rhine,* there were other award-winning dramas, but in the early 1950's her career came to a halt. She was blacklisted after her appearance before the House Un-American Activities Committee. She recalled that period, the McCarthy period, in her recent best-selling memoir, *Scoundrel Time.* The book has stirred up some old resentments among critics and friends. Her position has always been a controversial one. "I cannot, and will not, cut my conscience to fit this year's fashion," she wrote the Committee in 1952, offering by letter to testify about herself but not about anybody else. The offer was refused. In California recently, I asked her about that day she appeared before the Committee, and the story about a man in the press gallery who, after reading her letter, shouted, "Thank God someone finally had the guts to do it!"

Hellman: Whoever he was, it was the best friend of my—of my life, I guess, that morning. He—He sure saved—Well, I can't say he saved me. Maybe I'd have gotten through it anyway, but it was a very, very happy minute, because it just had not occurred to me that anybody on the press would be friendly to me. Certainly I knew the Committee wouldn't, and—and the audience wasn't.

Rather: And what happened after that? In brief, what did that cost you?

Hellman: Cost me—The whole Committee business and the years afterwards cost me all the money I had, cost me a farm. I didn't have a job for many, many years afterwards. It cost me a great deal. Once you survive something, I guess you tell yourself you took it better than you did.

Rather: It could have gone the other way for you, couldn't it?

Hellman: Exactly, it could have gone the other way for me, and—and did last long enough to make me believe it—it would be perhaps forever.

William Wyler [movie director]: I was told I could not engage

her. I went to see Barney Balaban, the head of the—head of
Paramount—President of Paramount Pictures.

Rather: Filmmaker William Wyler, who directed several Hellman
stories.

Wyler: And he took a list—took a piece of paper out of his desk
drawer, said her name was on the list. I reached for it, tried to get it.
He wouldn't show it to me. Whose list it was, I don't know.

Rather: How long did it last?

Hellman: It lasted about eight years, I guess. Economically, you
mean?

Rather: Economically.

Hellman: Yes. Yes, about eight years.

Rather: Well, this is not going to be comfortable for either one of
us, but we have to deal with it—

Hellman: Okay.

Rather: —as you fully expected, I would think.

Hellman: Okay.

Rather: Now, James Wechsler, the liberal columnist for the *New
York Post,* calls *Scoundrel Time*—and this is a direct quote—"A
dreary example of the revisionist writing of the McCarthy era."

Hellman: I don't think I rewrote history at all. I—*Scoundrel Time*
is about my personal experience before the House Un-American
Committee. I wasn't out to write history. I was out to say this is what
happened to me.

Rather: Well, what about the charge that, while you could see
what was wrong with McCarthy and that whole era in this country,
that you failed to see what was wrong with Stalinism?

Hellman: I came to see what was wrong with Stalin—Stalinism. I
don't—I think it's fair enough to say that, at that period, I did not
entirely see what was wrong with Communism. I happen never to
have been a Communist, for one thing, which is left out of this story.
I don't quite understand that argument. I mean, I don't really know
what has—one—one thing has to do with another. I am—I was not a
Russian. I was an American.

Rather: But I think you can see that the basic argument here is
that you applied a double standard. You applied one standard to
McCarthy in the United States and another standard to Stalin in the
Soviet Union.

Hellman: No, I don't think I did. I was injured by McCarthy, for one thing. I was not—I was personally not injured by Stalin, which is—is not—is not a very high-class reason, but it's a very—it's—it's a good practical reason.

Rather: Do you think we're in for another McCarthy period?

Hellman: No, I never have thought we were. I don't believe that McCarthy could happen again. I think maybe worse than McCarthy could happen again. I think that whole Watergate group was—was a much worse group than McCarthy, because I think McCarthy was rather a crazy man, and I don't think the Watergate kiddies were loonies at all, and thus, I think, were far more potentially dangerous. It was—It was colder stuff, I think, if that—if that matters. I'm not sure it matters what the motives are to villains.

Rather: After she was blacklisted, audiences did not see a Lillian Hellman story on film for over a decade. In 1962, William Wyler remade Hellman's first stage hit, *The Children's Hour,* a story, ironically enough, about the power of a lie. The film starred Shirley MacLaine, Audrey Hepburn and James Garner.

[Excerpt of *The Children's Hour*]

Rather: This is the stage at Campbell Hall at the University of California in Santa Barbara. A conversation with Hellman here is the final event in a special lecture series. Hellman has been teaching and talking on college campuses since 1961. Like her plays, she usually attracts a standing-room-only crowd. Hellman is often challenged by her audiences. A question about the women's movement, which she feels should concern itself more with economic demands, touches off a temperamental response.

Hellman: Can anybody who's worked since they were 20 years old think that women should be in a menial position? I don't believe you thought I thought that. I'm an old cook. I don't feel it's menial to cook. I also clean a house very often. I don't find that's menial. You can't have believed that either Dr. Coles or I felt women were—should be in a menial position. Because I said something was—its roots were economic, doesn't—doesn't mean that I think you or I should be put down by anybody, including you or me.

Rather: In the end, Hellman tries to back off from giving anybody advice about anything. She likes to sum it up this way—with a story about an old acquaintance of hers.

Hellman: I can't tell you her name, because it'd be too mean, but she's a very famous lady in America and I've known her since—we're about the same age. She's two or three years older, perhaps. About every year or two, she calls me up and asks me to lunch. And it took me about 20 years to figure out it's—the reason she does it is she expects some words of wisdom. And since she doesn't get any, she gets bored about half-way through lunch. And the last time she did it was about two years ago, and I thought to myself, "I—I'm tired of this now. I'm tired of the boredom you show with me through the years, and I've been very polite to you and you're very rude to me." She happened to be—It's rude, I think, to start to yawn in the middle of lunch when she doesn't—[Audience laughter]—when I turn out to have almost nothing to—wise to say. At that point she was telling me that she had just been interviewed and that she felt she made a very grave mistake; that she—she's been married three or four times, but that she now—she had talked to the interviewer about the fact that she had younger lovers. And I said, "Well, what's so wrong with that?" And she said, "Well, that's fine for you to say. You've been a much freer person than I've been, but it's not proper for me to do it." I said, "Well, why don't you look at it another way. Where would you find them older?" [Audience laughter, applause] I—I am proud to tell you I've never heard from her again. [Audience laughter]

[To Rather]: Yes, you possibly know I lived with the same man for 30 years and we didn't get married. And I—I don't see any sense to that ceremony unless there are children.

Rather: That was Dashiell Hammett.

Hellman: Yes. But then, I'm no great believer in ceremonies. Ceremonies make people stay together.

Rather: Hellman met Dashiell Hammett when she was 24 and he was 36. He was a celebrated writer of novels and suspense stories, including *The Thin Man.* She wrote once, "He was the most interesting man I've ever met." Their relationship endured until his death in 1961.

Hellman: We—We didn't make any real decision not to get married. We just—We started to a couple of times, and then kind of lost track, I guess, and didn't. And it finally would have been sort of silly, I think, to.

Rather: Did you talk of hav—having children?

Hellman: Yes, we did. I was pregnant once or twice, but they weren't terribly good days. Hammett was to go on the wagon for—forever, actually. He had been a very heavy drinker, and I was worried that—what was I going to do about the children? How was I going to support them? How was he going to support them? He—He was an extremely generous man with money, but he went on large binges. No, it just was one of those—when we could have had them, it didn't seem right to have them, and then after a while we didn't talk about it any more.

Rather: Hammett and Hellman's favorite play was *The Autumn Garden,* a story about middle age and broken dreams. She wrote it in 1951, the best time of their life together. Last fall it was revived at the prestigious Long Wharf Theater in Connecticut. A failure when it was first produced, this time it won an appreciative audience.

[Excerpt of *The Autumn Garden* . . . applause]

Hellman: For the first years of my life, I had a rule that I wouldn't lie to people about art. I'd lie to them about anything else in the world if they wanted it, but not about work. But I soon learned that that was a very bad game. I now, if I can't say anything, say, "I hope you have a large, large hit."

Jane Fonda: I came away with a sense of a woman who was very complex and very full of the most miraculous kind of contradictions. I don't think there's any other—

Rather: Actress Jane Fonda, who plays the part of Lillian Hellman in *Julia,* an up-coming film based on one of Hellman's memoirs.

Fonda: And she—she's not young any more, and yet she has something about her that is so flirtatious and feminine and sensual and, you—you know, she has a way of sitting, lounging in chairs, and the skirt kind of comes up above the knee and you see that she wears very expensive silk and satin underwear. And—And she has a way of lounging and of moving her body, and when she sat at the dining room table, there was just the two of us, but she would sit with a regal quality about her, like Nefertiti, and she would—I would be there, and she would talk looking out the window, and hold her cigarette and would move her head to the cigarette like this. There was something terribly feminine about her. And I've talked to a lot of men who know her very well, and they say, "Lillian, she's the biggest flirt in the world."

Rather: Are you vain?

Hellman: Can't tell you. Won't tell you.

Rather: Oh, come on.

Hellman: No. I'm certainly not going to tell an au—a large audience. I could get hit from right to left. [Laughter] I'm not crazy. [Laughter] Take you aside later and tell you. [Laughter]

Rather: Oh, I'd like to talk you out of that. Maybe just—just give an inch of yourself.

Hellman: Can't tell about—Can't tell you what—how—what I'm vain about. Vain about clothes, I think.

Rather: This ad: "What Becomes A Legend Most?"—advertising ranch mink. [Laughter] What in the world is that about?

Hellman: I don't know. [Laughs] I don't know.

Rather: No, I want to know why you did that.

Hellman: I don't know. I can't tell you. [Laughs] I can't possibly tell you.

Rather: Now, you're an intelligent person in command of your own feelings nearly all of the time. You know why you did that—

Hellman: No I don't.

Rather: —and I want to know.

Hellman: I got talked into it one bad afternoon. Do you—Do you object to it?

Rather: Well, no, but I don't quite know what to make of it.

Hellman [laughing]: I don't blame you.

Rather: I hear you talk, and watch you here. I find myself saying, "There are going to be millions of women who see this broadcast, envy this woman"—meaning you—"because you've had so much freedom."

Hellman: It's rather hard to judge one's own freedom. I suppose I have. I haven't always thought so. I guess I have had. I long ago decided that, for right or wrong—I have no idea whether it's true or not—that you have to pay a very large price for freedom, and if you were willing to pay it, then maybe you'd get it, and maybe you wouldn't. It's cost a fair amount to get it, I think, and I've lost a good deal along the way, but—But you play out your own nature, I guess, in the end.

Unfinished Woman

Peter Adam/1978

From *The Listener,* 101 (8 February 1979), 213–16. Originally broadcast as a BBC programme on "Omnibus," 8 February 1979 and excerpted from an interview conducted in late autumn 1978. Reprinted by permission of Peter Adam.

The mere mention of the name "Lillian Hellman" usually provokes instant strong reactions which might range from hatred of her irritable nature to warm affection for her personal vulnerability. There are those who mistrust her political motives, others who admire her as an example of courage and integrity. There is, however, more agreement about her status as a writer. With many honours and awards to her credit, Lillian Hellman is one of America's most important playwrights: she has written eight plays, most of which were long-running and critically acclaimed successes. *The Little Foxes, The Children's Hour, Watch on the Rhine, Toys in the Attic* and others have all been turned into feature films.

She has taken a hand in directing her own work, adapted three other plays and written the book for Leonard Bernstein's musical, *Candide.*

During the last ten years, she has published three remarkable volumes of autobiography: *An Unfinished Woman, Pentimento* and *Scoundrel Time.* She has given up the theatre, or maybe it is truer to say theatre people—a love-hate affair which lasted 30 years.

Lillian Hellman had great benefits from the theatre, liked and enjoyed many people in it, counted a few of them as her close friends, had pleasure in success and excitement, even in failure, but she had wandered through it as if she were a kind of stranger. The struggles with the theatre were those of a woman whose desperate need for privacy could not be reconciled with a profession which demanded teamwork.

Lillian Hellman: Around the time of *Candide,* I began to think,

"I don't think I like this business—there's too many collaborators, and there's too much talk of money, and too much talk of success, and too many pressures. I don't want to listen to how much money the play is losing, and what it needs and what I must do next. And I can't sit in this room feeling this guilty and this panic-stricken, and I don't have the interest any longer.

When I first started in the theatre, nobody could move me from what I thought. Since 1935, there has been a change. I do not think it changed so much in the theatre as it possibly changed in me.

Anyway, theatre has been only part of her life. There has been journalism, film scripts, political activity, Spain during the civil war, three trips to Russia, an interview with Tito and, finally, her famous refusal to testify before the McCarthy Committee.

Today, now aged 72, with her health deteriorating and her eyesight failing, Lillian Hellman spends most of her time on Martha's Vineyard, an island just off the New England coast. She lives in a house built after the death of Dashiell Hammett, who had shared her life for 30 years—"on and off," as she puts it.

Born in New Orleans, her Jewish grandparents having come from Germany and settled there, Lillian very early in life rebelled against her mother's aristocratic Alabama family, which she associated with the rich settlers who exploited the blacks and whose only interest seemed to be money. She remembers childhood as a "period of self-dislike marked by the rampage anger of an only child" and the early understanding that she "lived under an economic system of increasing impurity and injustice." Trying to understand the world of grown-ups, she fled from real life and took refuge in books.

This "stubborn, relentless, driving desire to be alone" would never leave her. During these years of passionate reading, spent hidden in a tree as often as not, she had the first intimation of sadness, the first recognition that there was so much to understand that one might never find one's way and that, for a nature like hers, the way would not be easy. When I asked her from whom she learnt most in her writing career, she said:

Hellman: I haven't the slightest idea. When I was very young— maybe because they did not know any better, and maybe because they were just pleased their child read—my mother and father forbad nothing. I read everything, from a dreadful magazine called *Snappy Stories,* which I borrowed from the elevator man, straight through Balzac, straight through everything that other people were forbidden.

Peter Adam: When did you first discover the desire to write?

Hellman: I suppose I was eight or ten years old.

Adam: Have you ever asked yourself the question, "Why do I write?"

Hellman: It is better, from my viewpoint, not to ask such questions. I think a great deal why, in my particular case, I wrote was accidental. Of course, there is no such thing as accidental. I wrote, in part, because I don't know too many other things to do, and partly because I know a few, but prefer writing. In part, because it is habit: I like to write.

As a young woman, she was openly rebellious against everything. But she knew that the over-proud, over-sensitive, over-daring attitude she struck was only covering up a frightened, shy human being. For a while, she worked at a publishing house and in a theatre as a publicity agent. Then, in 1925, she married Arthur Kober, a playwright, and they moved to Hollywood. There, she worked as a script reader for MGM studios. After five years, the marriage broke up, and she followed Dashiell Hammett to New York. There, they rented a house by the sea. At some time during this period, Lillian Hellman must have decided to become a playwright, but the precise moment is now lost under the chance circumstances which propelled her towards the theatre.

In 1934, when she was 27, she surprised critics and audiences with a play which brought her immediate success—*The Children's Hour.* The play dealt with the charges of lesbianism brought by a woman against her granddaughter's teachers. It shows how a lie can destroy people's lives. The play has twice been adapted for the screen, the second version stars Shirley Maclaine and Audrey Hepburn.

The Children's Hour carries many hallmarks of her plays to come: a highly-charged, melodramatic situation played out against a middle-class background. It received rave reviews: Broadway had discovered a new writer who could pack the stage with drama and passion. This was the first of many plays which would bring Lillian Hellman a great deal of publicity, fame and money, and keep her in the limelight for 40 years.

Adam: Those were good years.

Hellman: Yes.

Adam: You were young, and you had success—which was very rare for a woman of that age on Broadway.

Hellman: Yes, they were good, in terms of money and success. And very surprising, too. I never expected the play to be successful.

Hammett had taken off for Hollywood, for some reason I can't remember, so I was alone on opening night. And he was to send me some money when he got to Hollywood, because I had a giant hotel bill. But I guess he got drunk and forgot to do it (he was a very generous man, but he frequently just forgot about money or spent it), and I had about $18 the day *The Children's Hour* opened.

I sent the wardrobe woman out for a bottle of brandy, and began to drink it. And I think I was as sick drunk as ever I had been in my life. So I went to the opening night of *Children's Hour* with a new hat that would not stay on my head, because, evidently, I would not let it stay on, unable to balance myself in the back of the theatre; weaving around, getting in everyone's way; bumping into people, going outside on the street to get sick—not knowing what hit me.

Trying to go on stage, listening to this great applause and thinking, "What are they doing, and what's that for?" Everybody yelling "Author, author!" and a few people near me shoving me, and my absolute determination not to be moved. In the first place, I would not have gone on the stage, but I did not know what they were doing.

I guess, towards morning, I began to understand that we had a big hit. And I picked up some strangers. I even remember their names. And I went on drinking with them. Oh, there was no euphoria. It was a shame to spoil so fine a night with so bad a drunk.

Adam: Did you never get any pleasure from any of your opening nights?

Hellman: I cannot answer that truthfully. I do not remember any. I remember pieces of pleasure but bewilderment. I know certain facts. I remember the opening night of *Watch on the Rhine* on Broadway. It had been a big success in Baltimore, and we had come in expecting, therefore, to be a big success. At the end of the first act, I went back to Herman Shumlin, who directed it, and said, "It's just falling on its face, I can't stand it." And he said, "It's probably the biggest hit in New York this minute." And I said, "No, no, it's not, you don't understand. You've been in this office and you haven't seen." He said, "Please go away now, please go home to bed." But I was absolutely convinced we were a failure. It is an unhappy nature, I guess, to think that everything good is going wrong all the time.

It has often been said that many of Lillian Hellman's characters share her own nature—a tendency to cling on to the bad times and block out the good ones, but the years following the success of *The Children's Hour* were good ones. Lillian Hellman, living with Dashiell Hammett, moved between Hollywood and New York. She was now also a famous screenwriter. She mingled with the rich and famous, all those who made up the fat, loose years of the Thirties. William Faulkner, Nathanael West, George Gershwin, Tallulah Bankhead, Scott Fitzgerald, Gertrude Stein and Dorothy Parker, her lifelong friend.

But, among the glamour, were serious moments, too. For the politically conscious, these were disturbing times. She went to Spain during the civil war. This experience deepened her sympathy with left-wing causes. It prompted her to write *Days to Come*, a play about a labour strike. But it flopped—a failure which wounded her deeply.

Then, however, success came again: she wrote *The Little Foxes*, a play which gave her more trouble in the writing than any other. After eight versions, Hammett finally approved. *The Little Foxes* is the story of the avarice and greed of the Hubbard family, led by the powerful Regina—played on the stage by Tallulah Bankhead and later on the screen by Bette Davis—and it established Lillian Hellman as one of America's leading playwrights. It revealed her acute sense of realistic and historical detail, the result of painstaking research into the background. In her own words, "a play should have something to say, and should say it well." Or, as one critic remarked, "Her work is constructed with the rigidity and tensile strength of a steel girder— every dramatic hair is in place." Her Ibsen-like characters may not be lovable, but they are brutally alive.

Many of the characters in her plays are consumed by greed and avarice, so I asked her why she took such a grim view of society, of the world, of human nature?

Hellman: I don't think it's a grim view. I've written plays where the characters weren't consumed by greed or avarice. I don't mean to say there's anything wrong about writing about avarice and greed, because I don't think there is. Most of Balzac is avarice and greed.

Adam: You once talked about the "graveyard affection" you have towards your characters.

Hellman: It's my belief that you have no right ever to dislike a character: I mean I didn't dislike Regina. I may have disapproved of her, in a sense, but I didn't dislike. In a play, you can't write about someone you deeply dislike; the character comes to an end too fast. You can do it in a memoir, because you're going to dismiss the person quickly. Or you probably can even in a novel.

Adam: Are you sometimes surprised by what you have written?

Hellman: I go through two stages of rereading myself. One is to think, "Well, how did you get that much sense? You were only 16 or so! And what happened to you? That's strange, you write like a grown-up person." That's wonderful. And thinking, "Oh, my God, what nonsense! What made you write that way? What made you so young, what made you so awkward, what made you so. . . ?" I swing from one to the other. And, all my life, for this reason I have kept myself from re-reading or re-seeing work, because I know that swing and I know it's very painful.

It's very hard to explain to people that I don't want to know—it's over and done with. Whatever I hope I've learned, I've learned. Whatever I can't learn, I can't learn any more.

Adam: How important has success been for you?

Hellman: Oh, that is a loaded question. Come on, I'm not that big a sucker! It's important for everybody, and it's not of as much importance as everybody makes it. It's fine in dealing with head waiters and hotel managers. I don't mean to make fun of it; it is just fine. But it shouldn't govern a life, and I hope to God it hasn't governed mine.

Adam: I mean, failure in the theatre is, of course, much harder to take than—

Hellman: You didn't ask me what failure is like. Failure can be very cruel and awful and crippling. You asked me about success.

Adam: How about failure, especially in the theatre?

Hellman: Very, very bad, very crippling. But success and failure are not true opposites, and they're not even in the same class. I mean, they're not even a couch and a chair.

Lillian Hellman has never made things easy for herself. In life, as well as in her plays, she has always taken stands—an often ungrateful task leading to many misunderstandings. In 1940, she wrote the prize-winning *Watch on the Rhine*, warning a sleeping America of the danger of fascism, a danger she had first seen in Germany in 1929 and which she, as a Jew, felt doubly strongly.

Adam: You were always drawn into extreme situations—countries that were in upheaval. You went to Russia, you went to Spain during the civil war.

Hellman: Yes, I suppose there was a time in my life when I was a danger lover.

Adam: Have you had no fear?

Hellman: Oh, God, indeed! Maybe those are the only persons ever drawn to it. Of course, I suppose one is, in a sense, testing oneself about it.

Adam: You said, "Sometimes, I am a moral writer; sometimes too moral." Can you define what you meant by that?

Hellman: I think, particularly when I was younger, I took moral stands too sharply. I don't regret the moral stands as I regret the pounding I made of them very often, when it was necessary. I don't regret the moral stands. If wrong, they were at least myself being wrong.

Adam: And it coloured your writing?

Hellman: And it coloured my writing, of course. There are places in many of the plays where I don't wish I had taken any other stand; I wish I'd been perhaps a little less on the nose and a little less insistent about saying it twice instead of once. Or once instead of half once.

Adam: There is a very beautiful speech in *Watch on the Rhine*: "In every town, in every village, in every mud hut in the world, there is always a man who loves children and will fight to make a good world for them." Do you still share some of that optimism?

Hellman: Oh, yes, but I wouldn't say it that way any more. I think I would rather say: "In every village, in every mud hut, in every country in the world, there is a man intelligent enough to make a fight for a better world"—to have sense enough to figure it out; that something better has got to happen. "A better world for children" I do not think I would say any more.

Watch on the Rhine was written in Pleasantville, the 30-acre farm which Lillian Hellman bought with the proceeds from *The Little Foxes*. She and Dashiell Hammett spent 13 years there—the happiest years of her life. There she wrote her next five plays, among them *Another Part of the Forest* and *The Autumn Garden*. She raised poultry, farmed, fished, cooked and filled the house and gardens with friends and admirers. There were many glittering, brilliant parties, presided over by the always elegant Lillian Hellman, whose wit and sharpness became legendary. But the most important person among all this, as she has written in her memoirs, was Dashiell Hammett, who continued to spur her on to write.

Hellman: His effect on me was enormous. I've long had a belief, which is very possibly not the truth, that, without Hammett, I wouldn't have written. I've come to think, perhaps, that I would have written, but I would have had an infinitely greater struggle, and been less good, I think, without him. He taught me, in a sense, to write. And beyond that which many people have done for many other people, he took chances that very few people will ever take, particularly people they love. He told the truth. When I did something that he didn't like, he said it very bluntly and very sharply, and he really didn't give one damn if I liked it or didn't like it. And that, I think, is really the greatest gift anybody can give anybody.

Now, I may have exaggerated and taken too seriously, from time to time, his criticisms. People have accused me of that, and that is perfectly possible. There was a time when I thought that I would never have written anything without him. I don't think that's true any more. But I think I would have had a much harder time, so hard that I might have given up.

The McCarthy witch-hunts of 1951 and 1952 brought a cruel and unjust ending to this life. Although already an old and ill man, Dashiell Hammett, who was a member of the Communist party, was tried and sent to jail. Lillian Hellman, who was not a communist, was also asked to testify before the House Committee on Un-American Activities. It was then that she wrote the famous letter to the committee chairman—a letter so often quoted as an example of standards of integrity and courage, that it recently found its way into a Broadway play called *Are You Now, or Have You Ever Been?*

Dear Mr. Wood,
   As you know, I am under subpoena to appear before your committee on 21 May 1952.
   I am most willing to answer all questions about myself. I have nothing to hide from your committee and there is nothing in my life of which I am ashamed. But I am advised by counsel that if I answer the committee's questions about myself, I must also answer questions about other people, and that if I refuse to do so, I can be cited for contempt.
   To hurt innocent people whom I knew many years ago in order to save myself is, to me, inhuman and indecent and dishonourable. I cannot and I will not cut my conscience to fit this year's fashions, even though I long ago came to the conclusion that I was not a political person and could have no comfortable place in any political group.
   I was raised in an old-fashioned American tradition and there were certain homely things that were taught to me: to try to tell the truth, not to bear false witness, not to harm my neighbour, to be loyal to my country, and so on. It is my belief that you will agree with these simple rules of human decency and will not expect me to violate the good American tradition from which they spring. I would, therefore, like to come before your committee and speak only of myself.
                                                                      Sincerely yours,
                                                                      Lillian Hellman

Hellman: That letter, as you, Mr. Adam, know, had a very beneficial effect in many ways. It gave other people a place to stand, a legal place to stand, and was the first of its kind. Of that I am proud.

I have to tell you this: many years later (as even then), I would have preferred, and didn't have the courage to do, what two friends of mine, Leo Humer and Paul Sweezy, did. They went into an even worse committee and each gave his name, gave his address, gave his profession as writer, and to the next question, which was "Are you now, or have you ever been a member of the Communist party?"

said, "No, I am not now and I have never been; from now on, I answer nothing." And each rose and left his seat. This, to me, was an extraordinary and a correct position to take.

Lillian Hellman paid for her stand. Hammett was ailing in prison, and the Hollywood blacklist cut off half her professional life. She was forced to sell the farm.

Adam: There is a line in *The Autumn Garden* which says most people "haven't done anything to themselves; they've just let it be done to them." I mean, how much are human beings just reacting to circumstances, or are we in control of our lives?

Hellman: I believed, when I was young, that we were very much in control of our lives. And I cling to the belief that when we are young we should be. But, of course, one has to make all kinds of exceptions. They are where one was born, and who one was born to, was one hungry or well fed, was one sick or not sick, what world did one grow up in? Given a fair shake, one hopes that there's a large measure of control. Given an unfair shake, less.

Adam: Have you had a fair or an unfair shake?

Hellman: I had quite a fair shake. Not a brilliant one, but a fair one.

Adam: Do you sometimes wish you could have lived in a different time?

Hellman: No. No, I think this has been an enormously interesting time to live in. And, in spite of the fact that everything should have been much better, and it had a great deal of ugliness in it, it is a hell of a lot better, in many ways, than the world I was born in. No, I don't wish to have lived in a different time—I'd be dead, for one thing. I don't want to be dead!

Lillian Hellman now spends her summers at Martha's Vineyard, in a small house she built next to the mill house in which she lived with Hammett. Her drawing-room is filled with books, souvenirs and furniture from the sets of her plays. So much so that it could be the set for any one of them. There are still visitors. But, with her two closest friends, Dorothy Parker and Dashiell Hammett, dead, life seems to run in a more quiet vein.

She has frequently told reporters that she does not like to speak about her own writing. So far, she has discouraged anyone from writing her biography. She admires people who refuse to speak until they are ready. As she once said, "I have no enthusiasm for being a book-keeper of my life." But now, in an unremitting effort to be objective about herself, she has written about the world she had observed and thought about. The publication of her autobiographies and, especially, the making of the film, *Julia,* have again brought her back into the limelight. When I asked her about *Julia,* she said:

Hellman: It is very difficult always to judge pictures made about yourself, or even about your own work. You naturally resent any change that was made. I like *Julia* as a whole, but I have very grave reservations about some of it. I had meant the story to be a far more political picture of Julia and of the times than it turned out to be. I don't like myself, in the form of Jane Fonda, throwing a typewriter out of the window. I would have rather thrown myself out of the window than a typewriter—it was all I had! I'd have killed myself before I broke my typewriter.

I think the great virtue of the picture is that it does make the point that two women can be totally devoted to one another, and that each will do for the other what each wants, and believe it, even though she herself doesn't totally understand what is wanted. That, I think, did happen, and is a very good result, and I like it very much, in that sense. Maybe the others are small things, I don't know; I mean, some day, maybe four or five years from now, I can look at the picture and be more distant than I am now.

The film, *Julia,* was taken from two of her autobiographical books, *An Unfinished Woman* and *Pentimento.* The appearance of these two books was hailed by the critics as a literary event of the first order. They surprised anyone who had thought of Hellman only as a playwright. She revealed herself as a writer of masterly prose. Then, having dealt with her youth, her friends, her career in these two books, she wrote a third one about the McCarthy era—*Scoundrel Time.*

She kept a self-imposed silence until she was clear in her mind what her part in that "sad, comic, miserable time" had been. But *Scoundrel Time* did not convince everybody. Some accused Hellman of turning herself into a martyr. She herself knows better: "rebels seldom make good revolutionaries, because organised action, even union with other people, is not possible for them." For a long time, Lillian Hellman thought of herself as a radical, but she now painfully admits that she can no longer believe in radicalism or even liberalism. She has substituted for it "something more private, that for want of a better word, should be called decency."

When I asked her, when she wrote *Unfinished Woman,* was it to come to terms with the past or was it because she felt she wanted to pass on a message, she said:

Hellman: No, no. *Unfinished Woman* started out a totally different way. I was feeling bad about doing nothing and not knowing where to turn, and remembering that Hammett had been convinced that I should be a novelist, and I had been convinced I never should be. And I'd done a great deal of magazine work and pieces through the years: the Russian war, the Spanish war, the Washington march of Martin Luther King and the rest of it. And I thought I'd try it out. I got out those pieces to see what I thought of them, and maybe I could make a collection of them. And I began to use the pieces, and the diaries—to alter and usually to make longer. And that is how the *Unfinished Woman* began, and that's how it ended. I added to it, of course, my own childhood.

Adam: I was reading the other day that Simone de Beauvoir said she cannot write about her later years with the same candour as about her earlier years. Do you have the same experience?

Hellman: No, I have almost the opposite one. I can write much more easily about myself now. Dorothy Parker once pointed out to me that I had never, in my whole life, written a love scene. Which is the truth. It isn't, God knows, that my own life has been sexually very pure; it hasn't. It is that somewhere I shy away from sexual revelation. The roots of shying away—I've thought about it a great deal, naturally—don't belong to my generation, which was the generation that broke all the rules, and made all the fuss, and fought first, I think, for so-called sexual freedom. And, certainly, I did! It's something else; and I don't know what it is. It's just that I'm not quite able to do it. I find it easier to write about later years than I do about earlier years.

Adam: There is a line in your play, *The Searching Wind,* which says "the hardest thing in the world is to see yourself straight."

Hellman: Yes, it's hard, because most of us don't want to punish ourselves. And some of us wish to punish ourselves too much. I have, I'm afraid—and I'm not very pleased with it—an unpleasant tendency to wish to see myself so-called too straight, and therefore to punish myself with what I see. It's not a very pleasant quality. It looks like it has the outer shell of honesty, and doesn't have very much to do with honesty or dishonesty.

Adam: But you said, in *Unfinished Woman,* that, if you are willing to take the punishment, you are halfway through the battle.

Hellman: That is quite something else. I didn't mean punishment in that way. I meant, if you're willing to take the punishment that life will give you, or that somebody else will give you, or that society will give you. And I didn't mean willing in the sense of collaborating with it. I meant, if you say, "OK, so I've lost the job, or I've lost the person. It's terrible, I'm going to feel terrible, but there I am and there's nothing I can do about it." Then it is less bad. You're halfway through the battle to say it the way I said it once before.

Adam: If you could have changed the pattern of your life, would you have changed it?

Hellman: I would have hoped I would have done some less time-wasting things. And some perhaps less foolish things. No, I don't think I'd have changed it too much. It is too much a waste of time to think that way. Who would I have been, who could have changed it? It's better to have a future dream, it seems to me, than one that never has any chance of fulfilment.

Adam: What is your future dream?

Hellman: I suppose to live as long as possible, to live as comfortably as possible, and with as much work as possible. I don't think I expected very much, in that sense. I don't think I was a dreamer. I think it's one of the reasons success surprised me. It still does.

If I had dreams, they were other kinds of dreams. I dreamed of a farm, and I had a farm. And I dream of another farm, but I'll never have another farm. But I don't think I dreamed of success.

I know, as a little girl, I dreamed of being a beauty, but I wasn't a beauty, so what was there to do about it? I dreamed of being dazzlingly brilliant at college, and I was very undazzling! I gave up and decided not to compete. No, I do not think I have had dreams.

I had something called "happiness." Every American born in the world is dreaming of some vague thing called "happiness"; we're told it's our due, we'll have it. But I never knew what I meant by it, and I still don't.

Adam: In growing old, so much leaves us—strength, anger. What is one left with?

Hellman: You've got me! The hope for the best, I guess. The hope that not all anger has gone, not all strength has gone. You know perfectly well a great deal has. And I suppose you cling to the idea that a great deal has been. And you say a long prayer. I mean, some people come out just fine, I suppose, and some people come out not only physically crippled, but beaten up. I've asked myself this question almost every day for quite a while now, and I have no answer for it.

Profile: Lillian Hellman

Marilyn Berger/1979

This is a transcript of a five-part interview broadcast originally on KERA-TV Dallas/Fort Worth on 5, 7, 8, 9, 10 April 1981. The transcript is © 1979, KERA, Public Communication Foundation for North Texas. Used with permission from KERA-TV Dallas/ Forth Worth, Producer of "Profile: Lillian Hellman."

I

Marilyn Berger: Miss Hellman, you've written many plays and you've won many awards for your plays and yet, in *An Unfinished Woman*, you talk about the conflict that would cause you to work so hard in a world that is not your home, but that has been your life. If the theater has not been your home, what has been your home?

Lillian Hellman: That's not a fair question. I didn't. . . . I don't mean that you mean to be unfair, but I didn't intimate that anything had been my home. I simply said the theater wasn't.

MB: Have you felt more at home in writing the books than . . . ?

LH: Yes, I felt more at home in writing the books, but that doesn't mean I'm at home in them. I don't know what's at home in writing. All I meant was I was at *home* when I was writing the plays . . . *writing* the plays. What I meant by it was that I was not at *home* when the plays went into rehearsal and opened and we went through all the business of opening or closing or failure or success.

MB: In fact, Hammett said to you all the way back in 1937, I think, "The truth is you don't like the theater except at the times when you're in a room by yourself putting the plays on paper."

LH: Yes, exactly. I'd forgotten I'd written that, but that's absolutely true. That's when I liked it. I also liked, and still do like certain aspects of it. I like to see prose work. I like certain instincts that I have about the theater that still work well.

MB: You took pride, I remember, in discovering Patricia Neal when you were the director.

232

LH: Yes, that's what I meant about instincts. When my instincts in the theater are working, well I like it.

MB: Is it the working with that many people, the production, the money?

LH: I really don't know what it is. I don't think I can put my hand on it because it has nothing to do with. . . . I've liked a great many people in the theater as I said, and still do like a great many people in the theater. It's probably that I'm not by nature a collaborator. It also was in a much more conscious way, in a much more practical way, along about the time of *Candide,* a musical Leonard Bernstein, Richard Wilbur and I did, which is now a sort of cult show, as you know, and which was at the time it opened, a large failure and began to be a failure in Boston. I began *intensely* to dislike the talk about money and how one couldn't afford to rehearse another week or two and how much money had to be raised and what money one had to do to run, and I began to feel for the first time in the theater the pressures that money could bring on work, and to resent the idea that three years of my life was going down the drain for money just because money couldn't be raised to practice more, hold out longer. With *My Mother, My Father and Me* almost the same thing happened once again. We came in and the play opened in the newspaper strike and the pressure of money, no advertising and no newspaper reviews closed the show. Maybe it would have closed anyway. Perfectly possible it would've. But I began to think I just don't want to live this way. So much work and so much time, it's now absolutely out of my hands and dependent upon x amount of money being raised or not raised or. . . . I don't want my life to go this way any more.

MB: You said you're hard on yourself. We've talked about that. You said you took your successes for granted and worried so much about the failures. But don't the best people always run scared?

LH: No, forgive me. I don't think I said I took them for granted, did I?

MB: I have that quote.

LH: Have you?

MB: Yes.

LH: Oh goodness, maybe I better stop writing. I think what I meant. . . . I shouldn't have used the word "granted." I think what I meant was they didn't bring me the pleasures that I think they should have brought me, would be more accurate. God knows, I didn't take them for granted, because I never believed they were until I saw lines around the theater. And then it would take me weeks to believe they would continue. I was a kind of joke in the theater; that I never believed anything was successful even after it was.

MB: Now when your books are successful, do you get the pleasure out of them that you think is right?

LH: I get more pleasure. I get more pleasure, yes. I'm not sure I'm geared to get pleasure from. . . . I think my pleasures come from doing the work.

MB: Do you like the process of writing? Do you like sitting down in the solitude of a room and writing?

LH: Sometimes I hate it like everybody else, but most of the time I feel excited by it and pleased by it. Not always, God knows, but sometimes I'm semi-hysterical and sometimes tearful and sometimes depressed and think I've never written a word before, and I'm the clumsiest ox that ever lived and all those things that everybody thinks. But I'm not sure what success is anyway. If it means money, I enjoy the money. If it means fame, it's very nice to . . . about head waiters . . . .

MB: You said, "I like fame, but I don't like and I'm no good at its requirements."

LH: I'm awkward. I'm very awkward. When people pay compliments, I really mean to be pleasant, and I'm either so over pleasant that I scare them or I snap in some form. The one kind of compliment I remember with the very greatest pleasure that I ever had about a compliment was last year in San Francisco. My editor and I were walking on the street to an eye doctor where I was going and a very pretty young woman passed us. I noticed her because she was very pretty, and then I was tapped on the arm and it was she who had turned back to tap me. And she was carrying a very modest little package of flowers in a paper, and she said, "I'd like to give you these. Goodbye," and walked on. And I thought, "This is the nicest, pleasantest compliment I've ever had in my whole life. This woman doesn't want to show off, doesn't want me to know her name, doesn't want to tell me anything; just wants to say it her way and get off. It was very moving for me.

MB: Do you find fame intrusive? Does it bother you other than with head waiters?

LH: No, I don't find it intrusive. I wish it would intrude a little more.

MB: Does it bother you when people come up and say to you, "You're Lilliam Hellman." I mean, you know you're Lillian Hellman.

LH: It only bothers me . . . it only bothers me . . . I like it very much. Some people pick very odd times. One person picked the middle of Madison Avenue traffic about three months ago, right smack in the middle. The light changed while she was telling me and people were honking at us, and I thought one of us is crazy!

MB: Of course you did a good deal of writing in Hollywood. Is Hollywood the bad place for writers it's often made out to be?

LH: I don't think I can answer that question. It depends on who you are and what you're after. It wasn't a bad place for me, I have to say. But I had been lucky enough, by chance had been married to a man, and I went to Hollywood with him long before I wrote anything.

MB: And that was Arthur Kober.

LH: Arthur Kober. And I had a fifty dollar a week job reading scripts at Metro-Goldwyn-Mayer, so I saw Hollywood long before I was ever offered a decent job, which only came after *The Children's Hour* was a success. So I was prepared really for Hollywood, and knew I didn't want to live there really. But I liked movies very much, and I still like movies very much. I'm still very interested in them; was very interested in them then and didn't do what the rest of my generation did which was to think of it as whoring. I genuinely was interested in doing pictures, so when it came time to . . . after *The Children's Hour* was a success and I began to get large offers, I was protected by my earlier knowledge of Hollywood. I knew I didn't want to live there, but I knew that to some extent to write a script, one had to go there. I made a contract which allowed me, if it went over ten weeks, I didn't stay in Hollywood. I came back to wherever I wanted to go and then brought the script back again. So there was never a time when I was tempted to live in Los Angeles. My temptations are not swimming pools and cars is really what I'm saying. If they are, then I think it's dangerous for the writer, yes.

MB: You think writers could be very spoiled by what Los Angeles can represent?

LH: Could be, yes, particularly for a young writer and for an older writer. There's two classes I think could be spoiled. Luxury is a lovely thing and I'm not denying it to anybody, and I wanted it as much as other people wanted it. I didn't happen to want that particular kind of luxury. I wanted other kinds of luxury.

MB: You've presented an extraordinary picture of Hollywood in the '30's. You had some very unhappy times there and I remember your stories about driving home and how you hated the drive home. And then you present other pictures of going to the wealthy homes and sorts of parties they had. Are your memories of that time more painful or more happy?

LH: Well, there were two periods you see. There was a period when I was married and working at Metro and those aren't particularly pleasant memories because working for fifty dollars a week based on the fact . . . only . . . you were only paid fifty dollars a week if you could read two languages. You were paid sixty dollars if you could read three. And you sat, you had no office of your own. You sat with about 15 or 18 other people in a large room. And you were required to read, unless you came across something very remarkable, two and three manuscripts a day. This is slave labor, real slave labor. And it takes you an hour to drive home at night. That was not a pleasant life.

MB: You said it was in Hollywood that you learned to drink. Was that the period?

LH: Yes. Yes.

MB: And it stayed with you.

LH: I had drunk a little bit here, but not very much, not very much.

MB: You said you wanted to write for movies. How did you react to seeing yourself portrayed in *Julia* by Jane Fonda?

LH: I don't think that's the way I can answer the question. This sounds so simple-minded that I don't expect anybody to believe me. When I sold *Julia*, long before Jane Fonda was in the picture, it literally never occurred to me that my name was going to be used. I don't expect anybody to believe me, but it's the truth. When I read the script and there I was, I called up my agent and said, "Hey, let's get this out right away. What kind of business is this?" And he said, "I don't know what you're talking about. What are you talking about? What do you think they bought it for? There's nothing in the contract that says this. Why did you think of it now?" And I realized right in the middle of the conversation that . . . well, I don't know what words there are for that kind of lack of intelligence or blindness . . . but I stopped. I mean, there it was. There was nothing to be done about it. To come to your question, I was less, when I first saw a shot of the picture, less worried about Jane's picture of me, portrait of me, than I was about the total picture. The director and I had had some arguments about the picture; weren't pleased with each other to say the least, and I was much more worried about the picture than I was . . . I quickly forgot that it was me is what I'm saying. I was worried about . . . I liked Jane very much, of course, it was a very good performance. It's a very good movie, I think, in general. I have reservations about it, as anybody would have who . . . one doesn't like one's work touched, really, altered in any form.

MB: I've rarely seen a movie that seemed to follow quite so closely. . . .

LH: There were more alterations than you are conscious of. For example, there was a giant alteration at the end of the picture. We musn't talk about this as if it's *Hamlet* and everybody knows the plot of *Julia*. You remember what really happened was that I went to England to collect . . . to get a lady who was already dead, but who had previously told me that she had a child and the child was in Alsace; had never told me the name of where the child was, I mean with whom the child was boarding. She was, of course, too frightened to take the child with her on these very dangerous trips she was taking so she had boarded the child out. This was the, I think, wonderful scene of the movie in the Berlin restaurant, where she tells me she's had the child.

MB: Who was called Lilly.

LH: Who was called Lilly. And then I go to get the body and the truth was that I did not try to find the child. I was in a totally stunned stage and I have no reason for it except the stunness of what was happening. I was in a sort of semi-coma and I had no way of finding out anyway. I didn't know anybody to go to. Rationally I couldn't have figured out where to go to in Alsace, but even if I had known, I

think I was in too stunned a state. I returned to America with the
body, without looking for the child. The picture, on the other hand,
has me looking for the child immediately. I did not like this because it
was not the truth, and I didn't want to be that kind of heroine. And I
suffered terribly for not looking for the child and. . . .

MB: You did have word about that though, didn't you? You write
in your new *Notes to Julia* that you had word about what happened
to the child.

LH: I had gone to the funeral parlor for Julia and when told by
the funeral parlor man that the death certificate had been signed by
Dr. Smith, let us say, at such and such an address and then delivered,
he had called for it there. He, the funeral director, had called for it
there. I went to Dr. Smith at such and such an address and there was
no Dr. Smith, and I thought there was no such address of the man
who sent me the cablegram, who signed his name James Watson. He
was not listed in the London telephone book. And the funeral
director said he didn't know his name. So I literally knew nothing.
Hammett had always said when I got in my most nightmarish nights
about what happened to the child, "You are being very foolish to do
this. She would never have left the child without leaving the name
and address with trusted people in Europe. The only reason she
didn't tell you is you didn't live in Europe. She would not have left
her child without leaving the whereabouts with trusted people." And I
would say to that, "Well, where are the trusted people? They never
told me anything about the child. Certainly they would let me know."
And he would say, "I have no answer for that, but it's ridiculous to
think she would have not trusted . . . she trusted her life to these
people. She must have trusted her child's life." Well, two years ago
when I was in London, two and a half years ago, I had a telephone
call from a doctor whose name I changed in the notes, so it doesn't
matter what his name is on television either. Let us say it's McIntosh,
which it wasn't. In a quite angry tone, I had a telephone call at the
hotel. There had been an interview with me and he said that he was
the son of the doctor who had signed the death certificate. And why
had I used the correct address to harm his father; that I must know
that signing a false death certificate was a criminal act. Why had I
done such a thing? And I said, "I didn't do such a thing. I changed
your father's name and I changed the address." He said, "You did

not change the address. You did not change the address. And I have been very angry with you since the book came out." And I said, "Why don't you come and have tea with me and we'll talk it over because God knows, I didn't mean to. . . . Is your father living?" He said, "Yes, my father's living." And I said, "Did I bring your father any harm?" And he said, "I don't wish to talk about it." And I asked him for tea and we made a date for the next afternoon. He never showed up. He was also a doctor he said. About three or four days later I had another telephone call from him with no explanation about why he didn't show up. This time the tone was slightly different. It was still angry, but a different kind of angry. He said, "I'm sitting next to my father who's had a stroke, and he can't speak but he can write a little, and he's writing a message for you now. It will take him a few minutes. Have you patience?" I mean in a very unpleasant voice, and I said, "Yes, I have patience. May I come around and see your father?" He said, "No, under no circumstances." And I said, "I would like to change something I said the other day. I have cabled New York and I do realize that I did not keep a diary of those days, and it is perfectly possible. . . . I know I changed your father's name." He said, "There's no doubt of it. You changed his name." I said, "It is possible that the real address did stick in my mind and I did use it in the book. It is perfectly possible. I meant to change it, and didn't change it. And for that I'm deeply sorry. But you haven't told me if I brought him any harm by doing it." I had no answer to that. He said, "My father is now ready." The message in essence said, "I knew where Julia's baby was, as did James Watson, as did three people. We all searched for the child. The child was living in a very small town with anti-Fascist, anti-German fighters, a couple. The man was the mayor of the town. The man and his whole family were wiped out as the Germans walked through. There is no question the baby died with them. We went into it very carefully. I am sorry that all these years you didn't know it." He had read the story and realized that I didn't know it. "We should have been in touch with you. We didn't realize that you didn't know it." Well, I think I was as happy as I've been in many years, I can tell you. It's terrible to be happy at the thought of a child's death, but the relief of not being guilty was very great. And the message was very friendly. He said, "I'm sorry that I am too ill to see you and good luck and thank you."

II

MB: You wrote that you needed a teacher, a cool teacher who would not be impressed or disturbed by a strange and difficult girl. And you were to meet him, but not for another four or five years, and this was Hammett, your teacher.

LH: Yes.

MB: Was there something of the Pygmalion in your relationship with Hammett?

LH: Yes, I think so, particularly for me as a writer; not for me so much as a person. I think I said what I meant in that piece on Hammett that I did. He certainly had something to do with . . . with my development as a person, but I really meant as a writer.

MB: He really tore down some of the things you wrote, and you said the criticism hurt.

LH: Oh yes, indeed. He tore them to pieces. More important than tore them to pieces, I'm not at all sure that I would have written without Hammett because I had written and by the time I met Hammett, I had stopped writing. I had decided I was not going to be any good and that I wasn't going to be bad. It was he who teased me back into writing, annoyed me back into writing, baited me back into writing. And then watched for as long as he lived.

MB: You've written that *The Little Foxes* was the play that was the most dependent on Hammett.

LH: I'd done the ninth draft of *The Little Foxes* and I finished it and left it in a briefcase in front of his door. Went to bed at about 6 o'clock in the morning and got up about 6 o'clock at night, and he said, "Well, you're on your way. Now start all over again." I never hated anybody so much in my whole life.

MB: Well, you know, much is said in relationships between men and women who write or do some kind of creative work that it must be very difficult to take criticism, or that a relationship must be very strong to withstand criticism. Did you feel that? Or did you feel that it was such a natural part of your life?

LH: No, I felt various things. Sometimes furious. Often I hated him for what he said, but I'd quiet myself in a day or two and realize that it took bravery and great affection to chance saying such things. That he was chancing the whole relationship on the fact that he wanted me to be some good. And that I wouldn't have such courage with anybody. And he didn't think of it as courage. He just thought he was telling the truth, and that he hoped that I was good enough to fix things.

MB: Looking back, what do you think motivated him? To see you fulfill your potential, to make you. . . .

LH: He was very good to writers. I was not the only writer he helped. He was a very generous man to writers. I had lunch the other day with a woman he helped write her first book. She doesn't write very much any more, but she wrote two or three books. He was very good to writers, and in my case, there was . . . there was a great deal at stake, great deal of feeling at stake. I think he really wanted me to be some good and was very pleased and proud when he thought I was.

MB: In *Days to Come,* your character who you call Julie, says "I always wanted someone to show me the way, and I decided a long time ago there were people who had to learn from other people and I'm one of them." Is there some of you in Julie?

LH: Oh yes, indeed.

MB: And is there some of Hammett in Leo Whalen?

LH: I suppose so. I suppose there's some of Hammett in almost every character I ever wrote.

MB: Some in Kurt Müller?

LH: I suppose in every character. Somebody said . . . I think it was . . . I can't remember, I'm losing my mind. I think it was . . . Tolstoy said "everybody writes the same person over again in the same book." I suppose in everything I've written, Hammett has been somewhere, some form of him, some. . . .

MB: You know, Dashiell Hammett has become a legend and I think partly from your own memoirs. What kind of man was Dashiell Hammett? Tell us about him a little bit.

LH: I don't know that I can explain why he was extraordinary. He was a very good writer for one thing, I think. And while he was not of the very top level, he changed the face of much of American fiction, I think. He was a very important influence on American fiction, very important. He was a very remarkable looking man, which in his case, honestly had something to do with the whole thing, as it does with most people's lives, of course. He was an extraordinary tall and extraordinary thin and very distinguished looking.

MB: Very handsome, in a word.

LH: Yes, he was. I was avoiding the word handsome. I don't know why I was avoiding it, but he was very . . . he was. . . .

MB: Why do you avoid it? You've always said that intellectuals were the best-looking men you've ever known, and he was an intellectual in his way.

LH: Yes. I don't know why I avoid it. It sounds like an actor to me. You say actors are handsome. There was some self-discipline in the end. It was beyond belief. I've never seen anybody else . . . the fact that a man at that age enlists in the army and goes to the Aleutians for four years and is able to stand up to that climate and take that kind of beating and be cheerful about it and love it. He loved the Aleutians.

MB: How did you take it?

LH: Oh I spent the whole four years worried to death he was going to die of pneumonia. He had tuberculosis in the First World War. But he didn't. He came out okay. He came out looking awful, but okay.

MB: You depict him as being one of the most self-contained people I've ever read about.

LH: He is. He was. Not, mind you, in the drinking years, although they would often have long sober periods. He would often go on the wagon for six months at a time. He was almost totally self-contained.

MB: You wrote that you were a pretty good drinker yourself. How did you decide to give it up? Why did you?

LH: I didn't like it. I mean I didn't like being, and I saw it coming, and I didn't like myself. And I went to an analyst at what should have been the best time of my life, which was the week after *Little Foxes* opened, and I was blind drunk during the whole experience. And about a week later I thought, "there's something the matter with this lady. Something's very wrong with a woman with the biggest hit on Broadway, and this miserable and this drunk and I better go do something about it."

MB: Were you running away from success?

LH: I don't know what I was running away from. I suppose so. I don't think I ever. . . . I certainly wanted success. I don't think I ever, and I don't say this proudly because I think there's something very unpleasant about it. I don't think success ever gave me as much pleasure as it gave most people, and I'm very sad about that, very sad about it. It should give people pleasure.

MB: Do you think success came too early with *The Children's Hour*? Was it a letdown?

LH: No, it didn't come that early. Well, I was twenty-seven, well not late, but . . .

MB: You were a big success though for a . . .

LH: Yes.

MB: And everything that I've seen written about you said that you were a big success at a very young age, so let's call twenty-seven very young.

LH: Yes, I don't know . . . I don't know what happened to me. I mean, I was certainly drinking very heavily, but then everybody around me drank very heavily.

MB: Analysis doesn't always help drinking. In fact, it often does not.

LH: No, but it did in my case because one day the analyst said, "You will either stop drinking or not come back here on Monday morning. I can't analyze you this way. You're an alcoholic." And I said, "Oh no, I'm not an alcoholic." He said, "Yes you are. In my definition you are, and we can't . . . I can't go on this way. I'd just be taking your money and wasting my time." I thought it over over the weekend and thought, "Ok, I'll try." And I didn't have anything to drink for about six years. It wasn't bad after the first few months.

MB: That's extraordinary to be able to just say, I won't do it.

LH: No, it was hard . . . it was hard for the first . . . it was hard for a while, but then it stopped being hard.

MB: And then did you feel better without it?

LH: Well, I went back to my old drinking, which is what I do now, you know. A drink or two before dinner and some wine or something. I never wanted to be drunk again. Well, I did once. I did once actually about four or five years ago. I was up in the Vineyard and it was a . . . I had stayed up very late. It was a November, cold November night and I was by myself. And I thought, "I haven't been drunk since so many years, I think I'll just get very drunk tonight all by myself. So I got very drunk and there's a stair-landing up to my bedroom, a large stair-landing. And I got to the stair-landing and I thought, "You're never going to make the next steps, and why should you? You used to sleep anyplace you wanted, why don't you sleep on the landing?" So I fell asleep on the landing, very happily, very pleased with myself that I was young enough to just go to sleep on a stair-landing again. And I woke up with a terrible cold and the worst backache and my legs in some dreadful cramped position; went to bed for two-and-a-half days and thought, "that's the end of that. I'll never do this again. Age has descended!"

MB: You speak of Hammett still interfering with you and still dictating the rules after his death.

LH: Very often does. Very often does, and I often get very annoyed. Sometimes I break out laughing.

MB: How do you mean?

LH: Oh, I'll find myself doing something and hearing a voice behind me telling me what to do, or make fun of me, or tease me and I'll get very angry about it, and actually have conversations with it. And then I'll, of course, laugh about it.

MB: Do you sometimes measure what you do against what he would have thought about it?

LH: Sometimes. Sometimes I can't afford to. I know so well he would disapprove. Including possibly talking about him now.

MB: You've written about your life with Hammett that "It had settled into a passionate affection that was so unexpected to both of us that we were as shy and careful with each other as courting children." That's a lovely picture you draw.

LH: Yes, we had. Once the so-called affair was over . . .

MB: What do you mean, the affair was over?

LH: Well, once the so-called physicality was gone. . . . What a word! I'm just being nice for television. I don't recommend that it go between men and women. I sound as if I am recommending it. But once the worry about it and the feelings about it were beginning to disappear, usually people break up, I think. We had almost the opposite experience; in part, because he had stopped drinking. Wasn't only a question of a man and a woman who had known each other a long time, he was now no longer drinking; was totally on the wagon. It's a very hard relationship to explain, Ms. Berger, because it sounds as if, . . . when I write or when I talk about it, as if this was a totally steady relationship between a man and a woman who lived in the same house for many, many years. This is not the truth. I traveled a great deal. We almost always had different apartments.

MB: Was that for convention or because . . . ?

LH: It started out because I didn't want to shock my mother and father. Turned out my father not only wasn't shocked, but was devoted to Hammett. My mother wasn't, but my father was. But I think we both did it because we really rather liked it. This didn't stop our living in the same house together. It just meant that every once in a while he'd go to his apartment and. . . . We lived on the farm together, but once in a while if he didn't like my visitors, which was sometimes more than once in a while, he'd just go back to New York for two or three days and then come on back again. The last five years of his life we lived totally together when he was very, very ill; we lived totally in the same house.

MB: I think one of my favorite lines in literature, though, is what you said finally in that paragraph which was, "We knew we had survived for the best of all reasons, the pleasure of each other."

LH: Yes, we had great pleasure in each other. We had enormous pleasure in each other. I think more than . . . I'm no judge of other people's pleasure, but we had fun together. We had more fun than any . . . We had quiet fun. We amused each other and puzzled each other, I think, until the very end of his life.

MB: Would you say you were dependent upon him?

LH: Oh very dependent upon him. Very dependent.

MB: Do you think Hammett was dependent on you; finally, in the long run?

LH: I used to say that he wasn't and he used to say he was. I don't at, this minute, couldn't tell you whether he was or not. He was in the sick years, of course.

MB: No, I don't mean that. I mean otherwise.

LH: He used to say he was. I never saw any signs of dependency. I'm not a hundred percent sure that I understand Hammett to this day. I'm not willing to take my word for all that I saw. He was a very complicated man, and it's perfectly possible that he was very dependent upon me, but equally capable of walking out at any minute of the day and night and not returning.

MB: Is that necessarily an either/or proposition? Couldn't it be both?

LH: No, it isn't. It isn't. But I didn't know that. It certainly isn't. It's one of the things I have learned. You're wiser at your age than I was at your age.

MB: There are different kinds of dependence, and of course, what you were talking about in your dependence on Hammett was an emotional dependence, a loving dependence as opposed to an economic or financial . . .

LH: No, I was dependent, forgive me, I was . . . when I first met Hammett, it was five years before I did . . . I couldn't get a job. I had worked, but it was the Depression. . . . The Depression was ending, but I couldn't get a job. I was very dependent on him for five years. He supported me for five years, and I certainly thought nothing about that.

MB: You didn't? It was not uncomfortable?

LH: Nothing at all.

MB: Well, he was a very open person, though.

LH: Very open.

MB: He never used that dependence. . . .

LH: Oh no, never. I mean, it was never even discussed. It never was talked about. We didn't live the way most people lived. I mean, there weren't bank accounts and things. There was money on a table and I took what I needed. Later on, it was sort of a comedy of politesse that we played. Later on, as I said, when he came out of jail and the internal revenue department took away everything he ever earned. He never earned another nickel after he came out of jail. I, in turn, would put money in a safe and he would open the safe and take out what he needed. I never knew what he took or didn't take, which is almost going overboard in the polished situation of money.

MB: You know I sometimes think you still believe that he needed you less than you needed him.

LH: Yes, I think perhaps he sold me a bill of goods, and very wise of him too.

MB: Why?

LH: Well, I'm not sure it's perhaps wise to let people know how much you need them.

MB: Isn't that honest, though?

LH: Yes, it is. But it's also dangerous. They could take advantage of it all, and most of them do.

MB: Would he have?

LH: No, I think he was frightened I would.

MB: Would you have?

LH: I might've in certain ways. I might've. I wouldn't be too sure.

MB: Is this what you mean by the games men and women play with each other?

LH: Yes, in large measure. I'm not sure that. . . . I wouldn't be too sure. . . . I don't think I'd have meanly done it or taken anything away from him, but I wouldn't trust myself with too much knowledge of how people needed me.

MB: I think you're a person who sought limits. You wanted someone to limit you in some way. You were a spoiled only child.

LH: Yes, that's right. I did seek limits. That's right, I did. I did. I wanted somebody to say, "Nix, knock it off."

MB: You thought of marrying at one time and then you decided not to, and at one point you thought of marrying another man.

LH: Yes. Yes.

MB: Were you in love with Hammett and yet you thought of marrying someone else. Why was that? Was that the safer way?

LH: Well, Hammett was, as I told you before, not the . . . in his drinking days, not the easiest man to be attached to. And there certainly was a period when I believed that. I don't remember any great social discomfort. Maybe there was and I don't remember it. I'm not very conscious of people socially frowning at me, not conscious enough I think, half the time.

MB: You once told a story about when he was very sick at the end and was about to go to the hospital, and you were going with him and he seemed surprised that you were going. Tell me about the story.

LH: Yes.

MB: What happened?

LH: I find that . . . I'll tell it to you. I find it a painful story because I don't like him for it. It was the last time he went to the hospital and I, as I said in the piece that I've just written about him, I didn't want him to go and I lost my nerve. And the ambulance came for him. We lived in a house that I owned with a tiny elevator, and the stretcher was barely able to get in the elevator. So I had put on my hat and coat and watched the stretcher get in and said, "I'll meet you downstairs in front of the ambulance." And he looked up from the stretcher and said, "Oh, are you coming? How nice." And I thought, "If you were well, I'd . . . I think I'd put a knife in you. Here for all these years I hadn't moved, and it's a terrible, terrible remark you just made; insulting past belief." And I went down the stairs, almost unable to get in the ambulance. I've only lately begun to forgive him for the remark because I've begun to realize that it was very typical and very much his way of saying, "Nobody need to really do anything for me, and I won't blame you if you don't want to come to a nasty old hospital. There'll be no blame for you. Why should you come?"

MB: Did it make you think he didn't understand what you had between you?

LH: Beg pardon?

MB: Did it make you think he didn't understand what you had between you?

LH: No. Just made me angry. Just made me terribly, terribly angry. It still does as you can probably hear in my voice a little bit. But the pride in it is so . . . I have a great respect for pride, but the pride in it there is overbearing and unpleasant, I think.

MB: You're pretty proud yourself.

LH: Yes, I am. And I can also be overbearing and unpleasant.

MB: But you say you laugh sometimes when you are too insistent on doing things by yourself.

LH: Yes. Yes. Oh yes, I understand why he did it because of my own nature. That doesn't make it any pleasanter.

MB: You said Hammett was generous with writers and, of course, with you. His career as a writer was ending as yours began. Did that cause discomfort in your relationship?

LH: No. No. Because I didn't know it was ending in the first place, and neither did he. And then there was never any question that his career was none of my business. He made it quite clear that it was none of my business; was never anybody's business. He certainly never knew it was at an end. As a matter of fact, the last days of his life, an unfinished novel was on his bed. Dash had a mistaken belief that there was plenty of time for everything, and of course, there wasn't.

III

LH: Well, I have something to tell you, Ms. Berger, that's going to sound awful because . . . it's going to sound so mixed up. I'm pleased with what I did in front of the House Un-American Committee because it had good results and it led other people to take the same position, which was the first time anybody'd ever taken it. I am pleased with it, but I'm very regretful that I didn't take another one. I know that sounds crazy, because I know I've come out a kind of heroine for the position I did take. So it sounds as if the heroine wants to be even more of a heroine, which isn't what I mean. I have long wished. . . . I wished, even before I wrote that letter and went into that Committee hearing, that I really wanted to go in and say, "To hell with all of you. You're a rotten, stinking lot of unjust men, ragging me and everybody like me simply to get your names in the papers. You know full well I've done no harm, and you know full well nobody you've had in here's done any harm. You're a disgrace to your country and I won't stay in the room with you," and walked out. This is what I really would've liked to have done, and gone to jail for it. But I didn't have the nerve to do it. And there's no sense regretting it because I simply didn't have the nerve to do it. I thought I was going to jail anyway, but. . . . And everybody else said I was going to jail too. Hammett certainly did. He used to spend his entire time trying to persuade me not to write that letter that I wrote. He knew I was terrified of rats, as everybody born in New Orleans, Louisiana, was in my day, but I was . . . I have a particular horror of rats. So he used to describe to me rats in jail. Every single night of his life I got a little talk about rats in jail and how I was going. . . . He also knows that I have a neurotic . . . had a neurotic . . . have it to this minute, a neurotic horror of being pushed or shoved in a crowd or in any other place. So he used to describe to me how I was going to be shoved in jail and how I was going to turn on somebody and that night I was going to be dead. I'd get this lecture every night.

MB: Did you feel that you wanted to take that stand at the time, or do you feel it now that you wish you had taken that stand?

LH: It crossed my mind. Let me say this as honestly as I can. It crossed my mind that that's what I wanted to do. It never crossed my mind seriously that that's what I was going to do because I was already scared enough of what I did. That's to say it as truthfully as I can say it.

MB: The young people, students, have embraced *Scoundrel Time*. They have been your great readers, and yet they don't seem to know very much about the so-called McCarthy years. What's your view of that era? How do you see those years? How do you remember them?

LH: Well, I'm not sure that I'm the best judge. I was so involved, and in many ways punished, and living with a man who was so punished that. . . . Well, I'm begging the question now because I think I would have seen them, whether I was punished or not, the same way. They were all kinds of things. They were comedy. They were black comedy; they were really black comedy. Have you ever read any of the testimonies or the questions or the testimonies of witnesses? One is torn between laughter and tears. It's so truly comic. People were confessing to sins they'd never done; making up lies of meetings they'd been in when they'd been in no such meeting; asking God and the Committee's pardon for nothing but just going into a room and listening to some rather dull talk. They were. . . . That was one of the effects. And that, to me, was the saddest and most disgusting, as well as most comic. The effect was of a certain section of the country going crazy.

MB: Which section?

LH: Washington, the men involved in the committees. The committees that were involved were the HUAC and the Senate Internal Security Committee, which was the McCarthy committee. For their own reasons, their reasons being they could get their names in the papers every day by using more famous people than they were, and they were playing on, of course, the Cold War, the fear of our ex-ally, Russia, and they were led by, and I think in many ways paid for by, in some cases paid for by, not in many ways, what was known as the China Lobby. The China Lobby was a group of men who were out to restore Chiang Kai-shek.

MB: Well, this was an era, just to reconstruct it a little bit, that in 1945 when the war ended, we read at least, that the United States started demobilizing, cut down its troops, cut its defense budget . . .

LH: We're forgetting something. Forgive me for interrupting you here. We didn't so voluntarily demobilize as a demobilization was demanded, an absolute demand of the American people.

MB: And you say the Russians were devastated, as they were, and some kind of psychosis grew in this country when the Russians, in their own drive for some kind of self-protection, created a belt around the Soviet Union . . .

LH: Absolutely.

MB: The fall of Czechoslovakia was one.

LH: Absolutely.

MB: And . . .

LH: And their taking Poland and not being willing to give it up, and Finland, of course. We were very nervous characters, with certainly some justice, without question. That we were now facing a world we had never known before and had not expected. Whether some of that bargain had been made at Yalta, I suppose none of us will never know, but we were facing a new world and we had some of these men, the serious ones among them had some reason for fear of where the Soviet Union, once it recovered, would go. But these particular people we're talking about were not these people. They were on a much lower level.

MB: They were not serious people?

LH: No, they were not only not serious people, they were . . . It's as if one talked about, say a good college teacher and then one talked about one in kindergarten. These people were mostly un-known men, at this point in their lives. Nixon was a fairly unknown man. McCarthy was a very unknown man. McCarran, who was among the worst, was not unknown, but was not brilliantly known. They were men cashing in in a quite scandalous way on perhaps normal and expected fears. I'm not for a minute saying that we didn't have a right to be frightened of the imperialism of the Soviet Union, but we didn't. . . . It certainly didn't solve anything to bring a movie actor before a committee to express it. The committee wished to hear drama and these people supplied the drama. And the drama was full of lies. So they made liars out of rather simple-minded people; but simple-minded people trained in drama. And simple-minded people who were very, very frightened people.

MB: Actually, a third of the people who went before the committee at that time named names and the rest didn't. Now I don't know enough of the history to know if you were the first.

LH: Not to name names?

MB: Yes.

LH: Oh no, no, no. A great many people didn't name names. Oh no, no, no, that wasn't my stand at all.

MB: No, I understand that. I thought it was part of your stand and that's one of the attacks on you, that you represent yourself in the book as standing alone when . . .

LH: Oh no, no, no. Not . . . I don't think that's. . . .

MB: I'm saying that's one of the attacks. That's not a close reading of the book that shows that.

LH: You see, I was rather at the bottom of the barrel. I wasn't called until 1952. They'd been at this game for a long time, and many people didn't name names. The famous Hollywood Ten didn't.

MB: Oh, but they went to jail, and critics say that at the time you were before the committee, and you call yourself the bottom of the barrel, there really was no danger of your going to prison, but you say there was.

LH: That, I think Mr. Rauh and Abe Fortas who thought up the position would tell you, is not the truth. I was legal. . . . only on the grounds, it has nothing to do with heroics or not heroics. It has to do with legalities, which are never heroic one way or the other. The only difference in my position from other people's positions was that I tried not . . . I did finally take the Fifth Amendment. I tried not to take the Fifth Amendment. What I said was, "I will talk about myself freely. I will not give you . . . mention anybody else's name under any circumstances." That is a violation of the Fifth Amendment, and thus you are legally open to any contempt charge that can be brought. And this is what they were very frightened of.

MB: You were the first to do that. To say, "I will speak of myself . . .

LH: And it was actually not my idea. It was the idea of the very brilliant Abe Fortas, and was carried out, not only with the able . . . but with the thoughtfulness of the very famous Joseph Rauh. But

they were very worried I was going to get very nervous about my
going to jail on it. They had no legal grounds to stand on. There were
no heroics about it one way or the other. The heroics have been
thought up by people who don't like me.

MB: Why do you think they did not send you to jail?

LH: I think it was a technicality. At least we thought so that day.
The counselor, whose name was Tavenner, made a mistake. It was
an interesting day. I had written a letter two days before. The
committee had received it and had replied that they would not allow
the position. Thus, Mr. Rauh very brilliantly had the letters mimeographed, I guess in those days, or Xeroxed, I don't think
Xerox . . .

MB: Mimeographed.

LH: Mimeographed. And carried a whole stack of them with him.
I didn't know why he did it. They had not been very willing to
advertise my appearance, the committee; so the room was almost
empty except for six or seven sort of middle-aged southern ladies in
the background, who were obviously very anti-me. Then suddenly
the room began to fill. I have no idea why, to this day. And suddenly
the press boxes . . . the press box began to fill. I haven't any idea
how. Maybe Rauh did it; I don't know. So they, having refused to
accept the letter, there was nothing for me to do except to take the
Fifth Amendment. There was no place for me to go. Once in a while
I slipped on the Fifth Amendment, and made Rauh very nervous
because it, for the moment, made me so angry that I was violating it
once. I violated it once and he got very upset with me for doing it.
Then Mr. Tavenner, the counsel for the committee said, "I would
now like to read a letter that Miss Hellman has written the committee." And he read my offer out loud. Somebody in the press box,
God bless his soul, I've written all this, said, "Thank God, somebody's finally done it." At this point, Joe Rauh sprang up and
distributed all his copies, and Mr. Tavenner said, "Sit down, Mr.
Rauh. Sit down immediately." And Mr. committee-man, whoever it
was, I've forgotten the head of the committee at that point, said, "You
go on like this and we'll put you out of the room in a few minutes."
And Rauh said very pleasantly, "I don't think you can do that. You
see Mr. Tavenner read the letter, and thus I have a right to hand it
out. You cannot deny me that right. He's read it into it. He's read it

into the record. The record stands. I have a right to the record, these
gentlemen have a right to the letter." By this time I think they were
deeply nervous. They had made a legal mistake and whoever in the
press box had said it had swung the room, there was no question, in
my favor. The hearing was stopped within three minutes of the
handing out of the letter. And then something happened like I do not
know . . . legally know enough, nor do I remember well enough . . .
Tavenner . . . somebody. . . . One of the committee members said
something and Joe Rauh said to his assistant, "You get Lillian out of
here as fast as you can get out of the building. They cannot indict her
this time. There's no way any longer for them to indict her. Just run
out of the building now. Don't stop and talk to anybody. Don't let
anybody question her. Just go over to the Mayflower Hotel and sit in
the bar and wait for me." The assistant . . . I wasn't that old, but he
was very young, took me by the hand and we ran from the building
at top speed; must have looked like total fools running down about
four blocks to the Mayflower bar. Some legality happened. There was
no question of heroics. There was a question of legalities.

   MB: You know, I'm reminded that in *Scoundrel Time* you say
that, "what started in the McCarthy years ended up with Watergate."
And I think of your train of thought, I believe, going through
McCarthy, the wiping out of the China experts in the State Department, which was in part responsible for our going into Vietnam; the
climate that that created which led to Watergate. Is that the way you
saw it?

   LH: The way I saw Watergate?

   MB: Yes.

   LH: Oh absolutely. I think what happened, I don't wish to analyze
Mr. Nixon because I don't know enough to analyze him, but Mr.
Nixon came into prominence in a period of total amorality where you
said anything that furthered your career. He said it about Helen
Gahagan Douglas. He said it about anybody that came, Jerry
Voorhis, anybody that came into his . . . who fought him, disagreed
with him in any form. I don't think that changes in men. He learned
that it paid off quite well. It didn't pay off very well for McCarthy
because McCarthy was a drunk and besotted and a mess and was
going much too far. But if you kept your head, not unlike many other
people, and you don't see villainy as villainy, and I genuinely believe

Nixon doesn't see villainy as villainy, that there are people without any morals, who see only their part in this world and therefore almost can't be blamed since it's been left out of them. Whatever you do is ok because it benefits you; it doesn't matter much what it is. The pious words come out because you know the pious words are good salesmanship. You can't say, "I'm a villain." You have to say . . . because you don't think of yourself as one for one thing . . . and you can't say, "I've just decided to lie" at four o'clock in the afternoon, told a total untruth. So you say that total untruth is absolutely necessary for the country, and I think you genuinely believe it is.

MB: Do you think these are people in which a part has been left out?

LH: From my viewpoint a part has been left out. But they've always been, and they always will be, and they've been among the most successful people in the world always, I suppose. It must be quite comfortable to go through the world believing that you can do anything because you wish to do it.

MB: Well, I don't think you'd think that Mr. Nixon thinks he's one of the most successful people in the world these days.

LH: Well, he was for a long time. This was one of those accidents. One isn't saying they're always very bright, which is quite different. Sometimes they're dazzlingly brilliant, but nobody's saying Mr. Nixon's very bright. And there's a point at which. . . . There's often a point, thank God, for the safety of the rest of us, in which such people grow too confident. Thank God, for the safety of the rest of us.

MB: Are you frightened of another McCarthy-type era growing out of, perhaps inflation and the inability to take hold of the economy and the need for perhaps a leader?

LH: I don't think there could ever be another McCarthy time. There could be a worse time. I don't think McCarthy could be duplicated. It's too monumentally ridiculous now. One forgets that McCarthy could have only sprung out of a certain war hysteria, and we're not in a war hysteria. I think something worse could happen, and I think Nixon was on the verge of. . . . This is what so scared me in the whole Nixon era. I helped to form a committee called the Committee for Public Justice three years before Watergate, just based on that fear that we were headed for much worse than McCarthyism.

MB: How do you define that: much worse than McCarthyism? What is the. . . .

LH: Well, McCarthyism was bound, if you could live it out, God knows that doesn't excuse it from the harm it brought many lives and the ruination it made for many people, for thousands and thousands of people, but it was bound in the end to fail because it was too ridiculous and he was desperate to carry it too far. And nothing like that, I think, can last too long in America. I mean, in the end we have got some sense. But something worse could happen based on a seeming sense and seeming rationality and seeming need, which I think is exactly what a Nixon was doing.

MB: But that would, in the last analysis, deprive people of liberty?

LH: Yes. Yes. In a much more quiet and simple way since very few of us any longer pay any attention to the small laws that are passed, or even the larger ones. We can be deprived of a great deal without knowing it; without realizing it; waking up to it.

MB: You once said that America is almost dying to see a hero rise up. Are there any heroes left? When you say we yearn for one now, we're almost dying to see a hero rise up, do you mean by that a leader first of all?

LH: No, I don't really believe in the word leader. I resent the word leader. It comes, in my mind, too close to Hitler or Stalin or . . .

MB: Well, how about in the sense of Churchill or Roosevelt, leader?

LH: Well, I still don't like it. God knows they both were. But it's too undemocratic a concept for my taste, I think. It has overtones of dictatorship and dependence on one man and to one personality. I'm not crazy about such concepts.

MB: Well then, hero. You said we're dying for . . .

LH: Hero is something else again, I think. Hero is something else again.

IV

MB: You said that during the McCarthy years you learned what you could do without. What were those things you could do without? Obviously you had to give up the farm which was a tragedy in your life.

LH: Money.

MB: You could live without money?

LH: I did live without money.

MB: You even went to work in Macy's didn't you?

LH: Yes.

MB: That must have been an extraordinary time for you. How did you feel about going to work in Macy's?

LH: I didn't mind it. I was very pleased. I didn't do it under my own name.

MB: I understand that.

LH: I was very pleased. I only did it a half day. I was very pleased to have any kind of job. I didn't like the whole period, mind you. I hated coming down from having earned a lot of money to earning almost nothing. But I also found that one could manage if one had to manage. Well, you know it's silly for me to sit here and say this now because it always is crazy for survivors to talk about surviving. There's something almost callous about it. The people who didn't survive don't feel this way about it.

MB: You have strong feelings about not talking about things that were done right, about surviving; or when Hammett gave money he never talked about it. You said a lot of people would give money, but other people would talk about it.

LH: Yes. Yes, I do have. I do have because there seems to me something, well in this particular case, it's fine for me now to smile at that period. I survived it and came out very well. There's something callous about looking back upon it with amusement and pride because many other people didn't. I was . . . .

MB: You're a survivor.

LH: Maybe. Maybe chance did a great deal of it.

MB: You said Hammett was a survivor. You wrote that in " 'Turtle.' "

LH: Yes, I think he was. And I like survivors, but I'm not a hundred percent sure that, in my case, there weren't many other things at play.

MB: For example.

LH: Well I was, for example, in good health. I wasn't, at the time the McCarthy period came, I wasn't that old. I wasn't that old, but I wasn't that young. If it had come now, I'd be in hideous trouble. And I wouldn't survive.

MB: Those years should've been at the time that you discovered you were drinking too much. You've also written of what you called the celibate years so that what you said, "the years that are good for many women were not good for me. I didn't know that I wanted anybody; didn't even think about it much, but there suddenly was the wrong man of course, as could be expected, as usual." Do you want to talk about that?

LH: Well, they were in the post-McCarthy years.

MB: And you were living with Hammett?

LH: No, we weren't technically living together. Hammett was living in a cottage in Katonah and we'd had to give up the farm. I was living in New York. We saw each other two and three times a week, but he didn't want to live in New York and I didn't want to live in Katonah in a small, tiny cottage. I don't know. I made some kind of superstitious bargain that Hammett was getting ill, and we were getting to have less and less money, and I made some kind of idiot bargain that I would lead a very pure life if we were allowed to survive and had enought to eat and got through it. Doesn't sound like a grown woman, does it? And it wasn't a grown woman either.

MB: That sounds extraordinary.

LH: Sounds pretty silly.

MB: No, it sounds extraordinary. And you did survive. And you did have enough to eat.

LH: Yes, but I don't think we did it out of my purity.

MB: It was very hard for you to leave that farm and yet, in the story you tell about it, it was harder for Hammett.

LH: In many ways I think it was. In many ways I think it was.

MB: Tell me the story of the day you saw the deer.

LH: That's a hard story to tell because it's so sort of weird and crazy. This was a giant place, you know, with all kinds of machinery and boats; three boats and farm equipment and animals. All of it had been sold and moving vans had been in and out and people had been there to collect what they'd bought. There were deer on the property. There always had been deer on the property, and once about ten years before, we had seen a deer in the rock garden which was immediately outside the house. But we'd never seen another deer close to the house. They were always in the woods, way in the woods. And you had to hunt for a long, long time before you found them. Three days before we moved, I had a work room with a long window along one wall. And I came down the steps carrying something and Hammett put up his finger to his mouth and said silently, "Come here and bend over. Don't be seen in the window." Well I came to the window all bent over, and then slowly straightened up. And there on the lawn were about ten or twelve deer, on the lawn right outside the room. Not right outside the room; maybe twenty-five feet away. And coming up the lake path into the lawn were about twenty-five more deer, large and small and medium. And as they came up, the first deer would move up to the rock garden and begin biting the bushes, nibbling on things, and we both stood there absolutely transfixed from about four on an April afternoon until it got dark. We must have seen at least; they kept coming and coming and coming. We must have seen at least a hundred, hundred and twenty-five deer. And they would come and go nibbling at trees and get tired of that and go down, disappear, and then some others would appear after fifteen, twenty minutes. It was the most mysterious thing I've ever known because it couldn't have been that they believed the place was empty. The place had been full of noise; full of cars and trucks and trucking machinery and pulling animals in the morning of that day. It was the most mysterious and beautiful thing I've ever seen in my whole life. And neither one of us moved for fear of scaring them until it got dark, which was perhaps six-thirty, quarter-to-seven. And I don't know where they were then. We couldn't see out any more. I don't know whether they . . . there was none there the next morning and none to be seen thereafter. It was as if a farewell party was being given. Certainly a great farewell gift was given.

MB: I was thinking that it was like a pageant. . . .

LH: You're being very nice to me. I had to let go of the farm.

MB: You did have to let go.

LH: The House Un-American Activities Committee had called me and I saw the handwriting on the wall. There was no way out. I knew my income would drop.

MB: And you sold it before you testified?

LH: I sold it one month before I testified.

MB: And you had the possibility of selling it to someone who would subdivide it and build a lot of houses, and you decided not to.

LH: Well, I didn't decide not to. I suppose one of the things that always makes me rather proud and very angry with Hammett is that the man who was going to do that guaranteed me half of his profits and guaranteed me that nothing would be sold in less than ten acres, which is not bad subdividing. And when I told Hammett (the man was my lawyer), and when I told Hammett that's what I was going to do . . . that's what we were going to do, he said, "No, no, no. Let everybody else spoil the land. Let's you and I leave it alone. Let somebody else do it. I don't want to spoil this land."

MB: So you sold it to someone for, how much money?

LH: Oh, I sold it for $67,000, for nothing. I sold it for nothing.

MB: A hundred and thirty acres for $67,000.

LH: Hundred forty acres.

MB: Hundred forty acres for $67,000. Did those people sell it and subdivide it?

LH: They subdivided part of it. It's only, oddly enough, been recently subdivided. I had a call from a real estate agent about it two months ago saying it was being subdivided.

MB: Do you have any idea what that land is worth?

LH: About $25,000 an acre now. Thirty-thousand dollars an acre.

MB: One of the things that I think women forget is that there is a price to be paid for the extraordinary freedom that a woman like you has. Do you feel you've paid a price?

LH: Yes. Yes, I've paid a price.

MB: What price?

LH: Well, I think I said it earlier, that there would have been safer, pleasanter ways to go. And as you get older, of course, perhaps you think . . . I don't think much about them really. Things turned out the way they did. Some prices, but I have no regrets for that price. Prices are to be paid for everything. There's no way to live without paying the price, and the price is. . . . It would be very hard for me to regret my life. It's turned out . . . I was very lucky.

MB: I think people who do well and work hard often say they're lucky, but it's a little more than luck.

LH: Oh yes, it's a great deal more than luck. I don't mean to underplay it. I worked very hard. I don't mean to say it's lucky in the sense of throwing dice.

MB: Was not having children a price you paid?

LH: Yes, it was certainly one of them. I myself should have said it. I hesitate always to say it because it sounds, I don't know. I back away from saying it. Yes, of course it was a price I paid. However, I could have had the children. Hammett wanted them, as indeed you know I was married once, and my husband wanted them. It was my choice.

MB: I didn't know that Hammett wanted them.

LH: Yes, he wanted them too.

MB: That must have been very difficult not to at a time . . .

LH: Well he wanted to because I was pregnant. I'm very fond of children and I would have had a nice time with children. That I certainly regret. But now they'd probably be grown up and unpleasant.

MB: You like them when they're children? But that comes as a surprise to me in that Hammett seemed, the way you described him, sometimes given to great silences, sometimes moody. One has some difficulty thinking of him as a father, although probably a good one.

LH: He has two children. He has two daughters.

MB: And was he close with them?

LH: Well, he left their mother when they were both, when one was nine and one was three; so he wasn't that close to them. But he certainly was close to them and devoted to them. He liked them very much, particularly one of them. No, he was very fond of children.

MB: You tell a wonderful story of his new bow and arrow and taking a child out into the woods. Was that near the end of the time that you were on the farm?

LH: Yes, within about two years. The child is now a rather well-known botanist; teaches at the University of New Mexico.

MB: What did he say then? "Things should go to the people who want them most."

LH: I said, to sum it up, not to bore you. Westchester County had just passed a quite good law saying you couldn't shoot deer any longer with a shotgun or rifle. You could shoot them with a bow and arrow, which meant nobody could shoot them because nobody knew how to shoot a bow and arrow. But Hammett went down and bought a very expensive bow and arrow and taught himself to shoot with bow and arrow. Bought me one too and tried very hard to teach me, but I never could learn.

MB: Yes, you once shot a tree behind you?

LH: I once shot a tree behind me. He did actually bring in two or three deer with bow and arrow which is extraordinary because it's very hard to do. He was in love with this bow and arrow. It cost an absolute fortune. It was very delicately done, specially made. And the child belonged to a quite well-known writer at the time called Hamilton Basso. Does that name mean anything to you? Quite good novelist. And they came to visit us one Sunday and the boy was fascinated with Hammett's bow and arrow, and he took him out to show him how it worked. And as they left, they all got in the car and Hammett said, "Go around and talk to them for a minute. Hold them for a minute." And I didn't know what he was doing, so I went around and talked to them for a minute, and I saw Hammett open the luggage rack and put in his bow and arrow. And I was furious with him. As the car drove off I said, "How could you do that. That bow and arrow cost you a fortune. You love that bow and arrow." And he said, "The child loves it more. Things belong to people who love them more."

MB: Have you ever found a place in your life that was like the fig tree? Where you felt that much at home and that wanted you that much?

LH: No, but I think you have to be a child to do that. I think you have to be a child to find that. You have to live in a fantasy world.

MB: You said, "It was solid and comfortable, and I convinced myself that it wanted me and missed me when I was absent." Did you not feel that way about your farm in Pleasantville?

LH: Oh, I loved the farm, but I do think that you have to be a child to think that a place misses you and needs you. I very much like the house I live in in Martha's Vineyard; very, very much like it. And I miss it, but I don't think I fantasy any longer that it misses me.

MB: You seem to have a way of hearing voices. I happen to have been reading *The Lark* last night, your adaptation of the play of Joan of Arc, and you speak now of talking to Nursie sometimes. Is Nursie still around? Tell me about Nursie.

LH: Well, Nursie, I'm ashamed to tell anybody this. . . . I wrote it so I might as well. . . . It makes me sound so nutty. All my life I've divided myself into two and sometimes three parts. And they talk. They put me in my place or they have little dialogues, and one part for many years has been called Nursie. When I get very, very upset, Nursie says things like, "Now dear, quiet yourself," or "Why don't you take a nice nap or a hot bath," or "Why don't you go play tennis for a little while and forget things. You're taking everything too seriously. I'd put down that scotch and soda if I were you." And I say, "Please go to your room."

MB: You say to Nursie?

LH: I say to Nursie. I said that when I wrote about Nursie recently that Peter [Feibleman] was staying with me in the Vineyard during *Pentimento,* and I was evidently so wildly cutting up that he tells me . . . his room was down the hall, and I always keep my door open because my workroom is around an "L." He, about once a week, would think I had a visitor whom I didn't want, and would always keep his door closed and never come out for fear of seeing the visitor and getting into some kind of intruding upon us. But it wasn't any visitor. It was Nursie because I was having great, great trouble with *Pentimento.* And I was growing very angry with Nursie.

MB: Do you make the words that Nursie says? In other words, when [Feibleman] was down the hall, could he hear both you and Nursie?

LH: No, I don't. Nursie doesn't speak out loud. See, that's the trouble. Even I'm not that crazy. It's bad enough I talk out loud to Nursie. And Nursie has been, in the last ten years, joined by a character called Madam. Madam is even worse than Nursie because she doesn't often appear.

MB: But she's a recent arrival?

LH: In the last ten years she's been around.

MB: And what does Madam do?

LH: Madam says things like, "Oh you two, please don't be so noisy. Oh you two have been doing this for so many years. Why don't you get used to each other. There are two sides to everybody. Don't you understand that? Don't you?" And then I say very loudly, which is what Peter was hearing, "Both of you had better go to your rooms and stay there. Your life depends upon me, kids. Get the hell out of here!" at the top of my voice. When I told him this, he said, "I think I'm staying with a crazy lady." And I don't blame him.

MB: Is Nursie Sophronia?

LH: No. No, no. Sophronia never talked that way. Sophronia was very sharp. Nursie is rather upper-class delicate. She rather teaches at a very good girls' school.

MB: Tell me about Sophronia. What do you remember most about her?

LH: Oh, I remember . . . I remember so much you'd be here forever.

MB: Sophronia was your nurse from the very beginning?

LH: Yes, and was a very, very . . . I have a lovely picture of Sophronia. I'm sure you've seen it in that book. A very handsome colored woman, whom I loved absolutely, devotedly all her life. She lived until I was about somewhere in my thirties, I suppose. My father used to say, "If we'd been able to afford Sophronia until you were sixteen or eighteen, everything would have been different. We'd have all been happy and you'd have been a different child. The worse thing that ever happened to us was we couldn't afford Sophronia any more." Sophronia was an absolute controller. I was desperately in love with her.

MB: Were you an uncontrolled child and an uncontrolled woman?

LH: Fairly uncontrolled, yes. Uncontrollable. I wasn't uncontrolled at all. I was uncontrollable.

MB: Were you looking for limits, and did Hammett provide them?

LH: I don't think I was. I think that was rather too mild a way of putting it. I told you yesterday that after *Little Foxes* and the very heavy drinking that I realized that something had to be done about me, that I wanted . . . that I was getting totally out of hand for myself and certainly Hammett couldn't have provided that. That would have been, in the first place, they were his drinking days and he had no desire to control anybody. He was much too busy himself. No, I don't think Hammett had anything to do with my desire to be controlled. As a matter of fact, I think he rather frowned on it.

MB: You talk in your new notes to the new edition of your books about aging, about anger giving way to age. Do you think often about aging? You've said you never were tired, or you never knew what the word tired was. Do you get tired now?

LH: Oh yes. What I think I said was I never knew what it was up until about seven, eight years ago. I sure know what it is now. Yea, sorry.

MB: But you try again tomorrow?

LH: Well, I try not to be tired, but I'm afraid it's not up to me any longer.

MB: You've written that emotions are not recoverable and that years blank out even the passions. In a way, do you think passion is like pain? If you've had a very bad pain, you can never relive it. Do you think the price we pay for that is we can't relive the passions either?

LH: I don't think anything in the world goes faster than, say sexual passion. Any memory goes faster, but that may just be me. I mean if it's just that, and nothing else.

MB: If there were one passion that you could relive, either a political passion or an emotional one, do you think you could choose one?

LH: No, because I don't think it comes in ones. I think it comes in a whole mesh, in a whole great football of mesh nets and hooks and eyes and scissors and . . .

MB: It's the fabric of existence.

LH: Yes. It's so much. It's not one event. One thinks of adventure that way. You know, I can think of adventures I'd like to have again; adventures in the sense of places as a rule, or moments of enormous pleasure in seeing something or listening to somebody. That I can relive, but no, I couldn't do that, no. Could you?

MB: There's some I'd like to.

LH: Oh yes. Like is one thing. . . .

V

LH: I'm not quite sure what strength is unless it's the ability to think for oneself, which is what I suspect it is—that's the only thing it is; to take nobody's word and think for yourself.

MB: You've pretty much done that?

LH: I wish I'd done it more, and I mean that. I don't mean to turn away, if you meant it as a compliment, I don't mean to turn it away. I'm grateful for it, but I wish I had done it more.

MB: Give me an example.

LH: Well, it's what I meant by wasting time. I don't think I've done enough thinking . I would like, very much, at my age to think that I had thought a good deal about . . . for myself. I don't mean about life, necessarily, but about books or writing or the way you live, or what I believed in or didn't believe in or . . .

MB: Haven't you thought, excuse me, haven't you thought about all of those things through the characters you've written about?

LH: Yes, I've thought about all of them. They're all, you know, slogans. But I don't think I've thought, in some cases I've tried hard to think with some kind of steadiness, steadfastness, but I think my mind has wandered from them a good deal.

MB: In some of the things you've written, you have people who have sought things perhaps all their lives as Julian did in *Toys in the Attic*, and once they get it, it doesn't work for them. Have there been things in your life that you wanted all your life and when you've finally gotten them thought, "That's not for me?"

LH: Trying to think. I suppose some people, yes. I suppose some people I wanted to know very well and then when I did, I thought, "What's that all been about? Something must have been the matter with me."

MB: Men?

LH: Sometimes men, sometimes women. Mostly men, I guess. Yes, mostly men. Sometimes things, but that I think is age. I sometimes look around the apartment and think, "Well, it was nice to have had that, but what made me buy it? I don't really care whether it's here or not. I'm glad I bought it. I still like it." It's almost as if somebody else had bought it; had gone to the trouble of it.

MB: You said that during the McCarthy years you got rid of things you really didn't need.

LH: Yes. I had been so convinced that. . . . Well, I had loved farming and I still love farming. That loss I regret the rest of my life. I could never farm again. I have a true feeling for farming I think. But I didn't need so much land, and I didn't need to live so well, and I didn't need so many things, so many clothes, so much food, so much of everything.

MB: Do you think in retrospect that your life as a dramatist would have been any easier had you been a man, not a woman?

LH: No.

MB: Was it easier because you were a woman?

LH: No.

MB: Neither.

LH: No, I don't think so. It might've had certain minutes where it would have been easier to have been a man and where I wouldn't have had to . . . .so the personal things didn't become quite so personal, if you know what I'm awkwardly trying to say. There might have been that if I'd been a man, but I don't think it would've made much difference.

MB: Another question that's been raised is whether your books, coming out at a time of a great movement for women's liberation, have been lucky in their timing.

LH: I think they have been.

MB: And have you found yourself being considered as a standard bearer for causes that you really having nothing to do with at all because you happen to be a woman and . . . ?

LH: Yes. Yes, I have found that and been amazed by it. But then I have to say that in a sense, I understand it because I'm sure that I also had such people when I was young. I don't remember who they were, but I'm sure I also had such people too who I admired because they had done certain things that I was about to do, or wanted to do. Sometimes my admiration was misplaced. Sometimes it wasn't. I am all for women's liberation. I am not, as I said before, not for the off-shoots of women's liberation. I mean, I believe it must begin with economic liberation. There must be equal pay for equal work.

MB: Do you think the women's liberation has gotten bogged down in the wrong issues?

LH: Very often, I think. I think the main issue must be economic.

MB: I think you once said the argument comes down to who's going to take out the garbage, and you don't mind taking out the garbage if you know you can walk . . .

LH: No, I think that's going to be what it is, though. If that's going to be what it is or what veil you wear or the way you wear a brassiere, or whether you wear one or don't wear one, then as far as I'm concerned it can stop there and set itself now back to equal pay, jobs for every woman who has to work . . . some kind of job for every woman who has to support children.

MB: You describe without any fuss an abortion you had done in your twenties. What do you make of the anti-abortion movement today, the right-to-lifers in this country?

LH: Well, legal abortion, of course, in my mind is a very necessary and very properly advanced movement for people who either cannot, which is, I think usually the case, or even if they do not want, which is almost the same case since the child would not be loved or cherished if it's not wanted or taken proper care of, as one sees by child abuse . . . constant child abuse, certainly from people who had never wanted the child. It's a very necessary, civilized, proper act. The other is very irreligious to me. I have just the opposite theory. The anti-abortion law is a very irreligious law to me. It's forcing on people that which they cannot properly cherish and understand.

MB: Are you religious in any way?

LH: No.

MB: Do you believe in God? You mention him occasionally.

LH: I don't know. I'm told I have a religious nature.

MB: Well, you went to many churches as a child.

LH: I went to many churches as a child. I'm told by many people that I have a religious nature, but what God is I don't know.

MB: You said that the so-called return to religion is dangerous, the Hari Krishna kind of sects, the . . .

LH: Very dangerous, I think.

MB: You called it self-serving personal . . .

LH: I don't know whether it's a return to religion as a return to cultism, and that's put on the basis of a religion. And religion is used in it, which is, I think, extremely dangerous. We've become a cultist country.

MB: Since you said that, of course, we've had the massacre in Guyana.

LH: Yes. Yes. Very sad to see the ignorant played upon, and very understandable and miserable, particularly sad to see it in a place like

Los Angeles where it happens every Sunday. And it's all over the
television and all over the city.

MB: You say people say you have a religious nature, but you
don't think you do?

LH: Yes, I think I do somewhere. Yes, I do. But I don't know what
religion it is, and I never thought how to define it.

MB: You use the word puritan about yourself a number of times
in your books. In what way are you a puritan lady?

LH: I don't know because so many people have said it. I don't
know what they mean. I've always tried to get an explanation. I don't
know, and I suppose I'm scared to get an explanation because it
sounds so unattractive, but I suppose I am because so many people
have said it.

MB: Could it be your sense of right and wrong which was
important between you and Hammett, for example?

LH: I suppose so. And yet he was no puritan. I don't know why
so many people have said it. If it's true, it's true. There's nothing I can
do about it. I don't even know what it means. I suppose it means
intolerant, really. And I suppose it also has nicer things.

MB: You said you don't like the word tolerance.

LH: I don't like it when it's used with the word forgive. I like it
when it's used in other contexts. I like the idea of say, tolerance of
naughty children or tolerance of bad living conditions. When it's used
that way, I like it. I don't like it when it's used along with forgiveness.
Since I think forgiveness is a very arrogant word.

MB: In a recent interview you said, "We live in a time of junky
words, junky ideas." What are those?

LH: Oh, I think you and I have been talking about them. They're
kind of a cult world, the me world.

MB: How we must all find love, we all need love.

LH: Yes.

MB: Do you think people don't know how to give love very well
any more, these young people? They're looking for it, but don't
know what it is?

LH: I suppose they know as much about giving it as anybody ever
knew about giving except I don't think people talked so much about
it. I'm not sure love can be analyzed, and it seems to me the minute

you begin the analysis you're in trouble. There are so many kinds of love. There're so many ways of loving; whose ways, your way, your mother's way, your father's way, so whose way? But I really meant all the cultism, which I think comes from the over self-examination. We're all in America brought up, God knows I was and I'm sure you were and almost all other Americans were, particularly middle-class Americans, in the great belief that we were all going to be very, very happy. Most other countries don't have such conceptions. It's very cheerful and it's very amusing and it's rather nice we have it.

MB: It's in our Declaration of Independence.

LH: It's in our Declaration of Independence. It's very nice that we have it. But we also pay a high price for it.

MB: The search for happiness?

LH: Well, we'd all like to be happy, but . . .

MB: You mean the expectation of happiness . . . ?

LH: The living in full expectation that that is due us and if we're not happy, we're in terrible trouble. Older people. . . . I happen to be very amused and rather pleased with it in Americans because I think it has a hopefulness and cheerfulness about it. But I think we pay a very high price for it.

MB: What is that price?

LH: That we find that it's very, very seldom there. And that we've never stopped to define it for ourselves. We've been so busy looking at ourselves that we've never defined what it means. Does it mean a good meal? Does it mean a good job? Does it mean a sunny day? Does it mean enough to eat for that evening? Does it mean a nice book? Does it mean ten minutes of good music? What does it mean?

MB: All of those things.

LH: All of those things and some of them should do.

MB: Are you happy?

LH: I think so, but it took me a very long time to realize that I'm not unhappy.

MB: But you're happy about many of the things that you've accomplished.

LH: I've long ago stopped thinking about what happiness is; taking for granted that there was no arbitrary definition of it.

MB: Happiness is in moments perhaps?

LH: Yes, I think it's probably as much as one can expect.

MB: You once said, "It's a sad day when you find out that it's not accident or time or fortune but just yourself that kept things from you." What does that mean?

LH: I'm referring back to the same things I've been referring to of knowledge or growth or learning. I used to think, I guess, that when I was young if I'd gone to school longer or if I'd taken an M.A. or a Ph.D. that I was sad that I didn't and it was my fault. But I don't think that anymore. I think I perfectly well could have done it myself and didn't.

MB: You grew up, of course, in two places: New York and New Orleans. Did this splitting of your life give you a certain ability to remove yourself from things and be on the outside and look in and then describe? Did that contribute to your writing do you think?

LH: I don't think so. I don't think so. It gave me a certain precocious quality, I think, as a child. I don't think it gave me any greater ability to look in one way or the other because life is not controlled by cities, really, for a child. It is controlled by one's family. As I told you the other day, I liked New Orleans much better than I liked New York, but I think it gave me a sharper look into more people in the sense of my family than I might have had in one place. But, no, I don't think it had anything to do with looking on the outside. I had a curious mind as a child. I was curious about everybody. My family used to say I was born within a question mark. I seemed to have spent most of my childhood irritating everybody with. . . . I had no other form of conversation except a question.

MB: You wrote in *Unfinished Woman*, "A woman who was never to be committed was facing a man who already was." This was when you were talking about Hammett.

LH: Yes.

MB: And you seem to yearn for that kind of commitment to an ideal.

LH: Yes, I suppose I've . . . Well, I don't know whether yearn is the right word. I terribly admire people who are committed people. But committed has nothing to do in mind with politics. I'm a great admirer of people who are committed, say to any work they do, whatever the work is.

MB: Well, you've been very committed to your work.

LH: In my mind not enough. I suppose I have, but in mind, not enough.

MB: How do you mean? Are you too hard on yourself do you think?

LH: I'm told I am. I don't think so. I'm told so.

MB: I mean, you've written what . . . nine, twelve plays, three books . . .

LH: Thirteen plays.

MB: Thirteen plays. Forgive me, I didn't add well.

LH: I think it's thirteen; twelve or thirteen.

MB: You've worked very hard.

LH: That's quite different.

MB: And you've gotten critical acclaim. Why are you hard on yourself? What more do you think you should be doing or should have done?

LH: I don't think fame or the number of things you've done mean that you're necessarily committed in a total fashion to what you do, and maybe I am and maybe I don't know it. And maybe I'm too hard on myself, and maybe it's one of the reasons I romanticize other people's commitments, I think of their commitments. Hammett swears that once we had a plumber come at the farm to fix something and I never moved from the room for two hours. I was watching him. And he, Hammett, was calling to me to come and do something, and I said, "No, I can't come." And he came out in the kitchen and said, "Why can't you come?" And I said, "But I'm watching him." And he said, "but you don't even know what he's doing. You haven't any idea what he's doing." And I said, "That isn't what I'm watching. I'm watching. I'm watching somebody committed." I suppose that's exactly what I mean.

MB: Miss Hellman, in your introduction to the *Letters of Chekhov,* you quoted Chekhov and said, "A reasoned life without a definite outlook is not a life, but a burden and a horror." Have you had a definite outlook and a reasoned life?

LH I've tried to. It's not definite enough, but I've tried to. I deeply believe in that statement. That statement influenced me a great deal because I read it when I was quite young. And I agreed with it totally. I've tried to. I don't know that I've managed it. As you get older, you will find as so does everybody else, it's very hard to know what you did deliberately and what you did by taste and what you did by instinct, what you did because you were five feet four or five feet ten or blonde or brunette or pretty or not pretty or rich or not rich. It's very hard to sort it all out and to say that you had one path and followed it, which is what most people do think, I think, has always seemed to me a shabby lie and I don't like to tell it; or to mislead, particularly the young people, into thinking it's there. You go in so many directions, and you realize as you get older, for so many different reasons and for such quirky, inexplicable reasons, and then if you're vain enough and don't seek the truth enough, you pat yourself on the back for all the good things and tell yourself that you alone did them and skip the rest. I have an almost terror of doing this. I don't like to say that I filled a reason because I don't believe I did. I tried for it, but I don't like lack of reason. It scares me. Unreasonable people scare me a great deal and make me perfectly furious. My worst angers are with unreasonable people.

MB: How would you like to be remembered?

LH: Well . . .

MB: For what?

LH: As a good writer.

Hellman at 75: Fragile but Furious

Wayne Warga/1980

From *Los Angeles Times,* 10 August 1980, *calendar,* 1, 6–7.
Copyright, 1980, Los Angeles Times. Reprinted by permission.

Martha's Vineyard, Mass.—

"I have no objection to Miss McCarthy calling me a liar, but she must say where I lied and how I lied."

Lillian Hellman is 75, practically blind, restricted by a severe bronchial condition, deeply depressed and at the center of a major literary controversy, one most people her age and in her condition would ignore, let die in the soothing breezes of summer. Not Hellman. The recurring themes throughout her plays and her books are honesty and honor—the foundation of her character—and they are the two things she considers most worth fighting for.

"I remember Dorothy Parker saying about me that if I get a cold I feel I've sinned against God. I've thought of that comment often in the last six months. I giggled then; I don't now. I thought illness was something to be apologized for. It's such a bore. I've felt something terrible. I've felt in a total state of misery and exhaustion. I haven't even been in the water, which is unheard of for me."

She is sitting in the sun on the porch of her Vineyard home, indulging her love for the ocean. She pauses, stares off into the distance across Vineyard Sound, lights another cigarette.

"The truth is, I don't feel well enough to go many places. I'm in such a state of anger."

Her fourth memoir, *Maybe,* has just been published, the reviews have been critical to respectful to admiring. A special paperback edition of her three previous memoirs is being published next month. *Watch on the Rhine*, which originally opened on Broadway in 1941, was revived last winter and is going to be given a major production at the National Theater in Britain. Warner Bros. is negotiating to buy the film rights to her remarkable series of memoirs. Her life has been rich, full and accomplished. She is the preeminent woman playwright of her time, as well as a major literary figure, though she did not begin writing books until she was well into her 60s. She has become an icon in the age of iconoclasm.

She is accustomed to controversy and adversity, and better than most she knows how to tough it out. It was Lillian Hellman who made her stand before the House Un-American Activities Committee, was subsequently blacklisted and spent part of the 1950s selling groceries at Macy's.

It is those years and the years before which contain the beginning of the current controversy: a defamation suit by Hellman against novelist and critic Mary McCarthy, "The Dick Cavett Show" and Educational Broadcasting Corp. in which she asks $1.75 million in damages and $500,000 in punitive damages. She has, until now, refused to comment publicly on the suit, and has refused all requests for interviews.

It is a suit which—despite pleas from other literary figures, including a long letter from Norman Mailer in the *New York Times* begging her to drop the whole thing—she intends to see through to the end.

"I don't understand their reaction," she says. "No lawsuits are pleasant. Ever. But there seems to be a feeling literary people should not file lawsuits against other literary people. They seem to think we can say anything about each other."

In a Cavett show earlier this year, at the very end of the second half hour of the show, Cavett asked McCarthy whom she considered an overrated writer. McCarthy said, "Lillian Hellman, who I think is tremendously overrated. A bad writer, a dishonest writer." Cavett asked next what was dishonest about her and McCarthy said, "Everything. I once said in an interview every word she writes is a lie including 'and' and 'the.' "

It is an old and deep difference, one that has divided the intellectuals of their generation since the 1930s. It began with the Moscow trials which cleaved the intellectual left and sent Miss Hellman and Miss McCarthy philosophically adrift from one another, and continued on through the Spanish Civil War. The differences burst forth again in 1949 when the Conference for World Peace took place at the Waldorf-Astoria with Hellman as one of the evening's major sponsors and McCarthy one of its very vocal dissenters.

To those involved these were not simple political differences but

highly charged matters of commitment and philosophy. The struggle
was at its heights during the 1930s and again during the 1950s, times
when political issues influenced friendships and created enemies.

According to Irving Howe, the co-editor of the political periodical
Dissent, and an expert on those years, "The question involved—of
one's attitude toward communism—is probably the central political-
cultural-intellectual problem of the 20th Century. I think for many of
us those disputes were the formative passions of our lives—for good
or bad, it's made people what they are today."

The 1950s were a time of particular rupture and turmoil because of
the House Un-American Activities Committee hearings, Sen. Joseph
McCarthy and blacklisting. These times were the subject of Miss
Hellman's 1976 memoir *Scoundrel Time,* a book that rekindled old
alliances and angers. In some quarters, Hellman was accused of
writing a rather disingenuous and romanticized memoir which made
it sound as if she faced down the committee when, in fact, her
opponents claimed she took the Fifth Amendment like everyone else
who was unwilling to name names.

What she did was write a letter to the committee, one that was
subsequently to become famous, in which she said ". . . I cannot and
will not cut my conscience to fit this year's fashions." *Scoundrel Time*
received excellent reviews and became a best seller.

"The attacks came from Diana Trilling, Alfred Kazin and some
others of the same age group," she says. "Kazin wrote in *Esquire,*
came close to saying I'd perjured myself before the House committee, but I think *Esquire's* lawyers got to it. They mediated it. That
would have been a large charge. By the time Miss McCarthy came
along, I had grown sick of being called a liar.

"She's always given my plays bad reviews. That was absolutely her
right to do. She's also been unpleasant to me the few times I've been
near her, but that is also her right.

"But I am not a liar and I do not believe it is anybody's right to call
me a liar in space without proving it."

Hellman pauses, wrestles with her anger, then reaches for her cane
and holds it before her, her hands crossed on its hook.

"I long ago learned literary ladies come in two classes. Not
necessarily writers, but literary ladies. They're either the nicest people
in the world, the most trustworthy or they're sort of low down in a

way that is hard to understand. They have no standards or low standards. It isn't the same with men. Maybe because the difficult literary ladies have had a harder time than the men."

There is, in addition to the political and philosophical issues, another matter to contemplate. Both are women writers who succeeded in times not notably hospitable to women. There was—and is—competition. Hellman's plays and memoirs have been extremely successful. McCarthy's have not—her most recent novel, *Missionaries and Cannibals*, was neither a critical nor a financial success.

"I just don't understand jealousy of literary work. I just don't. Somebody's good literary work helps me, it doesn't hurt me," Hellman says.

"I think Hammett would have thought she was not worth the trouble. He had great contempt for that whole group. He had great contempt for people who call other people names."

Dashiell Hammett, whose Abercrombie & Fitch watch she wears, though she can barely see to read it, died in 1961 but his influence and his nature live with her still, both as a comfort and as a bulwark. They were together for 31 years and when Hammett sat down to write *The Thin Man*, he took Lillian Hellman and turned her—with very little alteration—into Nora Charles. It amuses her still.

"S. J. Perelman gave me a schnauzer, who became Asta in *The Thin Man*. We used to argue about royalties. I'd say Hammett didn't appreciate me or my dog, and point out what he owed me. He finally suggested I should shut up about it, he'd been supporting me for several years. It took him a long time to get around to saying it, I must say."

It was an incident in which Hammett played a prominent part which was the beginning of *Maybe,* a book which deals with the intriguing process of memory.

"I meant to say I'd previously written about what I did remember," she says about it. "There's only x amount you remember clearly—or you think you remember clearly. By the time you're 50, let us say, you've seen and known so many places there is a great deal you do not clearly remember. I think most people are not willing to see that or admit it if they do see it.

"What put the idea in my head was something that once happened to me with a very famous man. The man was in a bad situation and needed money. Hammett was very ill and I went into his room to tell him I'd be back in a few hours because I was taking some money to the man who had called me to say he needed it.

"Hammett got out of his sickbed, locked the door, put the key in his pocket, got back into the bed and said 'Lilly, sit down. You're not going anywhere.' I was completely bewildered. I said 'What is the matter with you? You have given away almost every nickel you've ever earned to almost anybody who wanted it.' Hammett said, 'This guy is a baddie and you like baddies too much. So take your coat off. You're not going anywhere to give him anything.'

"I was furious with him, but he was too sick for me to show it. It happened only a few months before Hammett died. I never delivered the money.

"Flip-flop goes 20 years. The man who asked for the money has been partly a friend, partly an enemy, if that's the right word. The reason I have so often allowed him to be unfriendly toward me is that I always believed he had a right to punish me for the non-deliverance of the money. He asked for help and I didn't give it. I'd feel betrayed too.

"Three months ago the man and I really had trouble, trouble that he brought on. Dash had been dead long enough, time has passed and so I told him why I'd done what I'd done. He looked at me in amazement and said he didn't know what I was talking about, that he'd never asked for the money. He had no doubt. He truly believed what he was saying. He was not lying. I sat on a sofa and thought I was going to be sick. I'd forgiven this man for 20 years for what he didn't remember ever happened. I asked him if an entry in my diary would convince him it had happened. He said, 'I think you're crazy, but I don't believe you're a liar.'

"In about 10 days, when I'd found the history of the day when Dash had stopped me from getting the money, I sent the day, the date, where I was, where he was, why he had asked me for the money and so on. I have never heard from him since. There is no question in my mind that he really did not remember the whole episode. But I had based a whole relationship on it."

She cannot work now, has been unable to write on the typewriter with special large type she brought with her to the Vineyard. It is, she says, partly her vision, partly her anger over her health which prohibits her from working.

"I finished the new book by postponing an eye operation last September. Whatever was going to happen I was going to finish. It's the first time any work of mine has gone off by itself and I've said 'I can't help you, kid.' I couldn't help feeling strange. You should have strong emotions about your work. It isn't that I didn't have them this time; I couldn't afford them. I want always to go back to the theme of this book. To memory. To what is memory? Where does memory fit? Who and what influences or changes memory?"

Memories—plus diaries and careful research—are the major components of her books. Following years in the theater she came to writing books, after "floundering around for a very long time.

"I don't know what directed things. The theater never suited my temperament. I wasn't unhappy with it, not until *Candide.* Then I became actively unhappy with it. I suddenly found I was acting like a dummy. Because I'd never done a musical before I was being told I didn't know the theater, was being talked into changing things, I rewrote 12 to 18 hours a day, patching things up, even putting aside the most primitive knowledge I have about the theater. I was being crazy modest. I had always fought for my work. I had looked for trouble even when there was none. During the Boston rewrite I was miserable. It wasn't that the show failed—it was an artistic success— but I had pushed aside everything I knew. We weren't ready to open. It was a mess. I was a mess. It was a hysterical period and I vowed never to get involved with such hysteria again.

"Of course, I then did *Toys in the Attic* and there was no hysteria. It went very well. I went my own way. I was with my own producer. It was a big success. Then *My Mother, Father & Me,* which was an adaptation. It opened during the 1963 newspaper strike. We got bad TV reviews and that was all we could get. I thought, no, no, I don't want any more of this.

"I don't basically have a theater imagination in spite of the fact I have a very decent theater technique. I started a play last summer, but I didn't go on with it. I like the theater. I find myself still very attracted to it."

Her health makes it impossible to live year-round on the Vineyard, so most winters are spent partly in New York, partly in Palm Springs or Los Angeles or wherever the climate suits her. She doesn't much like Los Angeles, no longer enjoys New York and would prefer to spend the rest of her life on the Vineyard, near the ocean. She lives in a small, modern home next door to the big home she once shared with Hammett. It is along the beach front, one of those places where the kitchen is the busiest room because its owner loves to cook and takes considerable pleasure in the rituals of mealtime.

She has fished all of her life and she owns a charter fishing boat— *Julia*, after the story and the film. She has access to it two half days a week, but has not yet fished this summer.

"But I will," she says, "I will. Water is wonderful. Life goes on in it all of the time, all year around. There's always movement."

In the living room of her home, a comfortable yellow room with empire furniture—and the sofa from the set of *The Little Foxes*— there are shelves of reference books, scattered reading material and some editions of Hammett's books in foreign languages, an old black-and-white photo of Hammett, shirtless, standing in front of a great scudding cloud not quite as white as his hair. There is also—a recent addition—a tape recorder and some cassettes of books on tape, a collection of *Walden*, Thoreau and Defoe's *Journal of the Plague Years*.

Last year at this time she took an accidental overdose of medicine which caused a serious reaction and when she recovered she had lost 30 pounds. Then, last spring, while she was in San Francisco, her bronchial problems became so severe she had to be hospitalized.

"I was told I had emphysema. Then I was told I didn't. Then there are the eyes . . . glaucoma and cataracts and now a third disease has set in. It so horrifies me. If I could get over the anger at what has happened, maybe then I'd be better able to handle it."

She is in her living room, sipping a martini, about to eat the dinner she has been going back and forth to the kitchen to inspect. It is being prepared by the two young women who live with her, who take care of her and her home, but Hellman is clearly in charge, determined—no matter what—to control her own life. She is like an aging lioness, frail, weary and wounded, but raging with spirit and fight, refusing to give up, patrolling her territory, willing to defend it at all cost.

"I've always had a theory that there's no preparation for sickness or death. I don't want to know. I never told Dash he had cancer. There was no point. He never knew."

Lillian Hellman Hasn't Gone Fishin'

Phyllis Meras/1981

From *Providence Journal,* 5 July 1981, sec. H,
9. Reprinted by permission of the Providence
Journal-Bulletin, © 1981.

Lillian Hellman celebrated a birthday last month. The playwright and writer of memoirs whose 45-year-old melodrama, *The Little Foxes,* starring Elizabeth Taylor, is having a successful Broadway revival knows she is older than 70, but is not certain exactly how much more. Her father, she says, had inherited an old European method of accounting that complicated birth dates.

Then when, at 24, she met the detective story writer Dashiell Hammett, and sensed that they were falling in love (which they did, sharing a life together for three decades until his death in 1961), she learned he was a dozen years older than she was.

"And I thought it might hurt his feelings to have me that much younger, so I told him I was two years older than I was," Miss Hellman recalled before lunch the other day in her bright and airy living room overlooking Vineyard Haven harbor on the island of Martha's Vineyard, Mass.

But even that wasn't the end of the story. The last time her name appeared in *Who's Who in America* she subtracted a year, and maybe another one or two in subsequent editions, she says.

Lillian Hellman freely admits that the onset of years is disturbing to her, principally because of an eye problem that began a few years ago and has made writing increasingly difficult. The author of a dozen plays, including *Watch on the Rhine, Another Part of the Forest, The Autumn Garden, The Children's Hour,* and four volumes of memoirs—*An Unfinished Woman, Scoundrel Time, Pentimento* and *Maybe,* she longs to be writing more, but is writing less.

"I can, of course, type without seeing, but I have a hard time reading back what I've written, so I've been trying to learn to dictate. Dictating the dialogue isn't hard, but the prose is."

Impatience about everything but writing, she admits, has been a hallmark of her life. Now she finds that same impatience creeping toward her writing, too.

"And I have always had nothing *but* patience about writing. I've trained myself to say, 'This version doesn't matter, the next one matters,' so I often wrote something as much as eight or nine times. It gave me pleasure to think, 'Oh, I don't have to worry about this. I'll do it another time.' But now someone has to read back to me what I've written and that's difficult."

"And then there's something else that makes dictating and reworking difficult: I always went on the assumption that I could tear up two-thirds of anything I was writing and that I would be able to remember what was good and that what wasn't I would be happy to forget. And I frequently *would* tear up what I'd done. Sometimes I'd save four or five pages, but that would be all. Why did I work that way? Probably I thought that to go back and rework was crippling," Miss Hellman mused.

"And I suppose its origin was also a real fear of laziness," she continued, lighting one of a non-stop series of cigarettes. "I guess I thought I would just recopy, not reinvent. I'm paying for that now, but don't be depressed by me. It will pass. I've done some 15,000 words of what may be a new book. It's about children I've known, and my editor is encouraging about it—perhaps much too encouraging."

Looking as cool in a pink-and-blue Madras skirt as her living room that blends yellows, and somehow invites the roses and honeysuckle outside inside, Miss Hellman moved with the aid of a cane to the dining table that offers a view of her effulgent garden.

"I was born in a city," she said, "in New Orleans, but I love the country and I love farming. I have two vegetable gardens here on the Vineyard. But real farming is out the window for me now, of course. I ran a farm for 19 years. Hammett and I had a farm in Pleasantville, N.Y."

The cane and a slow step are not the result of her septuagenarian status, she emphasized quickly. They came from a fall in March in Washington when she had gone to attend the opening of *The Little Foxes*. (Both the play's timelessness and the star's interpretation of the role of the seductive Southern predator, Regina, have been heralded by theater critics; Miss Hellman is generally pleased, too. After Labor

Day, it goes to Miss Hellman's birthplace, New Orleans—and she with it—if there has been no serious damage from the spring accident.)

A trouper to the last, despite her mishap, which occurred as she was leaving the hotel lobby on her way to the play, she stayed through the first act. Then the company manager suggested that she go to a hospital to be sure she was all right, and she was taken to George Washington University Hospital—the same one, she noted, where President Reagan had been taken after the assassination attempt.

As she toyed with a light lunch of cold chicken tarragon and a beefsteak-tomato and Bermuda onion salad, mention of President Reagan brought political thoughts to mind.

McCarthyism in Hollywood in the 1950s sent Hammett to jail and blacklisted Miss Hellman, as she explains in her 1976 memoir *Scoundrel Time*. She remains a strong proponent of the need for political and social commitment of writers, however.

"It's almost impossible to write without some sort of beliefs, isn't it?" she asked. "After all, a writer doesn't live in space. And commitment doesn't have to mean propaganda. In any case, most good writing is a kind of propaganda whether the writer did or didn't know it. (Miss Hellman's *Watch on the Rhine* was an outcry against Nazism; *The Searching Wind* was about the behind-the-scenes political appeasers of World War II; *The Children's Hour* dealt with lesbianism while it was still a taboo word.)

So of course she had some thoughts about today's world:

"I think we are being run by ignorant and selfish men just now, but things will be much better after a while. We have one virtue in this country: If we don't like things, we change them. The main thing is to see that these people don't get us into a war. Unless they do that, we don't have to worry too much. They'll just go out the way the rest have gone. It is too bad, though, that liberalism seems to have passed away from this country. I think that's a sad thing, though perhaps it's really there somewhere, quietly.

"I think the immediate future looks very grim, but there will be better things someday. If you don't believe in the future, you have no right to live."

Miss Hellman also has opinions about contemporary American literature:

"It may be second-class, but second-class isn't so bad after all," she says. "I don't think France or England or Russia have come out with anything better in the last 50 years, except for Joyce and maybe Pritchett, and Beckett in France. But we have a great many very talented people here, too. I think Pynchon is a man of enormous talent."

Although it is primarily as a playwright that Lillian Hellman is known, her first writing was of short stories and poems. "My first play, as a matter of fact, was written as a sort of a joke with the critic and essayist Louis Kronenberger. It got bought, but it was never pro- duced. But when I was a child, I went to the theater a lot. Kids in New York, where I spent much of my childhood, used to do that on a Saturday afternoon. And then I married a man who worked in the theater, Arthur Kober. (The late Mr. Kober, a humorist who wrote for *The New Yorker,* had once been a theatrical press agent and was, himself, a prize-winning Broadway playwright. His comedy *Having a Wonderful Time* was named the best Broadway comedy of 1937.)

"But I think I had an instinct for the theater from the beginning. I haven't written a play now since 1962, though. It's not that I minded the form, that isn't why I stopped, but I minded what the theater had become. I got tired of talking about money all the time and I got tired of the idea that a play could be ruined by one or two critics in just a day or two. I liked plays when I was actually doing the writing, and I liked them when they were in rehearsal, but I don't think I was ever very easy in the theater itself, though of course, like most playwrights, I approved the director and helped with the casting."

"Do I use people I know in my writing? Anybody who's around a writer and doesn't think he's being used is a loon. But I've always changed anyone I've used and I think of only one person who has recognized himself. I changed people not for gentlemanly reasons, though, but to avoid lawsuits. I don't see any great virtue except the scandal if you use people's names in your writing or make it evident who they are. I can write about you perfectly well without using your name."

Her failing eyesight has, of course, diminished Miss Hellman's ability to read not only her own work but other writers', and she is disgruntled about that. She has tried to find talking books that are appealing through the Library of Congress. "But there's very little

Dickens and not the Shakespeare you want. No Balzac and only *The Gambler* of Dostoevsky's."

The telephone rang and she moved slowly to answer it, remarking wistfully that she feared her accident might force her to forego her favorite Martha's Vineyard summer pastime this year. "I love boats and I love fishing, but I don't think I could pull in anything over a quarter of a pound just now."

Lillian Hellman as Herself

Sylvie Drake/1981

From *Los Angeles Times,* 18 October 1981, *calendar,* 1, 6. Copyright 1981, Los Angeles Times. Reprinted by permission, with one paragraph excised at the request of the Los Angeles Times.

Her father once said of her that she lived "within a question mark." Her friend, the writer John Hersey, called her "an ambulatory chimney," a woman "so liberated that she is not at all afraid of the kitchen," who defines culture as "applied curiosity." The late Harold Clurman, who directed her play, *The Autumn Garden,* described her as a women of "excellent intelligence interested in life in the broadest context. . . .A moralist vitally concerned with the proper conduct of life. . . ."

These are clearly descriptions by friendly voices (unfriendly ones also have piped up lately) of the person who is Lillian Hellman. They were sought out because Hellman is reluctant to define herself. In town recently for the opening of her play, *The Little Foxes,* at the Ahmanson, the grave and tiny Hellman deflected a request for self-description with, "You'd have to ask other people, someone who knew me well." Then, with a puff of her perpetual cigarette, she added, "I'm not sure they could."

True. At 74, her eyesight failing badly, Hellman is as much a paradox as ever, fiercely private and yet surprisingly accessible. In the sunny living room of an upper-story suite at the Beverly Wilshire Hotel, she inquired about the weather ("Is it warm out? Do you think I can swim this afternoon?") and answered questions with intense scrutiny and guarded thoughtfulness. She is at once recalcitrant and embracing, anxious to answer accurately, yet oddly embarrassed about being a focus of attention.

"I don't terribly like being interviewed," she acknowledged. "It's silly to say because it sounds fake-modest, but I'm not crazy about talking about myself."

Why should she be? She has said all she wants to say in three volumes of memoirs, *An Unfinished Woman, Pentimento, Scoundrel Time.* In the past 18 months, she's also become the target of some of her peers who've accused her of lying in those volumes, or at least misrepresenting the truth. The allegations resulted in one lawsuit, to the tune of $1.75 million and $500,000 in punitive damages, against writer Mary McCarthy, Dick Cavett and the Public Broadcasting Service, when McCarthy on the Cavett show called Hellman a dishonest writer. For a woman who has spent most of her life tracking and trying to define truth, it was a statement that had to cut deep.

This and other, less virulent refutations of some of her recollections left her angered and profoundly saddened. And yet except for owning up to the frustration brought on by her troublesome eyesight, Hellman is in good health and spirits. She's back at work. The energy has to be carefully parceled out, but the recent revival of interest in her plays (*Little Foxes, Watch on the Rhine, Another Part of the Forest*) has revived a participatory interest in the world. Having successfully fought off bronchial pneumonia last year, lashed back at her critics and made grudging concessions to her dimming eyes, this four-foot giant in a sharp red suit talked like a woman wiser with age but not a jot chastened by events.

"I've never believed that I was one of those people who learn from experience," she said in a slow, faintly regretful voice. "I've never understood it. I learned about myself, I think, but if I'm wiser than I was at 20, it's also because I'm more frightened or more weary. I think I'm wiser. I can't afford not to be. At 20 we may be narrower in outlook, but also braver and more open. I don't find that people get necessarily better with age. Some do, but most of them get more rigid."

Hellman, who admits to having "puritanical streaks," does not appear to be among the rigid. Her views have broadened and if they seem softer and more accepting than they once were, she counts it an achievement. . . .

Decency in the conduct of life has been another of Hellman's preoccupations, perhaps most memorably illustrated by the celebrated letter she wrote to the House Un-American Activities Committee (HUAC) when called upon to testify during the McCarthy hearings (Hellman agreed to answer questions about herself, but

warned she would not do so about others. When this condition was
denied, she took the Fifth Amendment in self-defense.) Decency?
She finds it at least as elusive as truth.

"It may be that the most that you can do is for yourself," she said.
"You live each day by your own standards, even if you can't require
other people to do it. It's as close as you can come to decency, or
honesty, or even courage. Not many people do it. Not as many
people as I thought.

"Courage is another very hard word to define. We're so unable to
judge other people that we're apt to call a perfectly ordinary or silly
thing 'courage' and then pass up something that took real courage. It
so depends on the person or the act. The most you can do is look at
a total life. . . ."

What about political courage?

There is a puff on the cigarette and a long pause.

"It seems to me it's the same thing. You do what you can do and
hope it has some effect. You don't question the gesture. You just do
it. It will be as effective as it can be for that one minute of time. We're
certainly at a very difficult minute of our history now. Everybody of
any liberal persuasion is floundering around in miserable, unled
fashion. There are very grave dangers. . . ."

Does she consider herself primarily a playwright? A prose stylist?
Does it matter?

"I've written, of course, more plays than anything else," she
replied, "and yet the theater had almost ceased to interest me until I,
once again, began to function in it, such as attending these rehearsals
of *Little Foxes*.

"A couple of the last productions—not *Toys in the Attic,* that was a
great pleasure—the last play I did, *My Mother, My Father and Me*
(1963) and *Candide* (1956), I thought 'I don't want to hear any more
about money. I want to find something else to do with myself, where
I don't have to listen to anyone tell me we may not be able to come
into New York because there's not enough money in Boston. Or that
something desperately needs changing because the audience doesn't
like X, Y and Z.'

"I see nothing wrong with saying that you're tired of one form and
want to try another. I believe that's what happened to me. The
theater, as I've written, never held any great glamour for me. I had

my best times when I was alone. I didn't start out as a playwright. I started out as a short-story writer. I'd hoped to write novels, which I don't think I ever will. I don't think I'm a novelist. But there's no mystery to my leaving the theater. Most playwrights stay with it too long. I'm glad I changed forms."

About *The Little Foxes*: "I've enjoyed rediscovering it, though I must say I could do without seeing it any more."

About *Another Part of the Forest,* which has been handsomely revived at San Francisco's American Conservatory Theater and will get productions at the Seattle Rep and the Ahmanson this season: "I think it's a good play and I had fun writing it. The discovery of Pat Neal (who played Regina in the original production) was a great pleasure. She's just bought a house on the island I live on (in Martha's Vineyard) and we had a nice time this summer remembering her first reading. . . ."

About *The Autumn Garden*: "I believe it's my best play."

About *Toys in the Attic,* which won the Best Play award from the New York Critics' (1959–'60): "I think it has bad flaws that I wish I could remedy. I think most of my plays do. When I published the 13 plays, I tried to rewrite some of them and found it impossible to do. It meant taking the whole fabric apart."

Last year, Hellman published, *Maybe, a Story,* an examination of memory that comes as close as Hellman is likely to get to novel writing. The book had a mixed reception.

"It got wonderful attention, wonderful notices, from very literary people. But from people just under the very literary, it didn't. That pained me—not because it didn't get great notices, but because they didn't seem to understand eight words of it. I thought I had said clearly what the book was. Evidently, I couldn't have. The puzzlement must in some way have been my fault. I still don't know how."

Maybe, a Story is the last book Hellman was able to read before the serious onset of eye trouble this summer. She writes now by dictating on tape, a process that frustrates her more than it satisfies. She works almost entirely during the morning hours and when she's at her favorite spot, the Vineyard—usually May to October—she still spends afternoons at sea on a charter fishing boat she owns. Doctors won't allow her to stay in the cold of northern winters any more, so

October to January is usually all the time she gets in her Park Avenue apartment, before seeking warmer climes.

"I hate to admit I have anything wrong with me," she said with obvious exasperation. "I should start, but I don't like to."

Hellman was expected at the Ahmanson for an afternoon rehearsal and our time was growing short. There were two more subjects to cover: being a woman and being Jewish.

"It hasn't gotten down to the basic issue," she said about the women's movement. "I said once that I don't give a damn who carries out the garbage. It's not the point of proof. The question should be addressed totally in economic terms: equal pay for equal work. Unless it does that, it's never going to attract any but unhappy middle class women. It is a working-class-woman's problem.

"It's almost come down to being a dislike of men, rather than an acceptance of the pleasure of men. Men have brutalized women, certainly, but the issues have been strange issues, often meager, minor complaints. And the enmity is strange.

"Child-bearing and -rearing is a very important function of women and always will be, please God. Yet it's absolutely absent from the discussion—perhaps because it is in the hands of women with very little interest in bearing or rearing children. I think—I hope—that when it's in the hands of simpler women, if ever, it will straighten itself out."

And being Jewish?

"I myself make very anti-Semitic remarks but I get very upset if anybody else does. I wasn't brought up as a Jew. I know almost nothing about being one—I'm sorry to say—though not sorry enough to go to the trouble of learning.

"I've asked myself many times what I would have liked to have been born and decided a long time ago that I was very glad I was born a Jew. Whether brought up as one or not, somewhere in the background there was a gift of being born a Jew. I don't want it to alter my point of view about things any more than I would want being Catholic or anything else to alter my point of view, but I am glad of what I am.

"I felt absolutely violent during the Nazi period, certainly. I still do. I was in school in Germany when it first started. Later I saw Majdanek (a concentration camp in Lublin, Poland). I'll never recover as long as I live. I only went back once (to Germany) with Mike Nichols, who *is* German, as you know. He stood it much better than I. We'd gone to see the East Berlin Theater and stayed in West Berlin. I felt all I was doing was walking on the street guessing how old everybody was. There's no rational explanation, but I couldn't stay. I left at the end of a week."

Producer Richard Roth has bought the movie rights to Hellman's three volumes of memoirs and novelist Diane Johnson is working on a screenplay which Sydney Pollack, Hellman said, may direct. Had she any suggestion as to who should play the Lillian part?

"Not the slightest! I haven't the slightest idea," she said with the first honest-to-goodness laugh of the day. "Do *you* have any suggestions? It will, of course, have to be someone wonderful and glamorous and ravishing!"

Index